TECH MONEY

TECH MONEY

A GUIDE to the NEW GAME of TECHNOLOGY INVESTING

IGOR PEJIC

Diversion Books
A division of Diversion Publishing Corp.
www.diversionbooks.com

DIVERSION
BOOKS

Diversion Books
A division of Diversion Publishing Corp.
www.diversionbooks.com

For more information, email info@diversionbooks.com

First Diversion Books Edition: May 2026
Hardcover ISBN: 9798895151044
e-ISBN: 9798895151051

Design by Westchester Publishing Services
Cover design by Will D. Mack

Printed in the United States of America
1 3 5 7 9 10 8 6 4 2

Diversion books are available at special discounts for bulk purchases in the US by corporations, institutions, and other organizations. For more information, please contact admin@diversionbooks.com.

Disclaimer

Nothing in this book, nor any other content presented by the author and the publisher, is intended to provide legal, tax, financial, or investment advice. Nothing contained constitutes a solicitation, recommendation, endorsement, or offer to buy or sell any securities or other financial instruments. The author may participate in any investment described in this content yet receives no financial compensation for discussing and mentioning specific companies in this book.

We believe the information presented in this book to be true and accurate at the time of writing but do not guarantee the accuracy of every statement, nor guarantee that the information will not change in the future. The information is provided "as is" and it is important that you independently research any information that you wish to rely upon. All investments carry risk, and past performance is not a guarantee of future results. You may lose principal.

The content is gathered from publicly available information and the expertise of the author. It does not contain any insider information. Although the author exclusively uses sources he considers to be reliable, he cannot guarantee the accuracy and the completeness of this information. The content is intended to be used and must be used solely for educational and information purposes. It is very important to do your own analysis before making any investment and you should consider your own personal circumstances and speak with a professional advisor before making any investment.

Neither the author nor the publisher shall be liable for any losses or damages, including but not limited to financial losses, that may result from the use of the content or the information presented herein. All content is protected by copyright and may not be reproduced without the express written permission of the publisher.

Table of Contents

IV. GETTING THE TIMING RIGHT

V. GETTING THE COMPANY RIGHT

IX. FINAL THOUGHTS

Introduction

I SPENT MY ENTIRE CAREER WORKING with emerging technologies, but I almost didn't end up there. After graduation it came down to two job offers. One was at a tiny management consulting firm specializing in tech and finance. Sixty-hour weeks, no job guarantee, and a salary an intern might have rejected. The other was from a world-leading personal care company. Many of my fellow graduates would have killed for the latter position. Yet I couldn't imagine myself selling shampoo. Not that there is anything wrong with it, but tech lured me with its dynamism and its speed. I didn't shrink away from its unpredictability; I welcomed it. Little did I know how fast the ride would get.

In the 2010s, I witnessed in awe the hyper-fast ascent of smartphones. Robots took over factory floors. Sensors and computer chips made cars safer and payments faster. Gene editing promised to eradicate disease. And thanks to cloud computing, it was easier than ever to launch and grow a company.

Technological progress was the most equalizing and life-enhancing trend since the spread of capitalism. What I didn't understand back then was the force fueling this progress: The pursuit of big money.

In 2015, I came across a technology that fascinated me more than any other: Blockchain, the trust machine that had enabled Bitcoin but promised to upend countless other mega-industries. After years of intense research, I eventually published my first book in 2019. This is where my learning journey actually started. The promotion activities put me right at the center of a new tech gold rush.

Blockchain events brought together people that otherwise would never have been in the same room. In panels, gray-haired banking executives babbled along with unemployed crypto bros residing in their parents' basements. Listening in the audience were nerdy developers with thick, smudged glasses sitting next to dark web barons in white tuxedos. Within the same coffee break you could talk to genius Silicon Valley pioneers as well as eloquent impostors. Often, it was hard to tell them apart.

I soon realized most of those people weren't really there to revolutionize money. They were there to make money. Tons of it. And as fast as possible. The desire was palpable in every chat, every article, every presentation. It was what had brought together all those diverse characters, a deeply human appetite unleashed. Whether it's crypto or AI, everybody has a feel-good story of how they want to empower communities in Africa or save the planet from overheating. Yet once you strip away the storytelling and the PR talking points, you see that it is all about tech money.

The crypto world taught me more about tech money than all of my previous work combined. Yet the person I learned most from was none of those chatty neo-tycoons, but an inconspicuous accountant named Oliver. I met Oliver at a blockchain conference in London. He walked up to me after a book signing and started firing questions at me. His questions were hard to answer but intrigued me, so we chatted a bit. His story fascinated me. Our paths would cross a couple of times.

Oliver had no formal training in investment banking. His technology knowledge peaked at creating macros in MS Excel. He did bookkeeping. Not for tech-startups but for restaurants and hairdressers. And yet, when I met him, he boasted an impressive tech wealth. He was a master of tech money.

Many tech wonks his age had been privileged to have access to the first personal computers when they were kids. Not so Oliver. He had no childhood memories of tinkering with an Apple II computer or navigating Pacman across the screen on a Commodore 64. And he was too young to have witnessed the inspirational moon landing. His emotions toward tech ended with the question of how much money it could make him. At some point in the 1990s, he decided the answer was "a lot." Tech would reshape the world. So, he invested the $12,000 he had saved, occasionally adding a couple of hundred dollars here and there. Oliver bought every stock he could afford: email providers, news outlets, web browsers, web shops.

Though he wanted to stick with the internet companies long term, the growth became too excessive. He pulled out. "I never obsessed with financial metrics," he told me, "but companies were trading at 30, 40 times their revenues. Sometimes more. It doesn't take a finance MBA to understand investors will never see a payback. It had turned to pure speculation." History proved him right. After the bubble burst in 2000, Oliver came back and bought up those few companies still standing at a special discount.

This time, he kept them until 2007. It was the year he saw Steve Jobs waving the first iPhone onstage. Oliver immediately understood the buttonless phone was actually ushering in an era of pocket computers. The next day, Oliver dropped his tech portfolio and went all in on Apple stock.

Over the next several years, the only thing growing faster than his net worth were his interests. There was hardly a day Oliver spent less than four hours reading up on emerging tech and hardly a week in which he didn't mingle at conferences or meetups. His horizons now stretched beyond IT innovation. Biotech piqued his interest. In particular, it was a gene editing technique called CRISPR that made him open his wallet. It was a sensation within the scientific community, but little known outside of it. Oliver was so early he had made a small fortune and moved on years before CRISPR won the Nobel Prize in 2020. This time his pivot was to cryptocurrencies. When I met him at that conference in London, he owned some 500 Bitcoins, roughly worth about $2M at that time.

I don't think he ever bought into the decentralization ethos of cryptocurrencies. "Will it change the system? That's beside the point. It will go up. That's all that matters." He told me he didn't intend to keep those either. The next big thing, he was sure, were semiconductors. There would soon be a shortage in chip capacity caused by exploding demand. And chip factories were not quickly built, even if governments invested heavily. Today this rationale seems like a no-brainer, but back then only a few people were racking their brains about chip supplies. Yet before moving his money to chips, he still waited for Bitcoin's price to swell a little more.

So how could Oliver become so successful? How could an accountant see the future so clearly while so many tech wizards couldn't? The short answer is that he understood technological trajectories, could connect them to the broader economy, and had a feeling for mass psychology.

Many tech practitioners have that, too, but what set Oliver apart was that he had range and distance. He was extremely well-read in different areas. At the same time, his fortunes were not tied to one specific technology. And he was nonplussed by all the buzz and infectious enthusiasm swirling around. Contrast that to Mark Zuckerberg's 2021 decision to steer his entire Facebook empire into the metaverse. Taken from a science fiction novel, the metaverse is a virtual reality seeking to be the next generation of the web. The name of Facebook's holding company was changed to Meta. Ten thousand engineers were to work on the topic in the EU alone. What followed was a bloodbath on Meta's stock price. Not even its employees were spending time in the metaverse. Zuckerberg was forced to backpedal. But how could this blunder happen to such a proven tech visionary? Shouldn't he have become suspicious at the latest when his legless avatar played poker in the announcement video?

When you are too deep into a topic, sometimes you start connecting dots because you want them to be connected. Apple and Google had established themselves as the gatekeepers of the mobile phone. Meta could only break that duopoly if it won the next platform. VR headsets are one of Meta's fortes, so wouldn't it be great if people started moving to the metaverse using Meta's Oculus Rifts? Facebook needed the metaverse; its users did not. No wonder the idea of this virtual reality faltered fast. This is not to say the solid remnants of the technological potential—call them Web3—will not witness a comeback. But even if they do, the timing of the pivot was a disaster.

Being too obsessed with one tech often makes you smug. It also keeps you in a bubble of like-minded people. You develop tunnel vision. The more highly specialized the experts, the narrower the tunnel. Eventually you start losing commonsense judgment. In 2021, tech-millionaire Sina Estavi paid $2.9 million for a digital representation of the first tweet, a so-called NFT. Convinced that NFTs would revolutionize art and that he owned the *Mona Lisa* of NFTs, Estavi tried to auction his precious artifact one year after the purchase. The highest offer he received: $6,800. He had spent a fortune on a worthless entry into a database. When you think you are smarter than everybody else, you probably aren't.

There is also the other extreme. Rachel Siegel was a substitute teacher in New York City. One day she ended up at an after-party for a crypto conference, where she heard about Bitcoin for the first time. The crackling enthusiasm at the party infected her, so she started investing all the spare money she had into this new currency. Usually $25 from every paycheck. In less than five years her investment turned into millions. She quit her teaching job, bought a condo in the Caribbean, and jets first-class around the world.

These are inspiring stories that funnel even more money into the tech sector from people hoping to replicate them. Yet stories like these are not a blueprint. They are pure luck. If they indeed were a blueprint, Siegel and others would be able to repeat their success the way Oliver did.

Speaking of Oliver, I lost contact with him for some years until we met in 2023. As I was holding a keynote on future technologies in banking, I spotted him in one of the last rows. Same shirt, same glasses. Like always, he sat in a corner listening, thumping his temple with an index finger and taking notes.

After I got offstage, I jostled my way through the crowd, eager to find out whether he had gone big into semiconductors or whether he was still waiting for Bitcoin to hit its plateau. I told him I hoped he hadn't sold his coins. He hadn't. Oliver had kept to his strategy even as crypto prices plunged by more than 60% in a year. So, he lived to witness the resurgence. Since our last meeting, the price had gone up tenfold. According to my napkin calculations, Oliver should have been worth millions. Sadly, this wasn't the case.

An inexplicable failure of judgment left him with an almost empty portfolio. He kept all his Bitcoins in a centralized exchange that got hacked. All the visionary decisions of the past 30 years were wiped out overnight. Oliver had known about the risks of such exchanges. He had known that you should never keep all your capital in one asset class, nor all your assets in one place. Yet he was so busy figuring out the next trend that he didn't take the time to manage his risks. The tech sector punishes such mistakes much harsher than any other industry.

Oliver's extreme roller-coaster ride could only happen in the tech world. And that is why he was again rummaging around at an innovation conference hunting for the next big thing. "I've built all this from scratch, and I can do it again," he told me matter-of-factly, soaked in an optimism that had been a cornerstone of his success.

Oliver's story illustrates a central theme of this book: Success in tech investing is as much about timing, risk management, and perspective as it is about technical knowledge. Because I learned so much from Oliver, I set out to find other people like him. Eventually, I ended up interviewing more than 50 of them for this book. Each was unique, but then again similar in that they spend every day racking their brains over how to realize tech money. The interview partners ranged from astronauts to authors. From the White House to Silicon Valley. From some of the world's most successful VCs and stock pickers to finance professors whose quantitative analysis dwarfs that of both. From tech pioneers who have shaped our understanding of the internet to those entrepreneurs driving forward a world of AI and digital assets. I spoke to innovation heads of global banking goliaths, as well as to creators of ubiquitous models for thinking about tech that you will find in every PowerPoint. Most of the 100 subchapters are studded with their powerful voices. Not all of the people I spoke to have ended up being quoted in this book, but I am grateful to each one for sharing their views even off record. Though not attributed, readers will benefit from their wisdom as well.

This book is not investment advice. There is far too much of it out there. Nor is *Tech Money* an exhaustive list of things to consider when putting your dollars into the latest innovation. I will not tell you which stocks to buy, nor teach you a bulletproof strategy to become rich. There is no such thing anyway (though many advisors and experts claim to have it, so beware). While technology investing can be mastered, it is anything but simple and straightforward, instead filled with new risks and surrounded by loud and buzz-brimming debates. *Tech Money* is an attempt to bring some sanity into this excited and agitated world. It is a robust strategic foundation for everybody investing in technology, highlighting patterns and tech trajectories, explaining how tech assets are fundamentally different to traditional assets, and teaching successful strategies to hit the sweet spot of large upside potential and manageable risk. The book helps you to decide not on gut feeling or expert sentiment, but with clear-minded thinking based on empirical evidence and long-term strategy. In other words: *Tech Money* teaches crucial, often counterintuitive, lessons that will help you surf the waves of progress.

I unpack these lessons in 100 charts. To be clear, charts and graphs are never neutral or objective. Like text, they carry a certain perspective. They highlight some things, hide others, and leave blanks for the readers to fill. Just as much is said between the bars of diagrams as between the lines of text. Yet charts are a perfect complement to written words as they are unmatched in clarity and speed. Messages can be conveyed in split seconds. Dimensions become clear at a glance. Lengthy descriptions can yield to focused interpretation on a single chart. And visuals not only help messages travel faster to your mind, but they stick around longer.

I

THE FUNDAMENTALS OF TECH MONEY

OLIVER WAS THE MOST IMPRESSIVE CHARACTER I HAVE MET. But there were others, less distinct yet highly successful in riding the waves of new technological revolutions. They were all optimists, sucking up information like sponges, with an extreme breadth of knowledge. They all seemed to know intuitively where the technology and the market were going. Of course, the right decisions didn't *come* from intuition. They came from a subconscious understanding of tech cycles and their logic. In this book, my goal is to make this logic explicit. I am convinced that everybody can apply these principles to become a successful tech investor and, over time, generate market-beating returns. Whether you are a private investor, venture capitalist, or an executive, there is no reason to be caught off-guard by the rapid changes. The world of technology might be speeding up constantly, but innovation and progress are still occurring in cycles. And the telltale signs announcing them are still discernable.

But even if you are the best surfer of tech waves, you will wipe out at one point if you fail to build a diversified and resilient portfolio strategy. So, before going on the hunt for emerging technologies and the companies that will be driving them, you must decide where you want to go and by which route. You can call it a strategic framework. Or a risk tolerance assessment. Call it whatever you like, as long as you understand the odds and the possible rewards of the various strategies that lead to tech money. Getting the next big technology right, for example, is more probable than finding the next tech giant. And it requires significantly less time and effort. And less discipline too. But if you do engage in those more sophisticated strategies—and you do it successfully—returns don't just rise. They go exponential. This part sets the stage on how to think about the trade-offs. After all, for most people, it will not be an either/or question, but one of allocation. What part of my portfolio do I want in low-risk strategies vs. more ambitious ones?

Regardless of the strategy, you must build the right mindset of a tech investor, one that will let you play on, even as you sometimes lose. Remember: You're not in for a game, but for the entire championship. Or, in investing terminology: Always account for multiple possible futures.

Finally, this introductory part asks a fundamental question, on which the value of each of the book's lessons rely: What exactly is a tech company? At its core, technology represents the practical application of scientific principles to meet human needs or goals. This is a very broad definition. And frankly, not of much help. Nor can official sector categorizations reliably tell you where to look for the next Amazon or Google. That's why I have a proposal in chapter 4 on where to draw the line.

1

Technology Alpha

THE FIRST CHART IS ACTUALLY A FORMULA, but it goes to the very essence of this book: Measuring the success of your tech investments. As long as there has been investing, people have been trying to beat the market. In other words, they seek to pocket higher returns on their capital

CHART 1

Calculating Technology Alpha

$$\text{Alpha } (\alpha) = \text{Portfolio return} - \text{benchmark return}$$

$$\textbf{Technology Alpha } (t\alpha) = \textbf{Tech-portfolio return} - \textbf{S\&P 500 return}$$

Chart: Igor Pejic

than their peers. We all know this as the term *alpha*. The investment world might boast thousands of charts, metrics, and formulas, wrapped in smart-sounding jargon. But how successful you are as an investor can all be boiled down into this one figure. This number can be positive or negative. If, say, you earn a 10% return whereas the market made 7%, your alpha is positive. If you earn 5%, it is negative. The mathematical expression can be found in the first line of the illustration above.

Entire industries exist with the sole goal of finding alpha. Whether it's fidgety stock traders hiding behind two rows of flickering screens, prim fund managers poring over their product's past performance, or math wizards plodding through a company's financials. There is nothing wrong or surprising in wanting to earn a higher return than the overall market. The problem is, only a select few succeed.

No matter how many screens you stack up or how much starch you apply to your collars, study after study shows that most active investors—retail or professional—end up below the benchmark. The longer the investment horizon, the less likely investors are to beat the overall stock market performance. In other words, they earn a negative alpha. Read part 6 for more details.

Such studies have given birth to the so-called *Efficient Market Hypothesis*, which says that you cannot find any underpriced securities. Rather, stocks and bonds are always priced adequately because investors have already incorporated all of the available information into the price. There is no room to be faster or smarter than the collective intelligence of all investors. To give you a simple example: An announcement that a government plans to subsidize chipmakers will have a positive effect on companies producing chips, therefore sending their share price up. But by the time the news reaches the investor, the market has already factored this development into the price. Even prior rumors of such an announcement would be reflected in the pricing. So this view holds that it is impossible to outperform the market solely with publicly available information.

This is why a huge portion of today's invested assets is in passive funds, which are funds that track an index like the S&P 500 or the Nasdaq. This is a battle-tested strategy for long-term accumulation of wealth. And it is one that works on autopilot. You don't have to pick stocks or take bets on technologies and macroeconomic trends. If, however, you believe as much as I do that technology will remain the major engine of economic growth, then the average return is likely not good enough for you. Innovation is accelerating. So is tech adoption. And there is no shortage of breakthrough technologies getting off the starting blocks that will upend our lives.

I argue that by skewing (parts of) your portfolio toward technology, you can beat the benchmark. I call this phenomenon *technology alpha*. The market benchmark will be defined as the S&P 500 returns. As the formula at the top puts it, technology alpha is the difference between the returns of your tech investments and the returns of the S&P 500.

The entire purpose of this book is to enable you to earn a positive technology alpha by choosing the right tech at the right time while avoiding the most perilous pitfalls. Though investing in technology is risky and history might not repeat itself, I am deeply convinced that technology alpha is the best road to achieving alpha in general, given a smart strategy and long investment horizons. All 100 charts in this book hold important lessons on how to get it done.

> *"If you tell me that many of my best performing Rule Breakers
> are technology companies, I would agree, but I also would want
> us to agree or define what we mean by technology company. I
> would say technology is so ubiquitous today. It is so important. It
> is ever changing and generally improving. And so for this reason,
> it's not surprising that the world beaters, the Rule Breakers of*

this past generation, no doubt this next generation, *are going to be companies that are masters of making technology helpful for human flourishing."*

—DAVID GARDNER, co-founder of the Motley Fool
and author of *Rule Breaker Investing*

2

About Change Vectors and Scenario Planning

WE ARE ALL TRYING TO TELL THE FUTURE. Retail investors, hedge fund managers, VCs, day traders. Each of us has our own investment hypotheses, a vision of what tomorrow will look like. And each of us is convinced that our version is the inevitable way things will play out. That conviction hardens the more we research and the more numbers we crunch. Most of us will be wrong. That's a fact. So simply trying to figure out the most likely future is negligent in traditional sectors like retail or manufacturing. It is fatal in the technology world. Exponential progress and countless interdependencies diminish the odds of correct future projections. Hence, your investment strategy should always be built to succeed in multiple possible and likely futures.

The mono-dimensional approach might work for prognoses and forecasts, things that will happen in the next few months. But this is not what tech investors should be aiming for. The best tech investors don't chase quarterly results. They also don't try to guess outcomes decades in advance. That's a space best left to science fiction authors. Instead, there is a sweet spot of hitting the right nascent technology. In other words: Successful tech investors get in early on the trends that will balloon over the next couple of *years*, rather than months or decades. This is the only area where beating the market is plausibly possible because this is where the market becomes inefficient. Still, keep

CHART 2

The sweet spot for technology investors

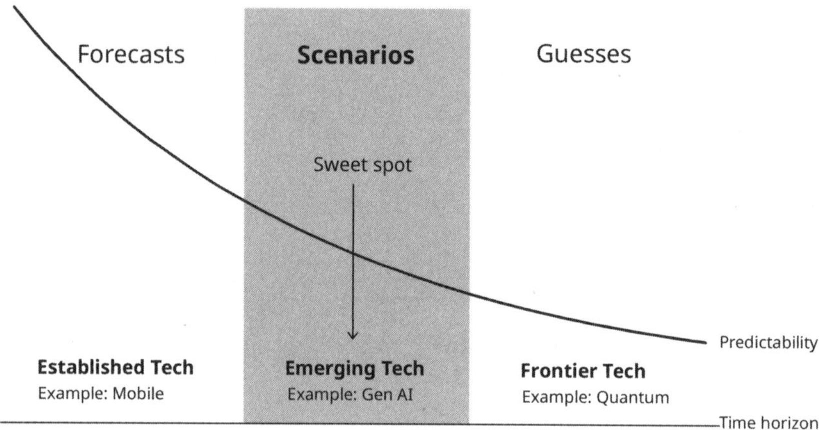

Chart: Igor Pejic

long-shot technologies on your radar. Those might turn into acute scenarios overnight.

To be prepared for the most likely of these mid-term futures, companies and professional investors have long resorted to scenario planning. It means they identify and rehearse strategic options for various possible futures. Scenarios can be very broad. For tech investors a scenario might be that a certain technology makes its breakthrough, that adoption for another one is killed by regulation or a competing tech, or that a certain company or group of companies benefit or are disrupted by an innovation.

So how do you build and assess scenarios? Listen to professional fortune tellers, aka experts? You might want to read chapter 44 about experts before doing so. My suggestion is to keep your future in your hands. To do so, start by pinpointing so-called change vectors. These are the raw material from which scenarios are formed. Change vectors are not technologies, but rather directions in which the market and the world are moving. Many change vectors are well known. Think miniaturization (gadgets getting smaller), automation (letting software and robots do repetitive or heavy tasks), decentralization (distributed computer infrastructure), or datafication (measuring and recording everything). Change vectors are the direction in which things are going for the long haul. Those changes usually transcend industries or technologies. Miniaturization and datafication, for example, have been enablers for the recent AI boom, but they also drove countless other technologies such as wearables and the Internet of Things (IoT). The trends I mentioned are all solution drivers, but demand drivers are just as important. Say a shrinking working population or diminishing natural resources.

At the very least, scenario planning helps to stress-test your investment strategy. At best, it results in a portfolio that performs well in many if not most of the plausible futures. You don't need to have the precision of a surgeon or a physicist. Vector trajectories are messy and bring unforeseeable side effects. Yet they lay out clearly the lines along which technologies and markets move.

3

About Risks, Rewards, and Exponentiality

SO HOW CAN YOU GO ABOUT ACHIEVING technology alpha? Before we answer that, we need to look at a defining characteristic of the technology sector: Exponentiality. Whereas in most industries linear progress is the rule, tech is defined by a mix of seemingly unpredictable phases of breakneck growth, long periods of stasis, sky-high expectations, bitter disappointments, and much more. Frequently, valuations are rooted in hype more than in earnings and profitability. Game changers occur overnight. Or never at all.

Is technological progress thus completely arbitrary and chaotic? No. Different? Yes. Trickier to forecast? Certainly. But technological adoption passes through cycles that are well understood by researchers studying the history of technology. They are hard to detect early, but there are indicators.

In investing, exponentiality also means that humans are very poor in judging risks and rewards. They tend to underestimate both. Hence,

CHART 3

Tech investment decision map

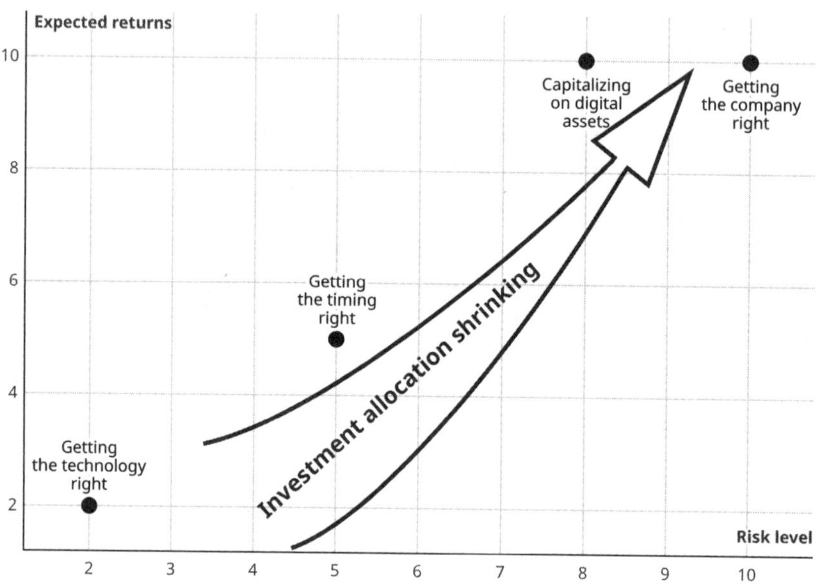

Baseline = S&P 500 performance

Chart: Igor Pejic

containing your risk is crucial. There are two ways to do so. First, investing only a portion of your assets in technology. For example, a conservative investor might keep 80% of investable assets in bonds and broad index funds and only 20% in tech-specific investments.

Second, select the strategy that fits your risk appetite. In the chart you see the different approaches and the trade-off between risks and returns. The basic aim should always be to separate those technologies that will fail from those that will succeed. The best case is to spot tech that will be truly transformative to the economy. Investing in a winning technology is no alchemy, yet it will beat the benchmark. If you had anticipated the AI wave, you would have had quite a ride had you invested in a fund covering the entire semiconductor sector or a general AI ETF.

From there, alpha and risk jump exponentially. Getting the timing right can mean the rewards are multiple times higher. Had you bought your semiconductor fund in 2015 and held it long enough, you would have beaten the average market benchmark. But if you got in shortly before ChatGPT hit the market in November 2022, your total returns would have gone through the roof. But had you waited too long, you would have probably done worse than investing too early. Needless to say, hitting the right timing is much trickier than just hitting the right technology. You have to pour money into a tech either shortly before or at the beginning of its growth trajectory.

To win the ultimate jackpot, an investor must not only pick the right tech at the right time but choose a specific company that will benefit from it disproportionally. Say an NVIDIA over Intel or Texas Instruments before the AI frenzy broke out or an Amazon before the e-commerce boom swallowed countless retailers. From today's perspective, the rise of these giants might seem inevitable, but just think of how many companies selling stuff online went bust. And of the survivors, none even came close to Amazon. You wouldn't expect to guess the right number in a game of roulette, and there are many more tech companies than fields on a roulette table. It's not to say that it can't be done or shouldn't be attempted, but keep in mind that hindsight bias is one of investors' biggest enemies.

Recently there was an alternative route for obtaining an exceptionally high technology alpha: Digital assets. In particular, their largest subcategory cryptocurrencies. Led by their front-runner Bitcoin, these assets take the tech sector's exponentiality to a completely new level. Historically, they have performed better than any one asset class, but the stellar growth has routinely been contrasted with sharp declines. If tech stocks are a different ballpark to regular companies, then digital assets are a completely different universe to tech stocks. They don't just work by different rules but by different laws. Each digital asset has its own mechanisms and economics, which magnify the extreme complexity of the crypto sphere. Investors not willing to dive deep in order to understand the asset class *and* each asset individually should keep their fingers from cryptocurrencies. It's a huge pity, but it's better that way.

As you will see throughout the book, exponentiality is baked into every aspect of the tech world. Risks, returns, venture capital, adoption—just to mention a few. AI had been around since the 1950s. For more than 70 years, it had close to zero private users. Then, in 2022, their number skyrocketed to 100 million within just two months. Apple put that many iPhones into users' pockets within three years, despite smartphones being a completely unknown technology and despite coming with a hefty price tag for customers. Decline can be hypersonic too. Ask Nokia and Siemens about their phone businesses. Exponentiality is what makes tech unpredictable and that is why the market for tech investing can never be truly efficient. Exponentiality is thus the main enabler of tech alpha.

4

___

What Makes a Technology Company?

THE TERM *TECHNOLOGY* has suffered from higher inflation than any fiat currency. Whether you read the press release of a carmaker or the mission statement of a paper printing company, there is more talk of technology than about constructing SUVs or printing billings. Talk of technology likely even tops sustainability and diversity in quarterly earnings calls. Save yourself the time and ignore these companies bragging about their tech strategy right away.

But how about companies that legitimately revolve around technology? Many bank CEOs, for instance, claim they are tech companies with banking licenses. They do have a point in that the vast majority of a bank's resources are invested in tech. So where do you draw the line? With banks, it is easy. You either have a license, or you do not. But tech is not regulated in any sense. How about a company that uses technology? Too broad. A company that creates tech tools? Too narrow. How about those listed on the tech-heavy Nasdaq index? Not precise enough. It would include the retailer Costco or the beverage manufacturer PepsiCo.

A much better guide is the number of engineers and software developers a company employs. Yet a look at the chart for this chapter will tell you that this indicator only goes so far. Yes, Big Tech companies

CHART 4

Number of tech workers per company

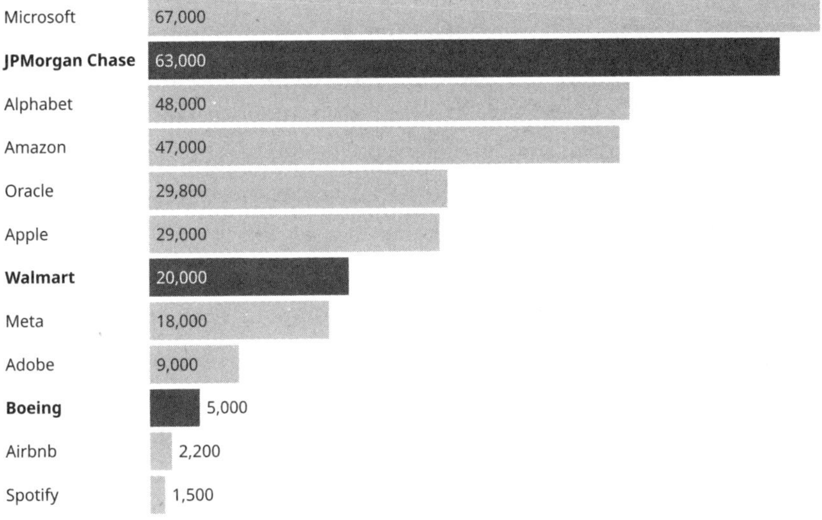

Non-tech companies in bold and dark gray. Tech companies in light gray. This is not a complete list of the largest employers of software developers.

Chart: Igor Pejic • Data from: Outtalent, JPMorgan, Boeing, Walmart

dominate the roster, but JPMorgan Chase has more tech staff than any of them except Microsoft. America's biggest bank easily beats Alphabet, Apple, and Amazon. Walmart has more developers than Adobe and Meta, Boeing more than Airbnb or Spotify.

We seem to know intuitively that the companies in bold are not tech companies, but we need to do better than that. After all, investing in pseudo-tech companies will not yield technology alpha. In this book, I use the following definition: *A company qualifies as a tech company only in case its business model falls apart when you remove cutting-edge technology.*

To make this definition more operational, it helps to break it down to a couple of questions that you should ask about each presumable tech company: Would the company's competitive edge collapse if you remove cutting-edge tech from the picture—i.e., would it lose significant market share against its competitors? Does the revenue stream of a company depend primarily on a unique technology? What is the ratio of a company's R&D budget compared to its peers? Are the business models different to the competition? Do those models involve network effects or platform economics?

The best illustration is Tesla. Unlike GM or Peugeot, it is a tech company more than a car manufacturer. Its design might be sleek, and its engine might work reliably, but that's not the reason people buy a Tesla rather than a Chevrolet. It is the autonomous driving module and Tesla's status as an electric vehicle pioneer. Hence, technology is the driving edge of the company. Walmart leverages technology at a fascinating scale, but if we were to wake up in a world without robots or the internet, the Beast of Bentonville would still be the undisputed number one retailer. Tech is a tool, but its core competitive advantage stems from somewhere else.

Working with a clear definition of a tech company is not semantic hair-splitting. All the rules and principles I describe in the book apply to tech companies only. They will work for Tesla and Amazon, but not for GM or Walmart.

11

WHY INVEST IN THE TECH SECTOR?

THIS ENTIRE BOOK RESTS ON THE ASSUMPTION that investing in technology is worthwhile. Nobody will doubt technology has captured the world economy and performed exceptionally well. As you will see in this part's chapters and charts, the recent high-tech age has birthed global corporate behemoths unseen in history. King Midas would be jealous of the wealth founders and investors have raked in. It has never been easier to become a trillion-dollar company. The hunt for unicorns heaves ever younger startups to billion-dollar valuations. And legions of tier-two tech companies, which still boast valuations of hundreds of millions, have entrenched their positions. But what does this tell us about the future? With such a track record, how much more room is there to grow? How do we know tech companies will not stagnate or even be cut back to size? After all, past performance is a poor indicator for the future. On the contrary, historic evidence shows yesterday's top performers are more likely to underperform today. Before joining the top 10 in terms of market cap, companies boast double-digit returns. Afterward, those fall close to zero and even below (see chapter 56).

Tech is different. As the charts throughout this part make clear, its growth is nowhere near its end. Even before we factor in emerging technologies, the potential to be tapped seems limitless. Collapsing software costs guarantee profitability. Tech's push into ever more industries guarantees expansion.

Big Tech is often compared to the corporate empires of the robber barons, America's industrialists of the 19th century. That comparison is misleading. The robber barons grew as big as they could only to suffer the unavoidable fate of having their empires shattered by trustbusters. Not so Big Tech. It operates in almost every country. It can enter almost every industry. It can blitzscale. Funding is never a problem. This breadth of possibilities lets them evade the trap of insurmountable monopolies that could be challenged. There is no ceiling in sight yet.

Even more: I believe tech is the *only* source of super-growth that developed markets have left. Over the past decades, growth and profitability came from three sources. First, there was the opening up of emerging markets. Tariffs and trade barriers were slashed. A deep optimism took hold. The spread of democracy and free markets seemed inevitable. It was "the end of history," as political scientist Francis Fukuyama so eloquently put it. People predicted ever closer ties between countries, fewer wars, and more stable investment environments. In the mid-2020s, it appears that vision has faltered. It turned out that the seeds of democracy and capitalism don't grow everywhere. Free trade agreements are ripped to shreds, flourishing absolutist regimes meddle arbitrarily into stock markets, and Europe is witnessing the most devastating war since WWII. It is hard to imagine international investments as a future growth engine any time soon.

The second historic driver was cheap money. Ever since the end of the financial crisis in 2009, interest rates hovered around zero. Neither companies nor individuals saw much sense in keeping their money under the mattress. US equities in particular had a bull marathon. They outperformed everything from gold and bonds to international stocks. Then inflation struck. Russia's invasion of Ukraine ended the low-interest prosperity. Within a year, interest rates shot up and suddenly stood at 5% in May 2023 and persisted at that level. Though inflation has been curbed, there is a long road back to zero. Even Warren Buffett admitted eye-popping returns are highly unlikely.

Yet despite the disappointment with internationalization and rocketing interest rates, the US stock market reigns supreme. This is due to the third historic growth driver: High-tech leaps. When Covid broke out in 2020, much of the world was pushed to use basic digital capacities. Internet connection, VPNs, and laptops with cameras—these were all long established, and most companies had them available. Yet only during the lockdowns did they unleash their entire potential, when managers could no longer insist on business travel and office commutes. Tech adoption that would have happened over 10 years was compressed into one. Zoom conferences, home office computers, and grocery deliveries catapulted technology companies to giddy heights.

Many experts predicted that overblown valuations would soon be corrected. After all, adoption was finished, so where should the growth come from? Pharmaceutical companies had their heyday with Covid vaccines, but after the pandemic they returned to normal. Not so tech players. They proved remarkably stable even as people once again started to leave their homes. So, how does one explain the continued outperformance of the tech sector?

The answer lies in tech's biggest strength: The industry never stands still. The Covid era was about spreading state-of-the-art technology across the economy. Now, more groundbreaking shifts have been set in motion. AI and blockchain are promising to unleash an automation wave across literally every industry. Privatization of spaceflight and advances of gene editing are cutting costs to a fraction of what they used to be. And physicists are working on their dream of an affordable quantum computer, a machine that will be 100 million times faster than today's computers.

If history teaches us anything it's this: People and companies will keep innovating. When they innovate, they disrupt. And this is why technology will always keep soaring back to the center of the economy. It might be overvalued at a certain point in time, but eventually it knows only one trend: Upward.

Won't technology be disrupted itself? Yes, but only by other technologies. The steam engine had to yield to the electric motor. Mainframe computers were replaced by PCs. PDAs by smartphones. Today, solar energy is challenging oil and gas. Investing in technology is like investing in change itself. The tricky thing is to seek out the right change.

5

The Global Economy Remade

SMARTPHONES ARE A DAILY REMINDER of how technology has come to run our lives. For investors, the equivalent of smartphones are corporate market capitalizations. They show the worth of a company by multiplying the number of shares with the share price. No other indicator makes it as crystal clear that technology is running the economy. Glance at the chart and immediately you will recognize how tech companies (highlighted in bold) have captured stock markets.

While 20 years ago only Microsoft and Intel made the list of the largest companies, today we count nine tech firms in the top 10. Tech's triumphal march is one striking thing. The other is the sheer size of those players. Whereas General Electric headed the list in 2004 with a valuation of $300B, NVIDIA in 2025 is worth roughly 14 times that much.

Of course, corporate valuations always reflect the expectations of future returns. The tide can turn quickly. When investors get carried away, an aura of too-big-to-fail takes hold. Sometimes a market shock dramatically shakes them out of their false sense of security. The bursting of the dot-com bubble in 2000 was such a shock. In 1999, no less than six technology firms were among the 10 largest companies. Only the strongest internet-related companies survived that shakeout. And most of the survivors never regained their past glory. Cisco and Nokia might still be around, yet they linger in a category best described as tier-two tech.

It took more than a decade for the sector to recover from the dot-com meltdown. But it did. And it did so in the most remarkable way. In 2019, tech occupied seven of the top 10 spots. Back then, Chinese tech giants

CHART 5

Top 10 companies by market cap (in $T) 2004 vs. 2025

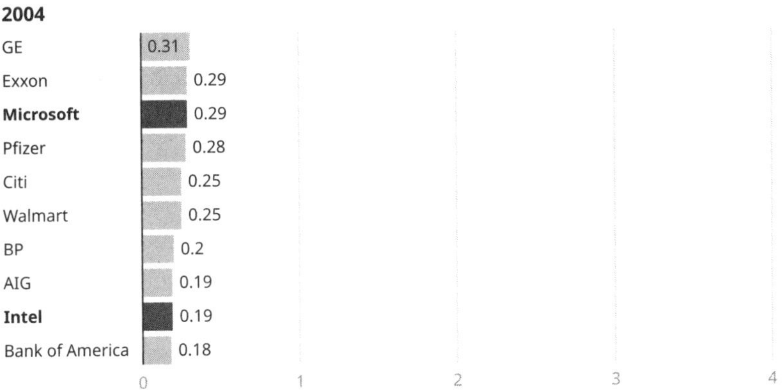

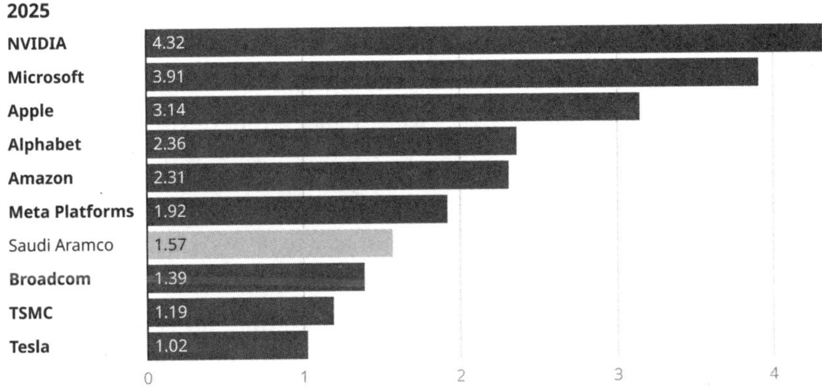

Tech companies in dark gray and bold.

Chart: Igor Pejic • Data from: companiesmarketcap.com; Economic Research Council

Alibaba (e-commerce) and Tencent (social media) made the list. Six years later, they had yielded their spots to semiconductor heavyweights NVIDIA and TSMC. Tech not only occupied nine of the 10 top spots, but corporate valuations exploded yet again. Microsoft, number one at the end of the '90s and again in 2019, almost quadrupled its market cap within six years. And it didn't even suffice to remain the largest company in 2025. The lesson: Long investment horizons are always good. In tech, they are imperative.

With such sky-high market caps, the inevitable question is this: Why should this insane growth persist? To answer it, look at the non-tech companies of 2004. None of them has failed in the last 20 years or committed a strategic blunder. On the contrary. Citi and Bank of America are still among the three largest banks in the US. Walmart is still the unchallenged number one address to get your groceries. And Pfizer had a stunning windfall when the entire world started jostling for Covid jabs. Yet this was nowhere enough to even come close to Big Tech valuations. The reason: Tech is the only sector with endless growth potential. There is only so much food a person can eat and only so many credit cards someone can max out. Technology, on the other hand, drives every single industry. Even more: It can *disrupt* every single industry.

Amazon sells stuff like Walmart, but it also rents out servers in the world's largest computer cloud, it produces smart speakers and reading devices, it films its own streaming content, and it runs an online payment channel. It is growing in multiple mega industries such as retailing, IT infrastructure, entertainment, finance, and many others at the same time. This approach makes growth not only limitless, but also faster. Increasing your market share from 10% to 15% is much easier than from 70% to 75%. That does not mean the tech sector won't be trimmed down to size in the near future, but it does mean that if this were to happen, there is plenty of room to roar back and outdo any historic records.

"This generation of tech companies especially has done a better job of staying ahead of the technology trends. Microsoft, in a different iteration, famously missed mobile, almost missed the internet. IBM missed the internet. Everyone said, why couldn't IBM do it? Because they were large incumbents and had great businesses, they were not as hungry to stay on the cutting edge. And I think that has changed and is materially different now. Just think about the AI transformation. Some of the companies investing the most in it are the Microsofts, Googles, Metas of the world."

—RICK HEITZMANN, founder and managing director at FirstMark Capital and CNBC's *Fast Money* commentator

6

Tech Titans vs. The World

MOST OF US HAVE A HARD TIME visualizing a trillion dollars. We know it has twice as many zeros as a million. Most of us will also know it is not twice that much, but a million times more. However, we are still struggling to intuitively comprehend the sheer scale of that number. What helps to truly grasp it is the comparison to something else. This is tricky for companies that have reached historically unprecedented scale like Big Tech. The only comparison that makes sense at this point is with states. Yes, entire sovereign states and their entire economic output.

To give you a sense of how large tech giants have become, the chart for this chapter compares NVIDIA's market cap with the GDP of each of the world's countries. All but three countries—the US, China, and Germany—have smaller GDPs. This means that the entire economy of countries such as Brazil, the UK, India, or France produces less output than it would take to buy one company. Equally striking is the trend: Just one year earlier, Microsoft headed the corporate valuation list. Back then, there were still six countries that had a bigger GDP.

Some commentators try to downplay this dominance, pointing to the British East India Company in the 17th–19th centuries. Not only that it controlled the corporate arena, but it also had its own army. It even outnumbered the British army at one point. All true, but Big Tech is a different caliber. While NVIDIA's software engineers and Microsoft's coders don't march across the globe carrying rifles, they are dominating markets in almost every country of the world. And they are joined by equally impressive peers. If you look at Apple, almost the same exact picture emerges. The iPhone maker has a market cap higher than all but seven countries' GDP. If you added up the valuations of the nine tech players that make the top 10 list, they would even eclipse the total economic output of China.

CHART 6

NVIDIA market cap vs. countries' nominal GDP

Bigger GDP ■ Smaller GDP

The comparison refers to 2025 GDP and market cap figures.
Map: Igor Pejic • Data from: companiesmarketcap.com; statisticstimes.com

To be fair, we are comparing the *output* of an economy with the *value* of a firm. The equivalent of a country's GDP would be the yearly revenue of a company. But this is beside the point. First of all, even in this comparison, Big Tech beats most countries. More importantly, the comparison in the chart shows the scale that private companies have achieved. This has only become possible thanks to the exponential age of tech.

7

Technology's Outsized Role in the Stock Market

INNOVATION UPENDS THE ECONOMY. Large tech stocks skyrocket. So the technology sector is sucking up ever more of the economy, isn't it? Actually, it is not. If you look at the number of people employed in the technology sector, they made up only 1.8% of the total workforce in 2023. Contrast that to health care with 12.8% or government with 11.8%.

Furthermore, the share is not even growing. Ten years earlier, it was already at 1.8%, and in 2032, it is forecast to be a meager 1.9%.

Maybe tech is simply a less labor-intense field, but it is the real GDP driver? Not quite either. While tech workers do contribute more to the GDP than their peers in other sectors, tech as an industry is not even America's GDP engine. In 2023, it accounted for 5.4% of the total economic output. Manufacturing contributed twice as much to the US economy. Finance four times as much.

In short: Technology companies have not taken over the economy. Nor are they going to any time soon. But they did take over the capital markets. Tech's dominance here is mind-blowing. IT companies make up 28% of the value of all publicly traded companies. The next sector is finance, reaching merely half of that.

CHART 7

S&P 500 by sector weights

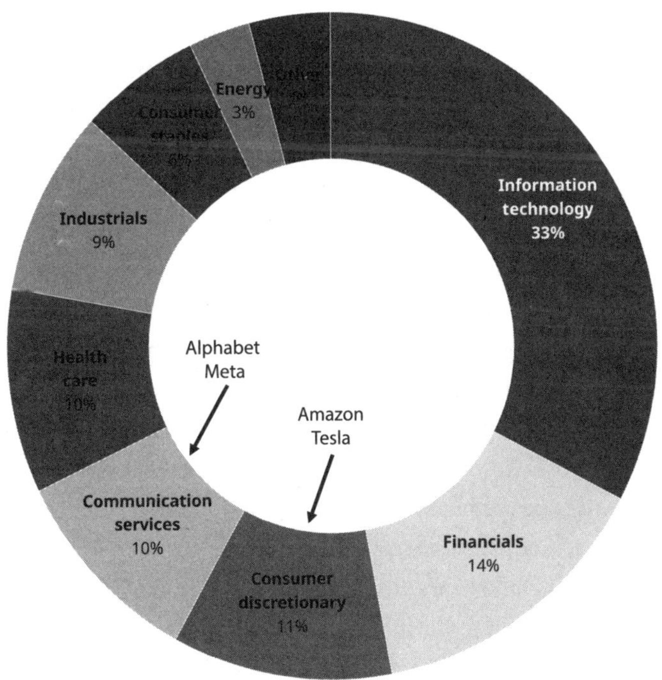

Data as of February 2025

Chart: Igor Pejic • Data from: Schwab

And here is where tech's dominance gets really mind-boggling. Many tech champions are not even part of the information technology index. Alphabet and Meta count as communication services. Amazon and Tesla fall under consumer discretionary. The outsized returns of biotech companies like BioNTech or Amgen are claimed by the health-care sector.

How can it be that investors seem to throw money at technology companies in such record amounts? And what does tech's dominance on Wall Street mean for your investment strategy?

First of all, tech companies being money magnets corroborates what I described in the introduction to this chapter: Investors see in them the major motor for future growth. These expectations have real consequences. Excess availability of capital accelerates technological progress and becomes a self-fulfilling prophecy. One person who has researched the impact of new technologies on economic growth like hardly anyone else is Alex Tapscott, the CEO of CMCC Global Capital Markets and the co-founder of the Blockchain Research Institute. He says, "The history of capitalism is the history of new technology innovations that begin as niche technologies. But as they scale and become more useful, they begin to disrupt the mainstream. They change how industries work. They open up new marketplaces. They enable new kinds of products." We've seen that time and again through history. Steam, electrification, the radio, transistors, and microprocessors. PCs. "In each of those different periods, there were humongous opportunities to invest in the market. There are also pretty significant risks. So, is it any wonder that technology is so influential in the business world?"

The tech sector's size in capital markets also gives it stability. Size itself is often reason enough to allocate capital to tech giants. To understand what I mean, look at Berkshire Hathaway. Warren Buffett's conglomerate soared to become one of the largest companies by buying up or investing in all types of businesses. And though Buffett has always shied away from tech, he made an exception for Apple. At one point it made up more than 40% of Berkshire's equity portfolio. A major reason: Berkshire has itself grown into a goliath. There is hardly any company outside of Big Tech whose performance could move the needle for Buffett's business. Many large asset and portfolio managers face the same issue.

8

Tech-Sector Returns in Perspective

SIZE IS GOOD IN MANY WAYS. Above all, large companies and sectors are more stable. But size usually also means that growth is slowing and might soon glide to a halt. Most gains have been realized. Like every organism, companies have a limit to which they can grow. And without growth, there are also no outsized returns. So to see if tech growth is behind us, let us have a look at how the technology sector has recently performed when measured against other sectors.

The results couldn't be much clearer. In 2023, the information technology sector saw a 57.8% return, whereas the S&P average was 26.3%. Keep in mind that a big chunk of the 26.3% was also driven by technology companies as they make up a large part of the index as we have seen in the last chapter. This makes the tech sector's outperformance even more significant. But could it be that 2023 was just an outlier? After all, one year earlier the sector *lost* 28.2%. So which year is the odd one?

This can best be answered by looking at the returns over a long stretch of time, say 15 years. In that period, 2022 was an outlier, the worst year on record. By far. It was actually the only year where the returns were significantly negative. Russia's invasion of Ukraine and the resurgence of the physical world post-Covid were exceptional events that led to a disastrous year for tech investors. But technology stocks did climb back impressively and continue to shoot up. As April Rudin, the founder and CEO of the Rudin Group, puts it succinctly: "Technology solves problems. As there will always be new problems, technology will always be coming back." She further explains that while there are hype cycles and eventually public interest wanes in a technology, it will be profitable as long as people are using it. "People are not talking about cloud computing as much as they used to, but still, it is raking in huge profits for giants like Amazon."

CHART 8

Yearly returns: IT sector vs. total S&P 500

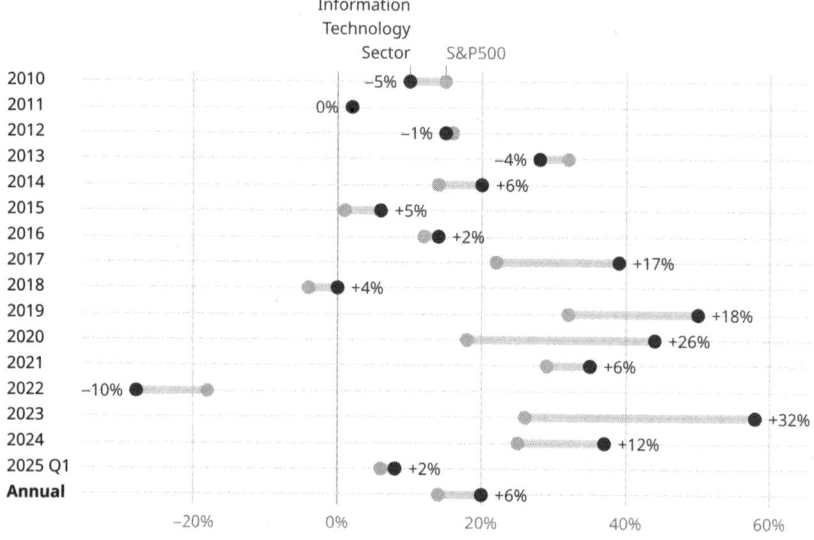

Returns represent total annual returns (reinvestment of all distributions) and do not include fees and expenses.
Chart: Igor Pejic • Data from: Novel Investor

I will discuss further what causes investor optimism in chapters 13 to 15. Before that, however, let us look at the impact 2022 had on the long-term returns of the tech sector. If we aggregate the performance over the last 15 years, technology stocks had a significantly better return than the general market. The annualized returns for the S&P 500 benchmark reached 13.9%. Impressive results, but tech even outstripped those. Its returns per year reached 19.8%. Apart from information technology, of the 11 sub-segments only one other (consumer discretionary) beat the overall S&P 500 index.

And don't forget what we have learned in the last chapter: The figure excludes many top-performing tech giants. Amazon, Meta, or Tesla have all been fueling the S&P 500 rally over the last few years, yet they don't even count into the 19.8% yearly returns. This is what I refer to as *hidden technology alpha*. Technology alpha is the difference between the market benchmark and the tech sector as measured by the official sector categorization of companies. *Hidden* technology alpha, on the other hand, also includes companies such as Amazon or Meta in the tech sector—i.e., all tech companies according to the definition in chapter 4.

Pinpointing hidden technology alpha is critical when selecting an investment vehicle. As for our following discussions, I will still use the information technology index as an approximation of how well tech does. It will keep things more consistent and avoid cherry-picking. But as we go along, keep in mind that the actual delta for tech vs. non-tech is significantly higher if you apply our chapter 4 definition of what makes a tech company. It includes all companies where tech is at the core of the business model.

9

The Rule of 72 and the Compound Effect

EVERY INVESTOR OUGHT TO BE FAMILIAR with the concept of compounding. When you take out a loan, you don't just pay interest. You pay interest on your interest. And when you reinvest your dividends, you earn a return on your return. In both cases, time works for those who are putting up the money. The capital snowballs. With every additional year, the effect gets disproportionally bigger. But humans are terrible at understanding exponential growth. They are also terrible at understanding the effect of time. It is why we are prone to cognitive biases that result in costly mistakes. Many people don't care whether they have to pay a 5.00% or a 5.50% interest rate on their mortgage. It seems like a small difference but easily ends up in a five- or even six-figure difference in total interest paid.

Investors might consider themselves more financially literate, but they fall for the same trap. Over the years, trading fees and fund manager costs can add up to a fortune. The same is true for returns. We fail to grasp the huge impact slight differences have in the long run. As we just saw, tech's returns are substantially above the market, so the long-term gap is tremendous.

CHART 9

$10,000 invested over time

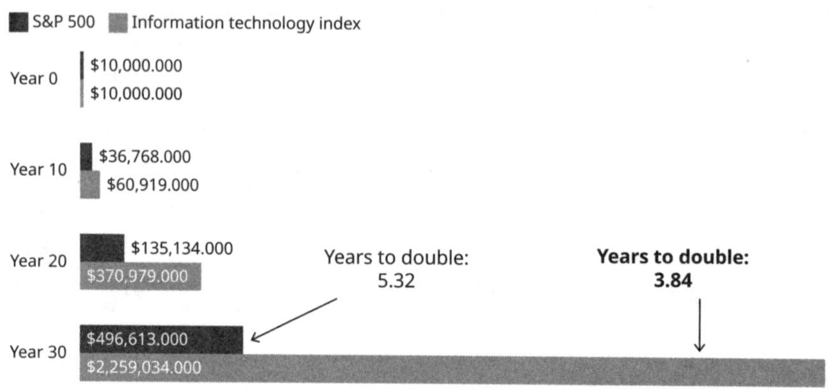

Hypothetical calculation assuming the annualized returns over the past 15 years as described in the previous chapter. Past performance is no guarantee for future results.

Chart: Igor Pejic

Luckily, there is a mental shortcut to make those snowball effects more tangible: The rule of 72. It is a quick formula that tells you how fast your investment will double in value, given an annual rate of return. You simply divide 72 by the return percentage and you get the doubling interval. So, for a 10% return, the calculation is: 72/10 = 7.2 years. That's how long it will take you to double your money.

The rule is an approximation. For the precise calculation, a more complex formula exists, but for our discussion it doesn't make a difference. For equities, nobody can tell whether an investment will yield 9.5% or 11.2% in the coming years anyway. I shall mention, however, that the rule of 72 has to be adjusted for the tech world. The formula works best for growth between 6% and 10%. For every 3 points outside of this range you should add or subtract 1 from the initial calculation value—i.e., 72. Take for instance the annualized 13.90% the S&P 500 benchmark yielded over the past 15 years. The more precise calculation would be: Adding 2 (for the 6 points higher than 8%), so the formula is: 74 / 13.9 = 5.3 years. For the 20% returns of tech-investments, you would have to add 4 (20 − 8 = 12 and 12 / 3 = 4). So, the formula looks like this: 76 / 20 = 3.8 years.

So, assuming the trend of the last decade goes on, you would double your money with tech two years earlier than going with the general stock market. So far, nothing surprising. It only gets impressive when you look at that effect over a longer period. Let's assume an S&P 500 investor and a tech investor both stick with their average growth rates for 30 years. The tech investor would have roughly doubled his investment eight times and his peer five times. Had both initially invested $10,000 and reinvested their gains, the average stock market investor would have a portfolio worth $497,000, whereas the tech investor would boast a wealth of $2,259,000.

Of course, sustaining the 20% return in the future is anything but given. And we will discuss this problem in the next chapters. The lesson, however, is this: Even if you outperform the benchmark only slightly, over time the difference that accrues is counterintuitively huge. The rule of 72 is a good reminder that time and patience is everything in investing. If you stick with your strategy, even investing in something as broad as the "technology sector" can yield incredible results.

"Our brains do not think in exponential terms. It is really hard to even grasp. There is a silly experiment in which you take a penny and double it every day for 31 days. The outcome is $10,800,000. A couple days in, we are not even over a dollar yet and then suddenly it is in the thousands and beyond. That steep end of the curve is really challenging.

One exercise is to think about compounding is just to take a look at where you were three years ago. We don't often notice how far we have come in these incremental small changes if we look at them every day, but only from a distance."

—CARL RICHARDS, creator of the *Behavior Gap* and
The Sketch Guy column in *The New York Times*

10

Tech-Sector Behavior Across Business Cycles

THE RULE OF 72 ILLUSTRATES THE SIGNIFICANCE of long investment horizons. Yet it is not just because of the compounding that you should refrain from short-termism, but also because of volatility risk. Technology is much more volatile than any other asset class bar one: Real estate. And it is also highly responsive. Tech reacts much faster to macro developments than almost any other sector. Just think of how long it takes until a change in interest rates trickles down to house prices. Thus, the potential downside can be much harder to anticipate in tech.

This is not to say that downturns in tech valuations come out of thin air. They are not isolated. On the contrary. Macroeconomic cycles are the heartbeat of temporary tech returns. Macro cycles don't move in lockstep with innovation cycles. And their impact is different. Macroeconomic trends are usually felt more quickly on the share price but are less profound. This chapter's chart depicts the average sector returns between 1960 and 2019, split into the major business cycles: Recession – Recovery – Expansion – Slowdown.

In the analyzed 59 years, the US lived through seven recessions, which means that GDP fell for two consecutive quarters. During recessions, tech performed worse than almost any other sector. Returns were negative by 20%. After those periods of contraction, tech usually rebounds. In these recovery phases, it grows at 28% on average. In the subsequent expansion phase, it even performs better than any other sector, before returning to mediocrity in the slowdown phase.

Technology performs best when there is market optimism. These periods are so strong that they sustain the overall outstanding performance of technology stocks. Thereby they benefit from the fact that economies are continuously growing over the long haul. While

Tech sector behavior across business cycles

Average period returns between 1960 and November 2019

Recession

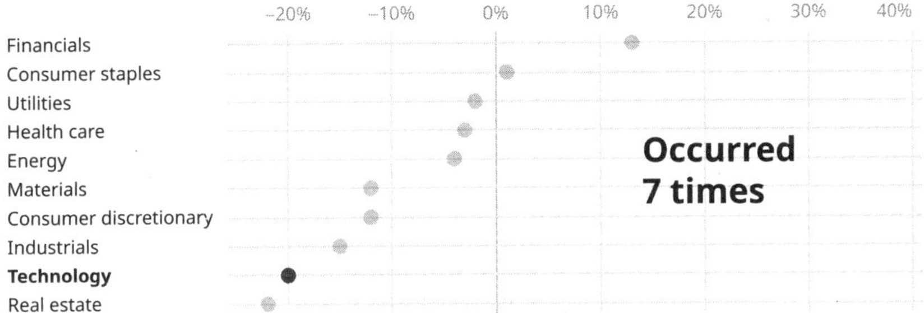

Recovery

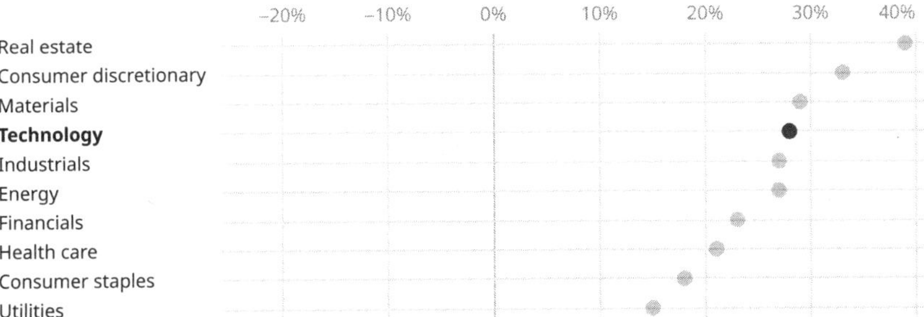

Expansion

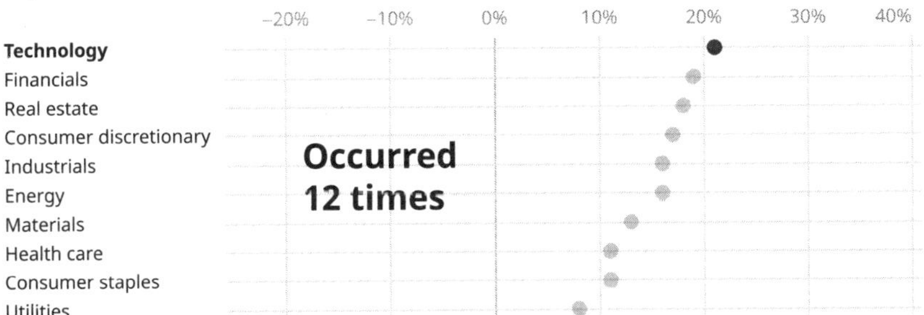

Slowdown

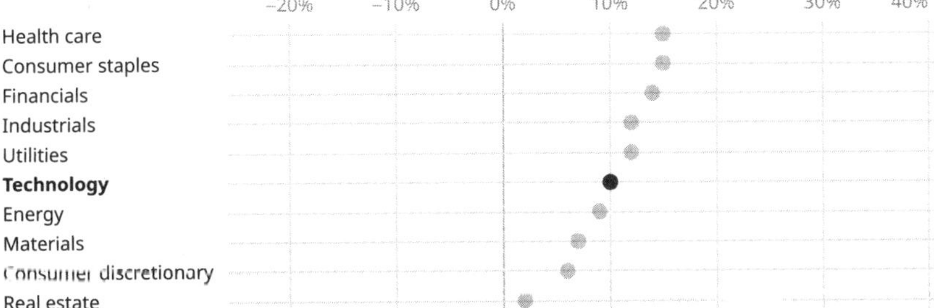

Chart: Igor Pejic • Data from: Kenneth French Data Library and SPDR Americas Research

there were seven recessions since 1960, there were 12 expansion phases. In other words: The economy grew 12 times beyond its pre-recession levels.

Tech does not only benefit from market optimism; it often creates it. This complex interplay enables outsized returns during the expansion phase. At the same time the chart shows that technology is everything but a recession-proof category. The gut reaction to the chart might be an urge to buy tech stocks during a recession. That would be a good strategy if you could predict the end of a recession. But you can't. Neither can top economists, at least not with certainty.

Nor can anybody predict the start of recessions. Hence, if you are looking to grow your money in the technology sector you should be willing to keep it invested for multiple market cycles. The only way to be successful continuously is to amortize tech's high losses with even higher returns. And as our expert comment in this chapter stresses, you always have to distinguish between the effect macro has on the share price and the effect on the balance sheet. Those are not the same thing.

"The way I've looked at technology in the past 20 or 30 years is that you have secular waves of technology that can last multiple years. And during that time you have different macro cycles, and tech stocks are very influenced by them. It's usually a slowdown and a recession that impacts tech.

But even in slowdowns and recessions, companies rarely pull back on most tech spending because they feel like it's going to provide productivity and opportunities to leverage fixed costs.

So tech spending cycles are relatively shallow, but the stocks react much more than the actual spending trends simply because they're high beta stocks against the market. So, typically, in a market that's going down, high beta would go down more regardless of what the fundamentals are.

So I think the hard part for investors is to separate the fundamental strengths of the innovation cycle from the fact that

*there's beta and there's high multiple. You have to understand
that in down markets those things will be bigger than the secular
drivers. You just have to risk manage that accordingly."*

—SAM RAHMAN, portfolio manager at
Hedgeye Asset Management

11

The Misunderstood Cost of Volatility

EVERYBODY THINKS THEY UNDERSTAND VOLATILITY. Most don't. Or at least
our brains don't until we actively switch on our neocortex. We compare the gains and the losses of an asset, and if the gains are higher, we
assume it is a sound investment. We even assume it is a better investment
than an asset appreciating slowly, but steadily. And here most of us fall
into another cognitive trap, a shortcut that makes us underestimate the
downside. Investing as a discipline has grown to unnecessary complexity.
But in the case of volatility, a spreadsheet might not be the worst idea.

What we fail to take into consideration is this: When an asset drops
by 10%, it needs to gain 11% to recover. A 10% loss of 10,000 leaves you
with 9,000. But 10% of 9,000 is 900. We all understand that principle
when we reflect on it, but that's not how our brains are wired to work in
the split-second assessments we have to make when glancing at datasets

For regular downturns it might not be a big deal, but for volatile
assets it is. Try to give your knee-jerk answer to this: If it takes an 11%
appreciation to compensate a 10% loss, what would it take to come back
to the baseline after a 25% loss?

You are probably not rushing to a conclusion, since we just reflected
on this bias. And this is exactly *not* the natural way we are looking at
investment opportunities. You might have guessed it: The answer is
counterintuitive. It's 33%. A 50% hit requires a 100% recovery. And so on.
Have a look at the chart with the historical performance of the S&P 500's

S&P 500 information technology index (SPLRCT) performance

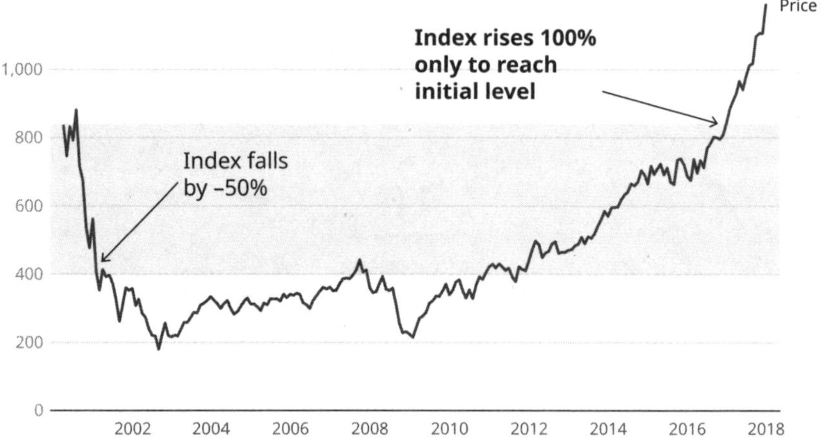

Chart: Igor Pejic • Data from: Investing.com

information technology segment. It crashed by 50% after the bursting of the dot-com bubble and it took 15 years to build a 100% appreciation to get where it was before the crash. The returns needed to offset the losses to grow exponentially. Hence, technology investors should pay special heed to this cognitive trap as they wrestle with much nastier volatility.

There is another characteristic of volatile assets that hinders many investors to be profitable. Once again, it is psychological: Loss aversion. Historic studies show that, over long periods, riskier stocks are more profitable than more stable bonds. Their gains outmatch the losses. Vanguard examined the performance of these two categories over the last 100 years and found that each allocation to bonds reduced your profitability. Thus, investing in stocks would have left investors richer across various market cycles. *Would* because many don't make it until the end of their envisioned time horizon.

Holding on to plummeting stocks is extremely tough, especially since markets in free fall usually coincide with a crisis hitting the entire nation or even the world. And crises are by definition times of uncertainty. Put yourself in the shoes of somebody who has their savings in stocks during the outbreak of the Covid pandemic. Lockdowns keep spreading faster than the virus itself as millions of people are dying. No vaccine is in sight. Every day a new sector of the economy grinds to a halt. Those are extreme events, but they happen regularly. 9/11. The collapse of Lehman Brothers. The war in Ukraine. Every couple of years an unthinkable scenario shakes the world. In the last chapter we said that a promising investment strategy should stretch across multiple business and technology cycles, meaning decades. So, if you invested for the last 25 years, you already witnessed four "once-in-a-lifetime" events. The psychological distress during those periods is enormous. Pursuing a high-volatility strategy makes it even worse. The result is many investment strategies abandoned at precisely the wrong point in time. "Volatility becomes something really hard if you're depending heavily on individual stock selection based on vibes, stories, or myths," reflects Carl Richards, creator of *The Sketch Guy* column in *The New York Times* and author of *Your Money*. "What you should ask instead is: 'If I thought this investment was a great idea at 100 and it's now at 50, I should be more excited, not less, because I can buy this great investment at half the price.' So it pays to remind yourself about the reasons for buying a stock in the first place before selling it. Check if your core assumptions are still valid and, if yes, you might be overreacting to what is happening around you.

12

Profitability Amidst Product Deflation?

THE MARKET-BEATING PERFORMANCE OF TECHNOLOGY companies can be explained by the optimism about their future. But optimism alone can make share prices jump only temporarily. Tech stocks, however, have been rallying for too long to be just based on empty promises. Rather, the sector has proven *sustained* profitability. The question is: How does it manage to pull this off in light of the price development of many products and services they are selling?

CHART 12

Consumer price index: Total vs. digital goods

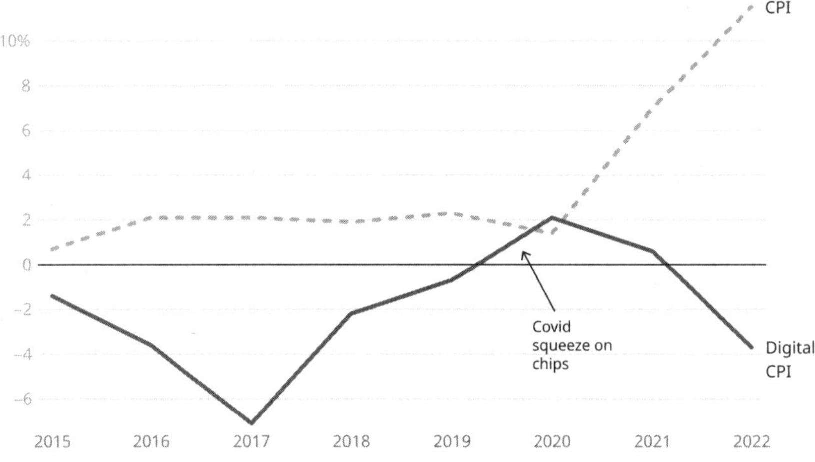

Data reflected until April 2022.

Chart: Igor Pejic • Data from: Innovation Frontier Project

Recently, most economies have been suffering from inflation rates not seen since the 1980s. At the pinnacle, in September 2022, some categories like out-of-home food saw price hikes above 90%. But one category is actually defying this trend: The digital economy. It doesn't matter whether we are speaking of smartphones, computers, household appliances, or many purely digital services: Their prices are actually shrinking. In the same period that food prices almost doubled, consumers paid 21% less for their phones.

Chart 12 confirms that tech deflation is not just supported by anecdotal and selective evidence. With the exception of 2020, high-tech kit got cheaper every year. And 2020 only saw a spike because of a global shortage of computer chips. Those are needed in any technical gadget, from cars to crypto miners and from phones to fridges.

Also keep in mind that the chart only captures the official deflation. The real one is impossible to measure. If the US Bureau of Labor Statistics examines food prices, it is comparing apples with apples. But how do you compare Apple's iPhone 14 to the iPhone 15? A better lens, a sleeker design, more processing power. None of those can be factored in, so you compare the latest iPhone in 2023 with the latest iPhone in 2022.

And despite the products getting better continuously, they are getting cheaper too.

Tech deflation is not a new phenomenon. For years tech products and services have been a moderating force on overall inflation. Just think of the free fall in prices for personal computers in the 1990s. Not to mention the panoply of services free of charge. Navigation, emailing, search, messaging, price comparison portals—you get the point. True, we are paying for them with our data and our attention, but at the end of the day we enjoy a host of services without our purchasing power being diminished. Without the mitigating impact of digital hardware and services, people would be getting significantly poorer.

That's good news for consumers, but what about the companies behind these services? If many of your services are free and those that you charge for are getting cheaper, how is it possible to keep up the profitability? After all, labor costs and rents are going up every year. Data protection standards get harsher and require more lawyers and documents. And on top, recently regulators have acquired a taste for levying record fines on Big Tech.

Partly, this paradox can be explained by a key characteristic of competition in the digital age: Platform economics, in which one or two winners take the entire market, before ramping up scaling effects the likes of Ford and Rockefeller would be jealous of.

Another explanation is that tech giants are moving away from those products that are increasingly under margin pressure—especially hardware—and moving toward the services business model. This strategy actually swallows a lot of the innovation budgets of tech behemoths. Sam Rahman of Hedgeye Asset Management points to Apple, which has grown its services segment to over 25% of the company. "Before, they had mainly hardware that was generating a margin of 35–40%. The margins of the services business are more like 65–70%." So, as the services business grows as a part of Apple, it moves the margins up higher. The investments they're making protect their core business but also allow them to invest in new initiatives and new growth areas. "The biggest part of Apple in terms of moat is the services business with the app store. Microsoft did the same with Azure, Amazon with AWS. They are not the same companies they were when they started out."

13

Putting Hopes in Collapsing Software Costs

WHEN CUSTOMERS ARE PAYING LESS FOR A GOOD, so are corporations. Thus, if both sides of the profitability equation—costs and revenues—move hand in hand, what is the problem? They often don't. New technologies have a healthy margin, but over time they suffer from commoditization. As prices come down, products get easier to produce, and new competition erodes the earnings potential.

This has been happening in the high-tech sector for basically all hardware. The plummeting costs of storage and bandwidth enabled databases, video streaming, and smartphones but eventually made hardware less profitable for the producers. Yet nothing was as consequential as the continuously eroding prices of CPUs. CPU is short for central processing unit. It can be thought of as the brain of any computer, phone, or smart device. CPUs are the chips coordinating the processing capacities of a gadget.

They are subject to a mechanism called Moore's Law. Put in simple terms, it describes how transistors get smaller and thus the chip performance goes up. It doubles roughly every two years. You could say it is akin to the rule of 72, only in technology terms. The continuous doubling results in exponentiality. Compare the power and price of your first PC with your latest laptop or smartphone and you will understand the principle. With prices tumbling and performance soaring, CPUs became commoditized and we could "waste" them, meaning put them into almost anything from fridges to fitness trackers. Today we have more smart devices in the world than people.

There has been one cost category, however, that has defied this trend: Software. In fact, the money it takes to build and maintain a computer program has gone up. Innovations such as the agile software development method or the proliferation of standard interfaces (e.g., APIs) promised to take down software expenses. Yet those gains have been

CHART 13

Who is using AI and for what?

Occupations using AI

Computer and mathematical	37%
Art, design, sports, entertainment, and media	10%
Educational	9%
Administration	8%
Life, physical, and social science	6%
Business and finance	6%
General management	5%
Legal	1%

AI usage by task

Develop and maintain software applications	17%
Program and debug computer systems	7%
Design and maintain database systems	2%
Produce and develop curricula and materials	2%
IT system administration and maintenance	2%
Produce and perform in film, TV, theater, and music	2%

Data and analysis based on millions of anonymized conversations on Claude.ai (The Anthropic Economic Index).

Chart: Igor Pejic • Data from: Anthropic

eaten up by the increased cost of labor. Wages for software developers were keeping pace with inflation, and even more. The other reason why software costs grow organically is the natural growth of entropy, which is jargon for complexity. With every new feature and every line of code, the interdependencies shoot up. Exponentially. For large programs, even miniscule changes can take months and cost a fortune.

But recently hope is dawning that we are approaching "software's Gutenberg moment." Generative AI is now at a level that it can radically disrupt the software business. Just as marketeers and translators can use applications such as ChatGPT to automate the majority of their tasks, so can coders. In fact, the AI firm Anthropic dug into the data to find out who is using its tool called Claude and for what tasks. Some professions like lawyers almost ignore it completely. Marketeers, artists, or researchers are more active users. But there is no doubt about the heaviest users of all: Coders. Software developers use the AI tool almost four times as often as the closest runner-up. They made up 37% of all queries, though they represent a meager 3.4% of the workforce. There is no doubt GenAI is a massive productivity booster for developers and thus tech companies.

But AI shouldn't be thought of in isolation, as managing partner at Fluent Ventures and author of *Out-Innovate* Alex Lazarow explains: "I think AI is part of a long-term trend to make it easier to scale. The SaaS-ification and the proliferation of APIs let you borrow the scale of much larger businesses. These things are in a trend where it is becoming easier and easier to build a startup anywhere. And AI is one thing in that trend." He recalls that he worked at McKinsey when PowerPoint came out and the legends of McKinsey were that 50 years ago you would have a 10-page slide deck that was drawn by hand. So, the decks were just 10 pages and were really concise. "And then PowerPoint happened, and now we're cranking out 100-page decks. With AI, things will be much easier to build, but customer expectations will go up. The amount of stuff that needs to get built will grow as well."

If software creation costs collapse, profits of technology companies will see a tremendous uplift. The operating expenses would be slashed. Tech giants spend up to half of their operational expenses on R&D (c.f. chapter 52), a large chunk of which could be eliminated with AI. That is a direct impact on the bottom line.

14

Growth and Revenues of Big Tech

WE HAVE SEEN TECH GIANTS' VALUATIONS break every ceiling. But is there any realistic hope for investors to recoup their high costs at some point? Tumbling software costs are a profitability promise whose impact on the balance sheet remains yet to be seen. And even if it does materialize, it will only truly be significant when coupled with large revenue growth.

Finance experts call this the jaws effect. If you plot the relationship of costs and revenues on a chart, it resembles the jaws of a shark. The larger the jaws, the higher the profits. In other words: If a company

CHART 14

Big Tech growth: Revenues vs. share price

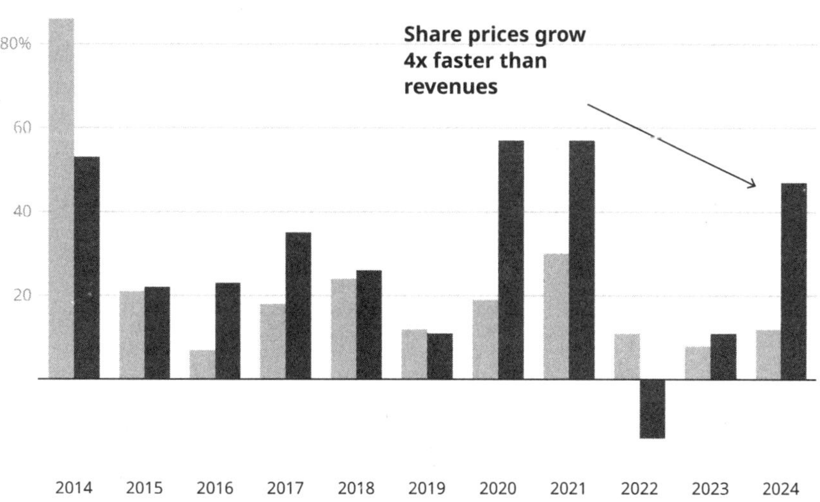

Combined revenue and share prices of Amazon, Apple, Microsoft, Meta, Alphabet, Tesla, NVIDIA.

Chart: Igor Pejic • Data from: Macrotrends; own calculations

has managed to get a good grip on its expenses, growth is all the more rewarding for shareholders because you get to keep more of every dollar earned.

With tech valuations reaching unprecedented highs, you would expect strong growth. To see if that is the case, I averaged the Magnificent Seven's development of sales and matched it with the development of their aggregated share prices. As the chart shows, Big Tech has no growth problem. Though it is slightly slowing, revenue growth per year is still solidly in the double digits. However, the revenues of large technology companies have not been escalating as quickly as the valuations. While in the early 2010s revenues were growing at a faster pace than the share price, 2024 saw a four times steeper stock price growth.

The growth trend of technology companies is challenged by many factors. Apple, for example, is heavily hit by people upgrading their iPhones less frequently. Tariffs against China hurt too. Alphabet and Meta suffer from US–China tensions as Chinese companies are spending less on digital ads abroad. Regulations such as the EU's Digital Markets Act and Digital Services Act limit the tracking of individuals and cut into the value of ads.

Plus, there is a natural limit on how many smartphones will ever be needed or how many hours a day people can stay glued to social networks. Every study suggests we are pushing those limits. Are corporate valuations ignoring these boundaries and thus treading on speculation territory? Not necessarily.

Though short-term growth is slowing, there is reason to be more optimistic for the long haul. Tech leaders are investing heavily into transformative general-purpose technologies such as AI and blockchain. If successful, they could also power a new foundational layer of the entire economy. Every industry will need AI algorithms, just as every industry needs phones, ads, or data centers. But the sales from these forays will still take time to materialize. For example, out of Amazon's 28% overall business growth, AI accounted for only 3%. The money AI services generate is still negligible, but the market has reached a consensus that they will explode at one point.

Second, Big Tech makes a credible point that it will be the driving force of any new tech revolution, because it has proven in the past that it can capitalize on its dominance. As the founder and managing director at FirstMark Capital, Rick Heitzmann, puts it: "Large tech companies are getting into markets where they can compound their network effect. So the Apple services business is now a giant in itself. It would be a Fortune 40 company if that was an independent business."

The third reason for the seemingly infinite tech optimism: the vast troves of data tech titans sit on. By now it has perhaps become a platitude that data is the new oil, but taking this metaphor at face value is shaping how investors make decisions. The explosion of generative AI has kicked the monetization of that data into high gear. More importantly, it did so in front of a closely watching public. The conclusion for many investors: AI algorithms can most efficiently be trained by our digital landlords—Big Tech. There is also another crucial reason for the optimism. More of it in the next chapter.

15

Sustaining Growth by Breaking Into Other Industries

GENERAL-PURPOSE TECHNOLOGIES (GPTS) give you pan-industry control over the infrastructure layer. But Big Tech has also used previous GPTs as a springboard to tackle entire mega-industries. Remember how the smartphone let Google and Apple capture the payments business? Or how the MP3 format let the iPod and iTunes upend the music industry? Many tech titans even have their very genesis rooted in new enabling technologies. Amazon used the internet to challenge booksellers. Google used it to syphon off ad revenue from newspapers and TV stations.

Those are all examples from the past. A very distant past by digital standards. But similar developments are going on today. Artificial intelligence is only the most recent example. It hands tech giants the tools to compete on hitherto inaccessible turf. Apple tried using AI to calculate credit default risks and thus threw down the gauntlet to the old masters of money. It works on capturing the value chain step by step.

Amazon revenue breakdown

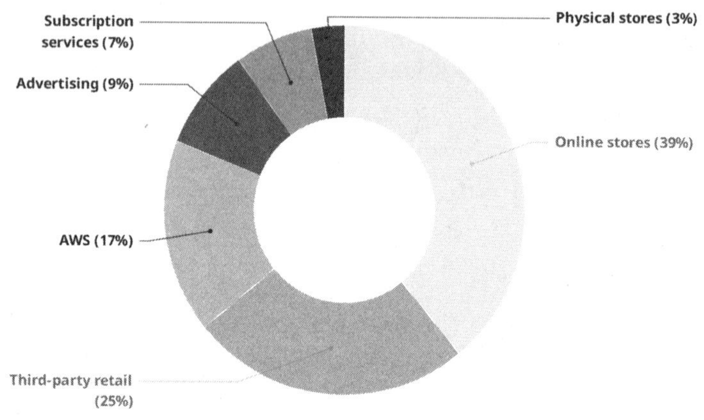

Apple revenue breakdown

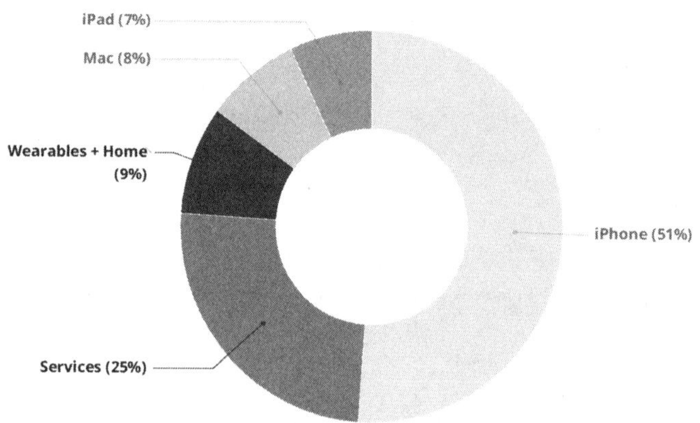

Microsoft revenue breakdown

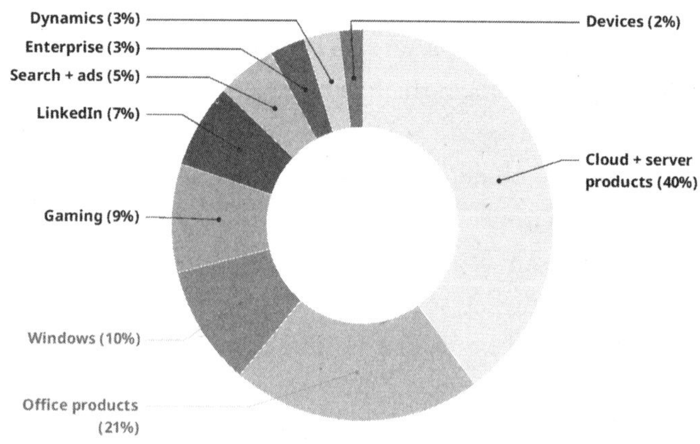

Categories in bold represent non-core business activities. 2024 figures for all companies.

Chart: Igor Pejic • Data from: Amazon, Apple, Microsoft, Visual Capitalist, Business of Apps

Amazon Go turns physical retailing on its head. Customers can simply walk out of the shop with their groceries in hand. No cashiers. No self-scanning terminals. Not even a tap with the credit card or phone. Thanks to machine learning and computer vision, the e-commerce giant is out to disrupt the entire cost structure of brick-and-mortar retailing too.

Innovation is a door-opener. It is a key that unlocks multiple arenas at the same time, allowing the largest companies in history to march on, growing and growing. Big Tech boasts an unmatched ability to tap into almost every industry, regardless of how far it is from its core business. Finance, music, cars, films, TV series, gaming. They even tried to go after core functions of the government. Facebook in 2019 attempted to issue its own global super-currency called Libra. It failed, but the project illustrates the brazen ambition. In earlier years companies like IBM and Oracle were happy to power different segments of the economy by building the infrastructure.

But how relevant are those nontraditional business lines, really? It depends on the company. Meta still makes more than 98% of revenue via ads. Alphabet earns money almost exclusively via ads and cloud computing. Yet Amazon, Microsoft, and Apple are very much diversified. Physical retail stores, ads, and subscription services now make up 19% of Amazon's revenue, and cloud computing alone accounts for another 17%. A fourth of Apple's revenues comes from services, which includes industries such as health, music, payments, TV, or news. If you count wearables too—an arena where Apple suddenly competes with luxury brands such as Rolex—then the iPhone maker earns a third of its sales in new industries. And a fifth of Microsoft's earnings hail from social networking, ads, and gaming.

These revenues come from technologies that have already become mainstream, things like mobile phones, sensors, or high-speed internet. They took a long time to build and so will revenues from AI or VR headsets. But the potential is there. What is also there is the proof that tech titans can tap into it. The (profitable) expansion to unrelated industries can be scaled to a point where it makes an important contribution to the bottom line. The crucial lesson is, despite the historic proportion of these companies, there is no growth limit in sight yet.

"At one point growth becomes a challenge. Take Tesla as an example. It has become fairly big, so the way to grow is by a new series of products. One is the robotic humanoid Optimus, which is a new product category starting from nothing. Then you have the robo-taxi possibilities.

And Elon Musk is invested in Neuralink that works on letting humans control computers with their thoughts, so he even sees what's coming after augmented reality glasses."

—ROBERT SCOBLE, publisher of *Unaligned* and *Scobleizer*,
former Microsoft strategist

III

GETTING THE TECHNOLOGY RIGHT

TELLING APART DISRUPTING TECHNOLOGIES from those that will fade into oblivion is the foundational building block of every tech investment. Even tech leaders have a hard time distinguishing between the two. It is a messy endeavor, one where crunching financial metrics is not enough. The solution is to understand patterns of technology adoption. Cycles, early trend indicators, and models such as the technology adoption life cycle are indispensable to grasp tech trajectors. We will discuss them in this part, as they belong in your tech toolbox. Yet while these models are easily applicable and often surprisingly reliable, keep in mind that they are heuristics, not laws of nature. Mental shortcuts that still might turn out to be wrong. Thus, even the best concepts and models must be analyzed in lockstep with other indicators. This triangulation is the only way to successfully and early on distinguish between technologies that will truly transform industries or economies and those that are just hyped up.

The first time you can tell apart those two with some confidence is when their adoption has reached a certain level. More precisely, when a technology has leaped over the chasm between visionaries and pragmatist adopters. Crossing this chasm is perhaps the most decisive point in a technology's journey. There are three ways to convince the pragmatist segment to adopt a technology. First, high-profile breakouts that set off a media frenzy. Second, efforts led by technology giants. Third, government-led adoption. We will learn what to watch out for in each of these to determine whether the technology's adoption can be sustainable. And we will also discuss whether a technology, once established, can fall back into the chasm. The electric car had dominated the streets a century ago, then yielded to gas-guzzling models, and is now set for a comeback. Or isn't it?

Electric cars are just one of many emerging technologies in which investors can look for growth. In fact, EVs are not even a particularly powerful tech. Chapters 25 and following show how to compare technologies in light of their potential for disruption and profitability. Platforms, transversality, and enabling technologies have become all-encompassing buzzwords sweeping across shareholder letters and LinkedIn walls alike. But used accurately, they can actually become the basis for comparing emerging and especially frontier technologies. The less market data is available about a new tech, the more important these techniques.

In the beginning of this book we talked about creating an investment strategy that will succeed in as many scenarios as possible. Keep that in mind as we look at the plethora of new technologies. They are all interdependent. They all compete for the same budgets and the same attention. You cannot build your investment theses by looking at just a handful of select technologies or even tech sectors. If you are a robotics fan eager to pour your money into drones, you cannot neglect what is going on in agentic AI, cybersecurity, and satellite communication. *Range* is what eventually makes a successful tech investor.

16

Telling Apart Tech Tops from Flops: The Chasm Where Technologies Die

GREAT COMPANIES ARE DEFINED BY GREAT PRODUCTS. But what is the difference between Ford's Model T and Sega's Dreamcast console? Between the iPhone and Google Glass? Hyper-successful products share many characteristics: Satisfying customer demand better than others, competitive pricing, clever marketing. But ultimately what makes them stand out is that they ride on the back of extremely successful technologies like the conveyor belt (Model T) or the smartphone (iPhone). The Sega Dreamcast, on the other hand, flopped after two years because it had ignored the nascent DVD standard. Google Glass failed to convince customers they should wear displays in front of their eyes because wearables failed in their attempt to dethrone smartphones.

CHART 16

The technology adoption life cycle

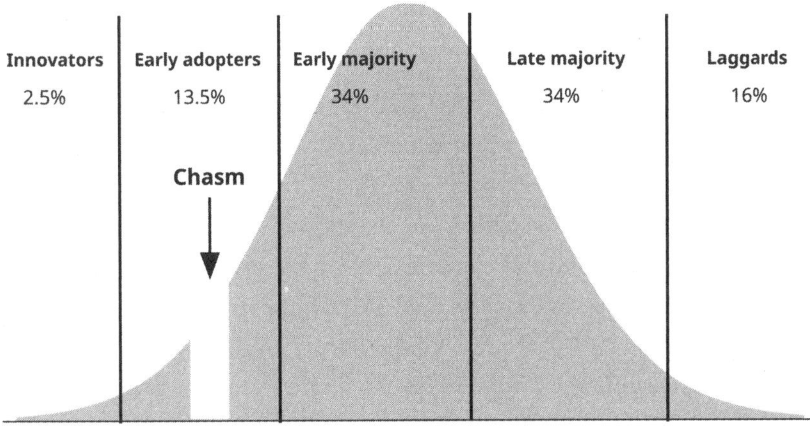

Chart: Igor Pejic · Data from: Based on *Crossing the Chasm* by Geoffrey Moore

So, the question really becomes: How can you forecast a *technology* that will be successful from one that will not? It is a critical question for investors and executives alike. There is usually no way to answer it from the start, but what investors can do is beat others to it. Meet the technology adoption life cycle. This tool—displayed in the chart—explains the trajectory of successful innovations.

No new technology will appeal to everybody at once. Instead, there are five different groups of people or companies: Tech enthusiasts (innovators), visionaries (early adopters), pragmatists (early majority), conservatives (late majority), and skeptics (laggards). People can be in different categories for different technologies. For example, many early adopters of mobile banking apps were people without access to PCs and laptops. That's why they were often quicker to use apps than tech aficionados. At the same time, they might not be the ones using ChatGPT to write birthday cards.

Many inventions are welcomed with open arms by tech enthusiasts and early adopters only to die painfully. They fall into the so-called *chasm*. In other words, they never get picked up by the mainstream market. The chasm is the most dangerous point for a technology. At the same time, it is a useful landmark for smart investors. The sweet spot of getting into a technology is located just after it has passed the chasm. It is when the large segment of pragmatists starts using it. When pragmatists adopt a technology, the conservatives will certainly follow. Laggards might still defy a new tech for a very long time. Yet they usually make up only a small portion of the market. Check the chart for the rough sizes of the categories.

The adoption cycle does not tell you anything about the speed of proliferation. The mainstream market can be convinced in months or in decades. There are some rare exceptions where technologies who cross the chasm don't make it after all (see chapter 24). Still, given that investing is all about probabilities, having crossed the chasm is the best indicator of whether a technology is worth your time and money.

The following rule of thumb is the best way to hit the sweet spot and lock in the best risk/reward ratio: Technologies meet the chasm usually between 10% and 15% adoption. This is the sum of most tech enthusiasts and visionaries of the total market.

17

Getting Stuck in the Chasm

WHEN FIGURING OUT WHETHER A TECHNOLOGY has crossed the chasm, don't believe the pundits. Don't believe the media buzz or your gut. Don't even believe the big capital flowing into a technology. Believe only hard figures on users. Or even better: Figures on *paying* users, also known as customers. Or best: Look at the number of customers in relation to the investments. If the ratio looks even remotely like the table below, run.

No failed hype illustrates this better than the metaverse. This elusive term means many things to many people. Perhaps the only thing they can agree upon is that it is a digital world, where people can socialize and play games with each other. In the future it might be a place where people also work and invest. An entire virtual economy so to say.

Some see the metaverse necessarily as an open and interoperable world built on decentralized blockchains and thus not controlled by a company or any other centralized entity. It is a setup defined by sovereign identities and digital currencies. This is referred to as Web3 and might be a concept that actually outlasts the metaverse idea.

CHART 17

User adoption vs. investments in leading metaverses

Metaverse	Money invested/market cap	Daily active users
Decentraland	$1.3B	38
The Sandbox	$1.3B	522
Horizon Worlds (Meta)	est. $100B	900

Daily active users. Methods of calculation may vary per metaverse.

Table: Igor Pejic · Data from: Coindesk, Cointelegraph, The Byte, Jarvis Jonson

Others define the metaverse as an immersive digital place. In their view, users have to don expensive VR headsets. Mark Zuckerberg is the leading voice in this camp. He saw in the metaverse the next chapter of the internet and went all in. Ten thousand metaverse jobs were to be added in the EU alone. And Facebook's holding company was rebranded to Meta. The estimated price tag: $100B. That was the amount shareholders fretted could be lost over the next couple of years. They wrote open letters to cap the money Meta poured into the pixelated space.

So what followed Zuckerberg's pivot? A lot. But here is the short version: First, almost every major brand announced how they were joining in, buying digital land, and running ads in different metaverses. Prices of metaverse coins and land soared. The media buzzed. Yet after the short-lived uptick, ridicule and humiliation set in.

The graphics looked like those in a video game from the '90s, with the difference that back then the characters had legs. VR sets necessary to access the metaverse cost a fortune and caused nausea. People had purchased land that nobody wanted to buy anymore. The most striking criticism, however, was delivered in the form of a question no metaverse advocate could answer satisfyingly: Why would anybody spend time in the metaverse?

It was revealed how the two largest metaverses, Decentraland and The Sandbox, had 38 and 522 daily active users respectively. Both worlds at the time fetched valuations above $1B each.

For Meta's walled-off version of the metaverse called "Horizon Worlds," reliable sources are difficult to come by. Company documents spoke of about 200,000 monthly users in 2022, the climactic year of the hype. This marked a stark decrease from the 300,000 users only months earlier. Not exactly what you would expect from an up-and-coming technology. Yet even these figures should be taken with skepticism. Social media companies have a long history of being accused of inflating user numbers, be that with bots or click farms. User numbers are directly linked to ad revenue. Independent, though admittedly not exactly scientific, sources counted around 900 daily users.

Either way, the figures are sobering, to say the least, and they fit the overall picture. Journalists reported that even Meta's employees rejected to spend time in Horizon Worlds. Is it any wonder, then, that hardly any user forked out $1,500 for a VR headset to play poker with pixelated avatars?

And it wasn't even the costs that choked off the idea of the metaverse. Tim O'Reilly is an influential internet pioneer who has popularized the concepts of open source and Web 2.0, and he is the founder of O'Reilly Media and AlphaTech Ventures. He told me how journalists kept asking him about Web3, so he looked into it and concluded that it was too early to get excited about it. "It came down to this notion about productive and unproductive bubbles, which comes from the Argentinian economist Carlota Perez." There are technological revolutions that are usually accompanied by bubbles, and the question you have to ask is—what is going to be left behind? "It was pretty clear that the dot-com bust was a productive bubble. There was all this new infrastructure that was built with all this new technology. And yes, there was a real wave of adoption that got ahead of itself. But I wasn't seeing that here. Most of it was about people getting rich because it was hyped."

The metaverse fell into the chasm—if it ever got that far. It almost took Meta with it. And though Meta's share price has recovered by now due to smart strategic decisions, buying into the metaverse wager would have cost you dearly. You have to understand who is getting into a technology and why. The adoption never reached beyond the innovator segment. The buzz was created by people and companies dumping money into it. Hence, before investing in a technology, it is not only crucial to track the adoption rates but to track them in relation to the investment volumes. There is nothing wrong with the money coming before the users, but if adoption doesn't follow quickly there's probably a bigger issue. The best way to find out what it is, is to simply talk to users and nonusers. Most importantly, find out what value the technology can add for them and whether there are insurmountable obstacles to using it.

18

Crossing the Chasm #1: High-Profile Breakout Moments

IN THE COURSE OF 2022, the metaverse craze fizzled out. Yet in November of that same year, another technology captured headlines and imaginations: Generative artificial intelligence.

OpenAI, a company heavily backed by Microsoft, launched a conversational AI application called ChatGPT. The app stunned everybody with how accurately it could understand natural language input as well as respond to it in flawless English (and almost flawlessly in other languages). By inputting as little as a few words, users could prompt it to produce essays, stories, poems, computer code, or simply answer questions. Translating a 10-page document from English to Spanish? A matter of seconds. Have them summarized? Just decide how long the summary should be. You can also tell the app to limit the answer to 500 words, to write it in Hemingway-style, or to add a bullet-point list of the highlights. The answers are almost instantaneous and if you don't like them, you can add additional instructions and context as you build on the previous exchange. The chatbot has a memory. It feels like a human-to-human conversation.

Little surprise the public went wild for ChatGPT. News anchors were wrapping up shows revealing that their scripts were written by AI. Students let ChatGPT write their homework. And teachers ran that very same homework through the app to have it corrected.

It took ChatGPT five days to get to one million users. In comparison: Instagram took 2.5 months and Netflix 3.5 years to reach this mark. Whichever way you look at it, ChatGPT became one of the most quickly adopted apps of all time. On its wings, generative AI as a technology simply flew over the chasm between visionaries and pragmatists. AI is such a versatile technology that it can be used by any company and any individual with internet access. Like electricity or mobile phones, it

CHART 18

ChatGPT single-handedly crossing the chasm for GenAI

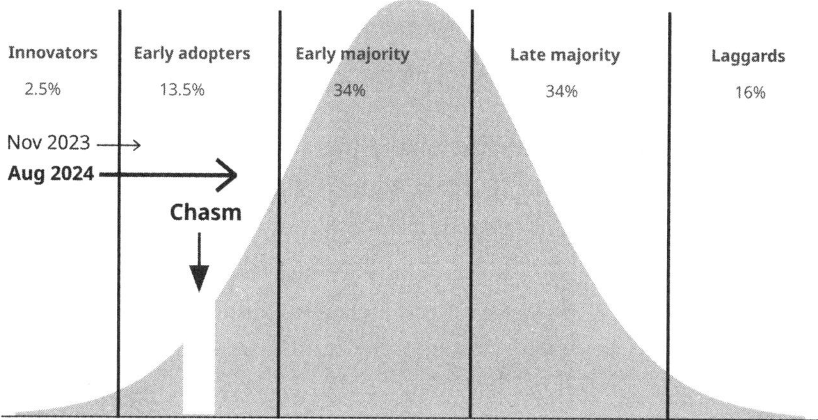

Chart: Igor Pejic • Data from: Based on *Crossing the Chasm* by Geoffrey Moore. Data on ChatGPT from Axios, Electro IQ, and Statista

thus has the largest possible addressable market. Such transversal technologies are the most powerful but usually take time to unfold and to gain a grip of the market. Thanks to the breakout success of ChatGPT, this was not the case. In less than two years, generative AI muscled its way past the chasm in the United States.

Researchers have been working on AI at least since the 1950s, whereas the metaverse was only taken up seriously in 2021. So, might it just take more time to be adopted? Maybe in a matter of decades, but there are issues with the metaverse trajectory. Since the 1950s, AI never had that media momentum. And yet the number of companies using it grew constantly. Insurers used it to find the right pricing for an individual, banks to determine the likelihood of a customer paying back a loan, spam filters to keep your inbox clean. This is what a healthy trajectory looks like.

Compare the metaverse also to Bitcoin, a very recent invention. The first coin was minted in 2009. Since then, Bitcoin has lived through a number of media frenzies and doom prophecies (often occurring simultaneously). Sometimes even systemically important players like Mt. Gox or FTX collapsed. But its popularity grew after each of them. As of the time of writing, there are more than 560 million cryptocurrency owners. Plus, millions of people hold those crypto assets via ETFs or own stocks of companies with large crypto exposure. Many finance mavens shrug off Bitcoin as a purely speculative asset. However, it doesn't behave like one.

Another important question is why the AI breakthrough was triggered by ChatGPT. It was certainly not the first powerful AI tool available to the public. Midjourney, for example, is an extremely potent software for image generation. Up to this day, Midjourney has one of the most robust models to create visuals. The trouble with those earlier applications was that they lacked accessibility and user-friendliness. ChatGPT's user interface is as simple as the Google search bar. You just type in your prompt or your question. It's free. It's versatile. If you wanted to create a Midjourney picture, on the other hand, you first had to sign up for Discord and then . . . Never mind. By now you have lost almost all interested users.

"You have a hint that the timing might be right when there is a big shift in the technology. For instance, it was really hard to have a digital bank without a mobile phone. And then all of a sudden, the mobile phone actually changed the economics of a branch bank and allowed you to do a lot of things like identity verification or fraud detection without the branch. We wouldn't have neobank unicorns without it. At the same time, it is not so exciting today anymore to build a neobank because we have so many of them. Just like it wasn't very exciting to do a CRM two or three years ago because Salesforce is pretty good. It might be pretty interesting today because I think AI is a paradigm shift that makes a new business model possible."

—ALEX LAZAROW, managing partner at Fluent Ventures and author of *Out-Innovate*

19

Breakthroughs and the Exponential Effect on Funding

MAJOR BREAKTHROUGHS SUCH AS CHATGPT work as a magnet for customers, companies, and talent. They also attract excessive capital overnight. For years, before the advent of ChatGPT, the money flowing into GenAI was fluctuating. One year it doubled; the next it dropped by half. Sometimes it stagnated. But with the watershed moment in late 2022, funding to GenAI startups tripled. A new hype cycle was kicked off.

A rising tide lifts all boats. Ever since the dot-com boom, numerous studies have proven that in a hype cycle it is enough to include the keyword of the day in the company's name to make corporate valuations go up. Investors work in gold rush mode. Wallets are opened up to everybody with a good story.

CHART 19

ChatGPT boosting application funding over infrastructure

A healthy investment boom is characterized by high initial interest in the application layer

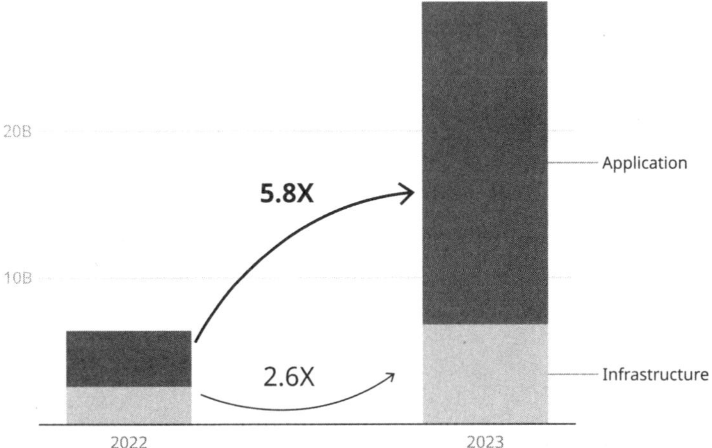

Chart: Igor Pejic • Data from: S&P Global

Much of investor behavior at this stage is driven by FOMO—fear of missing out on the next big thing. That goes for private as well as for public investors. Poor companies benefit from it disproportionally because hype often occurs shortly before the mainstream adoption chasm. This means the industry around a technology is in a hyper-growth phase. Rather than having consolidation, the number of players is shooting up. The final form of the technology has not yet materialized. Because it is difficult to pick winners at this stage, capital flows indiscriminately. Big investors take multiple bets, often backing direct competitors.

These bets are taken on multiple levels. AI's hype dollars went to companies like OpenAI that work on foundational LLMs. They went to startups that created applications on top of those LLMs. They went to chipmakers like NVIDIA. And they went to data center providers like Amazon or Microsoft. It would be easy to dismiss funding explosions as an anarchy. They are not. Pay close attention to the underlying patterns of money flows. They can reveal whether the technology's trajectory is a sustainable one. In other words: If it will make it past the chasm.

In the case of ChatGPT, applications got a much bigger initial funding boost than an infrastructure did. Only in the second year after its release was the trend reversed and infrastructure took the lead. This is a healthy trajectory because application investment tells you there is proven customer demand. Now consider the metaverse. After Mark Zuckerberg announced his pivot, professional and private investors started to write a lot of checks. But the money wasn't put into chasing the killer app of the metaverse. It went into developing VR sets, building blockchains on which metaverses could run, and most of it went into virtual real estate. The investment didn't advance anything of relevance to users. It was just sitting there locked, hoping that one day somebody else would pay more for it. If a hype is kicked off and more money is going into infrastructure, it means that the base is probably not there yet. It first has to be built, with the timeline and adoption remaining a guessing game.

Jackie Fenn, the creator of the famous Gartner Hype Cycle, highlights that hype is a useful and necessary contributor to an innovation's adoption. It alerts people to the fact that something has changed—a technology is making something possible that wasn't before. "The danger is when companies adopt an innovation early because they don't want to be left out, without fully understanding the risks and costs involved. The same behavior often applies to investors, who may feel pressure to add 'one of these' to their portfolio in a market that won't be able to sustain the rapidly growing number of providers."

20

Crossing the Chasm #2: Tech Titan Push

CROSSING THE CHASM CAN ALSO WORK the other way. Massive investments can improve the technology and drive up demand. Economies of scale effects are put to work. Production costs are slashed. This can eventually make the technology relevant to a more mainstream market.

To pull this off, you need the commitment of a global mega-player. In other words: A tech giant. The best illustration comes from Elon Musk's SpaceX. Apart from commercializing spaceflight, creating reusable rockets, and one day hopefully colonizing Mars, SpaceX also seeks to make available a stable internet connection from the sky. To offer this product, called Starlink, Musk first had to shoot up a large network of satellites into the earth's orbit. He did. And in doing so, he disrupted yet another industry and ushered in the era of mass production in space technologies.

For the past half century or so, the number of global satellites has been hovering around 1,000. Most of these were traditionally owned and run by the US government. Then came SpaceX. Within three years it sent around 3,400 satellites into space. In 2022, half of all existing satellites were under its control, 10 times more than that of the US government. In 2025, 75% of all satellites were owned by Elon Musk, and people around the world pay for Starlink internet. The best proof of demand came when the Ukrainian vice prime minister begged Elon Musk to activate Starlink following the Russian attack. Musk did so

Space satellite ownership by category

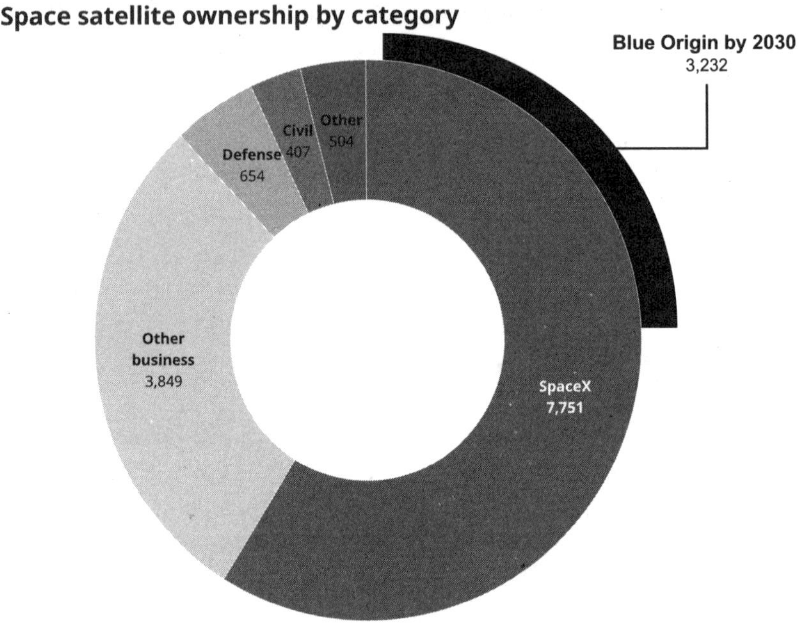

Satellites as of June 2025

Chart: Igor Pejic • Data from: Jonathan McDowell, Amazon, own calculations

within 10 hours, helping Ukraine defend itself by rebuilding connectivity after kilometers of internet cable had been destroyed.

In fact, the business model behind the internet from the skies has been so convincing that it has prompted another tech mogul to do the same. Jeff Bezos has committed himself to place 3,232 Blue Origin satellites into the earth's orbit by the end of the decade, an effort dubbed Project Kuiper. Starlink's radical advancements have also pushed other private providers such as OneWeb to innovate and expand.

This is a very common pattern with tech titans. UK-based payments infrastructure expert Daniel Jonas explains this by the engineering-based approach to innovation that characterizes the leadership of these companies. "Useful innovation means you are clearly identifying the problem to solve and understanding how to solve it. That's where Big Tech firms have been highly effective because they come equipped with an engineering mindset. By nature, engineers are very solution-driven."

The problem that is solved also includes leverage for their business model. "We have seen that work out in the past when they isolate a single revenue driver and then put the flywheel to work, taking the profits and investing them to further improve the platform or technology."

Though Starlink as a single project moved the needle for space tech, it had to pioneer a number of innovations to do so. Instead of a handful of large satellites, Starlink introduced constellations made up of many smaller satellites. Those satellites can be deployed much more frequently, they feature autonomous collision avoidance, and they can communicate with each other directly using laser links. And, most importantly, the cost of shooting Starlink satellites into the sky is a fraction of others thanks to SpaceX's reusable Falcon 9 rockets. We will look at this game changer in the next chapter.

A tech titan push can catapult a technology into a sustained period of growth. There are some signs that reveal whether the push will succeed. One thing to check is what this massive investment does to the cost structure. Will it make it easier for others to follow? And also, is it solving a truly painful problem? Then look at the business model. Is the value proposition clearly articulated and is it clear who will pay for the new service or function? The strongest sign that the push has succeeded is when others start committing to this tech as well, like Jeff Bezos in the case of space satellites. If those things are missing, that's a red flag.

21

Setting the Cost Reduction Spiral in Motion

WHEN BIG NAMES GO BIG ON A TECHNOLOGY, journalists report about it and competitors try to emulate it. More importantly, the massive size can reduce the cost calculation—in particular, when those scale effects are complemented with technological advancements. Again, SpaceX is the best case in point. It revolutionized the cost structure of spaceflight. It brought private sector efficiency to an industry that was exclusively in the hands of governments. While NASA's moon landing mission was instrumental in winning the Cold War, heavy bureaucracy precluded it from later triumphs. This is why Elon Musk's SpaceX and Jeff Bezos's Blue Origin hit fertile ground when they set out to privatize spaceflight.

It was in particular SpaceX's reusable launch systems that cut prices substantially and jump-started a new space race. The first-stage boosters of the Falcon 9 rocket can be landed and recovered. Obviously, such a revolutionary approach is not without its teething problems, but today even NASA uses the technology to cut its launch costs. It has inspired Blue Origin to build the completely reusable New Shepard rocket for suborbital flights.

If you wanted to shoot cargo into space in the 1960s with NASA's Saturn V rocket, it cost you close to $6,000 per kilogram. Instead of prices going down, they actually went up. The cost for one kilogram on the 1980s space shuttle was north of $50,000. Though the prices went down again, they never dropped below $6,000. Until SpaceX came around. Thanks to the revolutionary reusability of Falcon 9 rockets, costs

CHART 21

Costs to launch a spacecraft into orbit in $ per kg

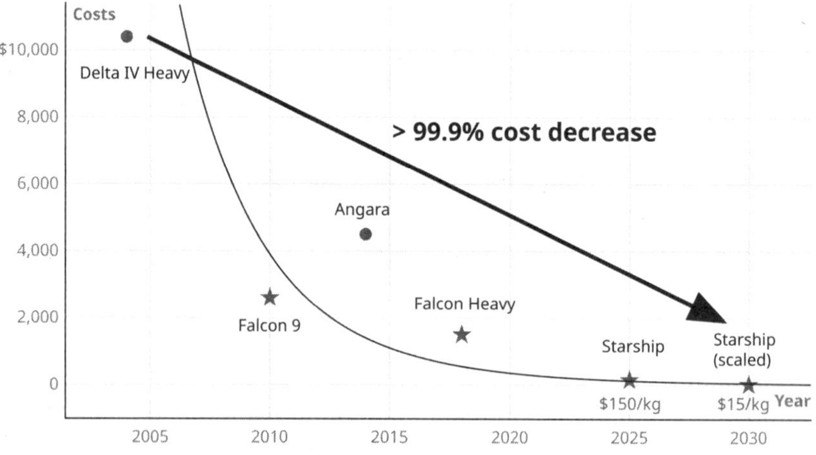

Star symbols represent SpaceX, circles all other players. Starship costs are estimates. Costs are inflation adjusted.
Chart: Igor Pejic • Data from: The Aerospace Security Project, Brian Wang

were reduced to a mere $2,600. The new follow-up model, Starship, will bring them down to $150, with further advancements calculated to push them all the way down to an eye-popping $15. That is more than a 99.9% decrease over the last 25 years.

If such major improvements are successful, they can move a technology into the mainstream. Something similar happened to blockchain. Bitcoin was the first blockchain, but it was mired in inefficiencies. Seven to eight transactions per second was the best it could do. This made it useless in terms of a currency. Its primary use turned out to be as a deflationary asset. As soon as more users wanted to send Bitcoins, the prices per transaction went into hundreds of dollars and took days. The major twist was to centralize the blockchain mechanism. And though many crypto lovers despise this idea, claiming that centralized blockchains are merely better databases and subvert the idea of decentralized control, you cannot argue with their efficiency. The Chinese digital yuan targets 300,000 transactions per second. Other improvements are layer two blockchains. Built on top of decentralized applications like Bitcoin, they take off the processing load and make transactions cheaper. It is shifts like these that enable a technology to cross the chasm toward mainstream adoption in the first place.

A technology that is still waiting for such a leap is quantum computing. But it does not always have to be a single event. The smartphone became accessible because for decades computing chips were becoming smaller and cheaper. Regardless of how a technology gets there, when choosing which one to invest in, the cost structure of the product must play a major part. Has the technology been refined to a point where the mainstream can afford it? The risk/reward ratio is most favorable right after the costs have spiraled down. Not only is this preceding adoption, but it also triggers other innovations that build on top of these advances. The expert quoted in this chapter is not only a highly successful tech investor but has been trained to go to space herself. She describes what the panoply of innovation can unleash for space tech by the lowered costs.

"The new space boom didn't happen suddenly, but definitely bringing in the private sector and making rockets cheaper has

made a huge difference. Space is going to get really interest-
ing. It's become less capital intense and there's a lot of things
you can do as a startup. I am talking about all kinds of space
tech, in particular areas like synthetic biology. Can you go to
Mars and actually build something sustainable? How do you
sustain human life? You're going to need to figure out how to get
oxygen and do recycling, combat radiation, and the impact of
weightlessness. And once you do it, many of these innovations
will make their way back to Earth."

—ESTHER DYSON, founder of Wellville and
author of *Term Limits*

22

Crossing the Chasm #3: Government Push

IF TECHNOLOGY GIANTS HAVE THE RESOURCES to push a certain technology
to success, so do governments. They can force unparalleled investments
and do so not only to commercially viable tech development, but also to
more basic research. The latter might not yield immediately applicable
results, but it unlocks game changers in the long run.

There are many historic examples where taxpayer dollars, and to
a lesser degree Euros or pounds, have resulted in technological revolutions. The aforementioned spaceflight would have been impossible
to start by the private sector. The military has often been the most
powerful innovator. Without America's DARPA (Defense Advanced
Research Projects Agency) we would live in a very different world.
The internet, GPS, drones, voice assistants, cloud computing, robotics, cybersecurity, and countless other technologies were funded by
defense-dollars. Wartime economies have been particularly productive.
Think radar, nuclear energy, or rocket launches. Wars send economies

in a mode of survival at all costs. The entire economy is redirected. Tech evolves at warp speed.

Today, governments in the Western world want to remake one of the biggest industries of all: Energy. They are splurging on green tech, whether that be subsidies for electric vehicles or green energy production plants. They are also taking a more outsized role than just handing out money. Many countries are completely phasing out coal. Cars with CO_2-emitting internal combustion engines will not be sold in the EU from 2035 onward, though it is highly doubtful if the ban will hold. The mandates are sweeping. The burden for taxpayers and corporations will be felt for generations to come.

Whether the green new deals in America and the EU are a sound strategy, only time will tell. But what can already be said is that they are reshaping mega-sectors such as energy and mobility. The ratio of renewables in the energy mix has been skyrocketing. Solar, wind, and geothermal are winning more and more market shares. Hydro-energy, on the other hand, has been growing steadily over the last years, but saw

CHART 22

Government mandates and the global rise of green tech

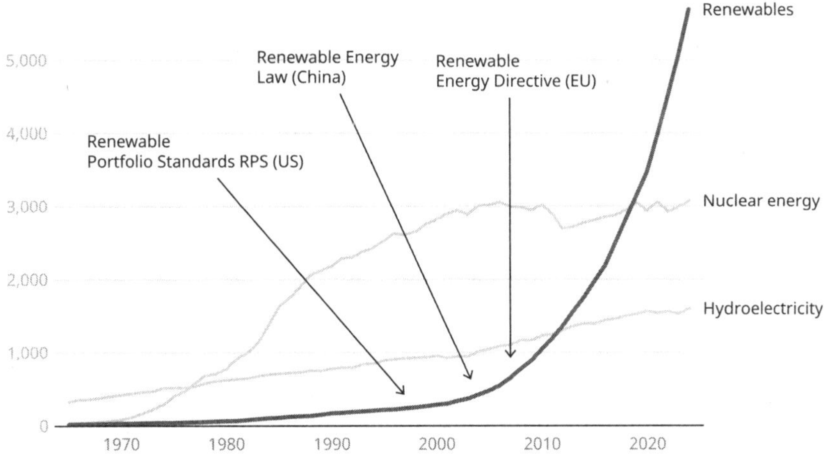

Renewables: Consumption; Nuclear energy and hydroelectricity: Total energy supply. All units in exajoules.

Chart: Igor Pejic • Data from: Energy Institute

no such explosion. Nuclear energy is equally eco-friendly but staying steady in terms of output. Why? Because neither nuclear nor hydro are promoted by governments, who are effectively choosing for the market which electricity to consume. So can a mandated technological push be sustainable?

I have mentioned previously many successful government interventions, yet there are also countless examples where government tinkering not just burned money but even delayed the ascent of a superior technology. We will see a couple of those in the next chapter. The good thing is, you can rather easily draw a line between them: Foundational research is usually a wise way to spend taxpayer money. Problems arise when governments try to be the arbiter, deciding which available technology *to scale*. Pushing adoption means picking winners and this is something better left to the free market.

> *"Government investments are generally politically (for capitalist governments) or control (for socialist governments) motivated. They rarely are looking to make a profit. If they subsidize investments, it generally means that they are either trying to accelerate investment in an area or are trying to get investors to invest in businesses that ordinarily would not make money. Some investors have done well with following government strategies, but they can be whipsawed when governments change over. Governments have done some good with their deep research funding, and when they lent money to Draper Associates when we got started, or to Tesla to build their first plant, but generally, money is better invested by the private sector."*

—TIM DRAPER, founder of Draper Associates

23

How Sustainable Is Government-Funded Tech Adoption?

WHETHER CLIMATE CHANGE IS AN EXISTENTIAL threat or not is hotly debated. For investors, it doesn't matter. At the moment, money is flowing freely. Investments into green technologies make shareholders greener either way. Green tech looks to have an assured growth trajectory. But does it really?

The critical question is whether growth can last beyond what is taxpayer-funded. And this is where it gets tricky. When a corporation pours billions into a technology, it's because it anticipates sufficient demand. The beauty of capitalism is that customers' needs tell companies what to do. And if managers are wrong, shareholders will soon start to write open letters. The course will be corrected. Governments are, per

CHART 23

Number of EV registrations per year in Germany

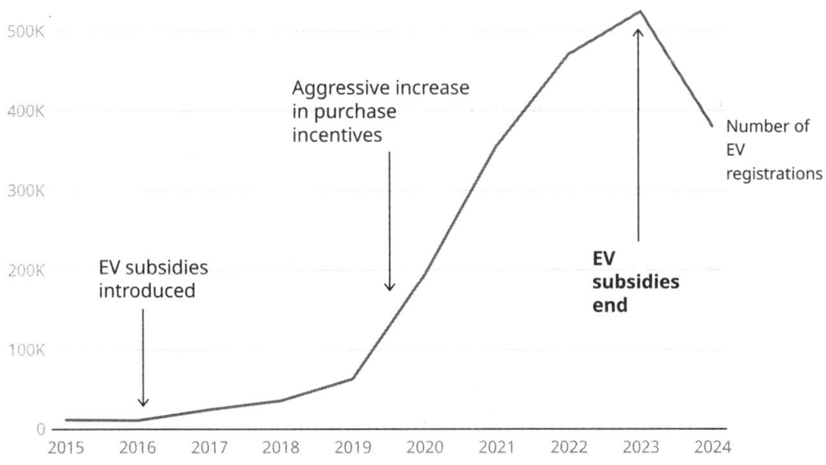

definition, not profit-oriented and thus can get this wrong much more easily than companies. There are first indications that the green new deal could fall prey to such a misfit. Renewables might be great for the environment, but they can't provide the supply stability of gas and oil. Industrial plants need to run even during cloudy days. And hospitals need electricity also when the wind is not blowing.

Nowhere is the mismatch more evident than in the demand for electric cars. As this chapter's chart shows, subsidies can drive the adoption of a technology, but as soon as they expire a slump is inevitable. In 2023, the German government abruptly decided to end the subsidies for electric vehicles. Afraid of a crash in demand, car manufacturers themselves jumped in to fill the void and paid parts of the subsidies. To no avail. Despite softening the blow, new registrations of electric vehicles fell sharply by 27% in 2024. Government funding distorts market demand and obfuscates a technology's weakness. When taxpayer money is redirected, the adoption halts. People that had already switched to the new technology might switch back to the old one.

Even worse, such a government intervention might preclude or delay superior technologies from developing and gaining traction. E-fuels are a synthetic alternative to fossils, created with renewable energy. They are better than electric vehicles in both their environmental footprint and the comfort for drivers. No batteries mean no long charging times, no waste of rare earth minerals, and no problems with discarding them. However, most governments have decided they wanted EVs. Their argument: Synthetic fuels are too expensive. Yet in a meta-study—i.e., a study of studies—Frontier Economics estimated that synthetic fuels might replace fossils as early as 2037. Increasing the synthetic component of fuel incrementally would have only a marginal impact on prices, while economies of scale would gradually bring down the e-fuel price and reach fossil fuel levels. Many car manufacturers openly admit they would like to go that route but don't want to commit significant investments into a technology competing with one that is pushed by governments.

Examples abound. In the 1980s, for example, the French government promoted Minitel, a precursor of the internet. When the World Wide Web took the world by storm, no government handout could keep

Minitel alive. Today, central banks are vying to push the adoption of a specific technology—central bank digital currency (CBDC)—and to onboard the entire banking system on it. Nick Anthony from the Cato Institute is studying how this type of currency destroys the natural competition in the market that brought us all this innovation. Without private actors, we wouldn't even have the technological basics to build CBDCs. Anthony argues that a similar problem applies to all government intervention and that such tinkering is unsustainable: "The market is far more flexible when it comes to adapting to technological innovation. Businesses rise and fall depending on their ability to adapt. In contrast, governments are much more locked in."

Examples like these prove that while states have a crucial role in foundational research, especially in vital areas such as defense, they are not positioned to judge which tech or which format is best. Hence, as an investor, I am very skeptical of jumping onto the bandwagon of government-led tech adoption. It may well deliver high returns in the short run, but long-term investors should beware.

24

Electric Cars: Can a Technology Fall Back Into the Chasm?

WITH A STRONG MISMATCH between a government's goals and customer demand a technology can fall back into the chasm. Mainstream adoption once thought assured can falter. But what if the technology has already made it into the mainstream? Can it still fail? It can happen. And it has happened.

Most of us know that the electric car was not a recent invention. The first EVs date as far back as the 1820s. What most people don't know is that the electric car was not some fringe experiment but actually dominated American streets. By the turn of the century, electric cars already made up about a third of all vehicles. This is, per definition, way past

CHART 24

EV market share over the past 200 years

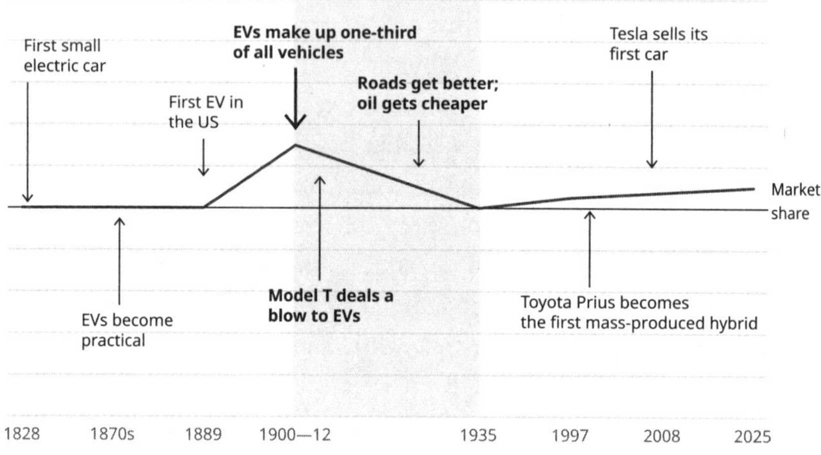

Chart: Igor Pejic • Data from: US Department of Energy, miscellaneous

the early adopters. The selling points were the same as of today's electric cars. They didn't pollute. They were silent. The constraints seem familiar to us too: Battery power and range.

People had accepted those constraints for a lack of a better alternative, but innovation ended that. What dealt the death blow to electric cars was not as much a new technology but a process innovation that made a competing technology cheaper: The conveyor belt. Ford's Model T brought down prices for gas-guzzling cars dramatically. The discovery of cheap Texan oil took care of the rest. The dominant technology in the 1920s all but disappeared by the 1930s. Automakers never gave up on the idea, regularly trying to improve electric cars. But the technology only started to fight its way back into the mainstream by the turn of the millennium. The first hybrid cars got popularized as a bridge technology and then Tesla Motors built the first competitive EVs, feeding off the emergence of high-capacity lithium-ion batteries. Tesla did not just produce great cars, but it drastically altered the image of electric cars and piqued interest with nontraditional buyer groups. EVs were no longer seen as an environmental statement, but as a modern car of the future.

When technologies fall back into the chasm, the trigger is usually a newer and better technology. But how you define "better" makes all the difference in terms of speed of replacement. As the expert in this chapter explains, there is a difference between sustaining and disrupting innovation. A sustaining innovation is doing the same things its predecessor does, just more efficiently. Think 128GB vs. 64GB storage. Change occurs quickly. No resistance. Disruptive innovation is more complex, involves trade-offs, and can appear ineffective. That is why change is slow. It took the internal combustion engine years to overtake EVs. And it might take EVs decades to again grab the top spot, if ever.

Scott D. Anthony is a professor at the Tuck School of Business at Dartmouth and a close confidant of the revered Clayton Christensen, with whom he has spent much of his professional life analyzing disruptive innovation. He confirms that a technology can fall back into the chasm even after mainstream adoption, namely when it is pushed back into it by a new technology. Yet this only applies to disruptive innovations. Anthony illustrates this with CD vs. MP3 technology. "A CD is what you would call a sustaining innovation. By almost every measure it is better than a cassette. MP3 technology was a classic disruptive technology, in that it brought new benefits (easy sharing) but had limitations (lower quality, difficult to use)." Like all disruptive innovation, it created a new ecosystem and enabled new business models. All of a sudden, you had Apple music players or streamers like Spotify.

The lesson for investors is this: The chasm is no checkpoint that, once passed, poses no danger anymore. A tech's trajectory might go the other way. It might also rebound, but it will usually take too long for an investor to pay off. So, once a tech falls out of the mainstream, it is better to get out. Much better: Get out as soon as the first serious signs of decline show. Stagnating growth? Suppliers offering new technologies? Declining margins? Run.

25

Transversal and General-Purpose Technologies

SAVVY INVESTORS BUILD THEIR PORTFOLIOS around transversal or enabling technologies rather than on narrow, domain-specific innovation. Both types can excel on growth rates, but ultimately the latter is limited in absolute volumes. There are exceptions for mega-industries such as health or mobility, but overall the upside potential is bigger for transversal technologies. The risks, not necessarily.

Almost all technologies listed in the chart are transversal. Some may seem domain-specific at first, but if you look beyond the surface, they cut across multiple segments of the economy. Space companies are in the exploration business. Yet they also benefit the military, just as well as civilian airplanes. They enable space tourism and shoot satellites into the sky, which are key building blocks of human communication and connectivity. Gentech is used to develop vaccines and treat genetic disorders, but it also lets farmers grow more resistant crops and it reduces CO_2 emissions by developing biofuels and renewable bioplastics. Even those at the very forefront of identifying disruptive tech are routinely surprised about what it ends up disrupting. Chris Wake is a founding partner at Atypical Ventures who focuses on frontier tech. Here is how he describes the task: "Our approach is to invest in plausible science fiction. This means looking at the entire spectrum of technical innovation and filtering a lot of that down to find places where technology is almost finally caught up to solve seemingly unsolvable problems. Sometimes the technology is solving a problem we didn't even know we had."

The chart lists the nine major tech sectors and their most important emerging technologies at the time of writing. These are where I see the largest growth opportunities in absolute numbers. Some of them have passed the chasm already (e.g., biotech); others still need to

General-purpose technologies (GPTs) of tomorrow

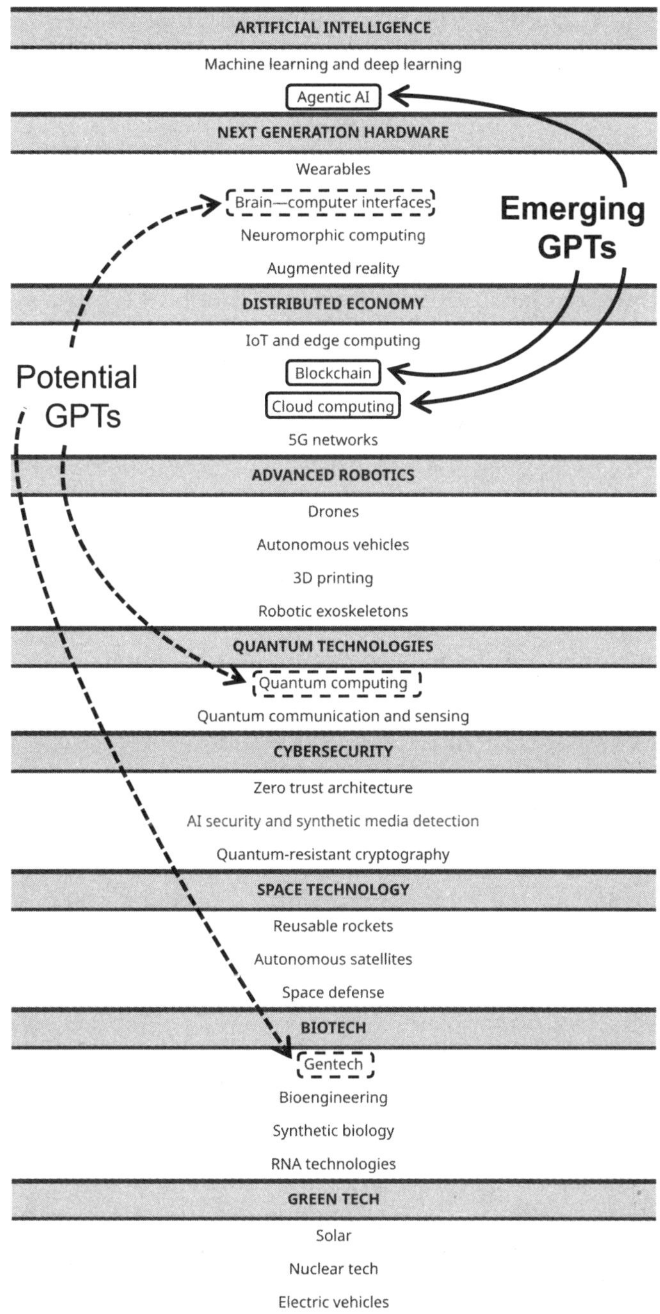

The list covers the most important tech sectors and technologies at the time of writing. It is neither exhaustive nor constant, but it allows us to pinpoint which tech is likely to be extraordinarily consequential in the mid- and long-term future.

Table: Igor Pejic

prove they can get there (e.g., quantum computing). I have excluded long-established technologies such as mobile. Those are transversal and sometimes still growing. And some of them may still be sound investments. Yet they have already reached a point at which they have become dominant. No further stellar returns are possible unless there is another breakthrough. Many sectors and technologies overlap or are mutually dependent. Tech is always recursive, meaning it builds on itself. So, the list is neither exhaustive nor definitive, and by its nature it is ever-changing. Yet it serves as a starting point to your own research. After you are finished with the research, draw up your own canvas with the next growth opportunities. But don't stop there.

Transversal technologies are generally good investment opportunities. Yet some of them are better than others. The best opportunities are so-called general-purpose technologies (GPTs). The standards for GPTs are very high. The steam engine, electricity, and the internet would qualify. Others, like 5G networks or drones, would not, despite their global significance. GPTs are foundational innovations that not only transform multiple industries from the ground up, but the economy and society as a whole. GPTs spark complementary innovation. They destroy existing structures. They heave global productivity on a new level. And they create tremendous wealth for those driving and funding the change. Here is Chris Wake again: "Solving foundational problems is great because those problems are not acute nor specific to a given industry or industry segment. Sometimes the market opportunity is ridiculously large."

Today, only three technologies can be seen as emerging GPTs. The oldest one, cloud computing, has been powering ever more computing infrastructure since the mid-2000s and thereby has revolutionized how data is stored and processed in every industry. I define it as emerging because it still boasts year-over-year growth rates north of 20%.

The second GPT currently unfolding in front of our eyes is agentic AI. These AI applications are making decisions and performing tasks completely autonomously, all but eliminating the need for humans. All types of white-collar and blue-collar jobs are at risk of obsolescence. Agentic AI is an extremely young technology, a frontier tech. Nobody can say what its impact on humanity will eventually be, but even its early applications suffice to categorize it as an emerging GPT.

Blockchain and digital assets are the third emerging GPT. Digital currencies already make up a significant portion of the world's money supply. Hundreds of billions of dollars' worth of real-world assets like bonds or real estate are recorded on the blockchain. Blockchains are also used to track mega-financing rounds for the largest corporate loans or to organize supply chains for giants like Walmart or Mercedes-Benz. The technology has also started to upend digital identities. And while agentic AI is set to redefine the nature of work from the ground up, blockchains do the same for the corporation. DAOs are decentralized autonomous organizations that can be built on top of them. They are companies without incorporation or staff.

The path is a bit less clear for gentech, brain–computing interfaces, and quantum computing. Unlike the long list of other transversal technologies, these three have the potential for large-scale transformation. Yet it will either take further technological breakthroughs until they are prime-time ready, or the path to adoption must be further accelerated. Gentech has already passed the hype stage and has started to disrupt industries like health, biology, and agriculture. The magnitude of the change still remains to be seen, but merged with the recent advances in AI optimism is justified. Brain–computing interfaces and quantum are more experimental but must be monitored closely as well.

26

Technology's Potential ≠ Mere Revenue Size

POTENTIAL CUSTOMER INTEREST IS FUNDAMENTAL. The willingness to fork out for a service even more so. But what separates simply successful technologies from those that make their investors exponentially richer is their ability to drive profit margins.

Amazon might deliver 17.2M packages every day, but that is not the source of its greatness. At least not when viewed from the prism of its shareholders. What is making the company a gold mine is Amazon

AWS revenues vs. profits

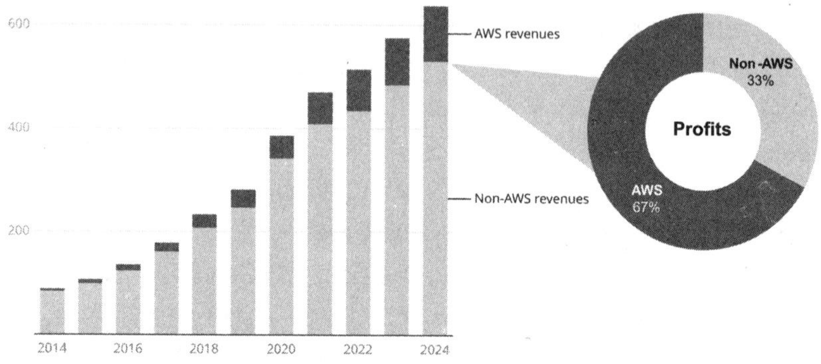

Chart. Igor Pejic · Data from: Amazon, Business of Apps

Web Services (AWS), its cloud computing arm that controls around a third of the global cloud market. While it contributes only a tiny part of Amazon's revenue, it rakes in 67% of Amazon's entire profits.

This high profitability ratio lies in the very nature of cloud computing as a technology. Building a mega data center incurs high initial costs, but once the infrastructure is set up and the services are running, it is easy to add new customers. While AWS must buy new servers if volume goes up, the software is already in place; the marginal costs are negligible.

Compare that to Amazon's core business of e-commerce. Of course, the marginal costs get smaller with every unit, but only slightly. You still have to pay for packaging and delivery, for search ads and warehouses. With software, on the other hand, marginal costs are close to zero.

Whether you churn out electric vehicles or robotic arms, size matters far less than it does for software and platforms. Just look at the other top 10 most valuable companies. Microsoft made its fortune with Windows, Google with its search bar, and Meta by connecting people. Apple might seem different at first glance, but its profitability stems not just from the iPhone hardware, but its iOS operating system and its app store. That doesn't mean that other tech cannot be profitable, but scale will play a smaller role and profitability curves are not exponential. And remember one more thing: The more profitable an innovation seems to be, the higher the incentives to bring it to market. And to push through. Scott D. Anthony reminds us how a disruptive technology will meet a lot of resistance. "It is important to remember that disruptive innovations start with limitations. Robo-taxis sometimes get stuck. Generative artificial intelligence hallucinates. Lab-grown meat can taste funny. The promise of profitability allows the would-be disrupter to overcome these limitations and reach broader markets."

In short: The higher the scale effects, the better the return. So, when deciding on which technology to invest in, always understand what it will do to marginal costs.

27

Beyond the Chasm, It's All About Profitability

SOFTWARE IS NOT THE ONLY WAY TO ACHIEVE low marginal costs. Biotech, for example, works through monetizing intellectual property. This means that you have high initial expenses for R&D and product development, but new units incur much smaller costs. Software and biotech companies fall under a category called technology creators. Those are highly profitable. Still, every metric shows that there is one type of company with an even more profitable business model: Platform orchestrator.

The least profitable type of companies are asset builders—i.e., companies that manufacture physical goods. Car manufacturers, shipbuilders, food producers. Then there are service providers. These include banks, consultants, or cleaning companies. Service providers have better balance sheets than asset builders, but their marginal costs are high, and they are limited in terms of growth. Not so the above-mentioned pharmaceutical companies and software developers. These technology

CHART 27

Corporate performance according to business model

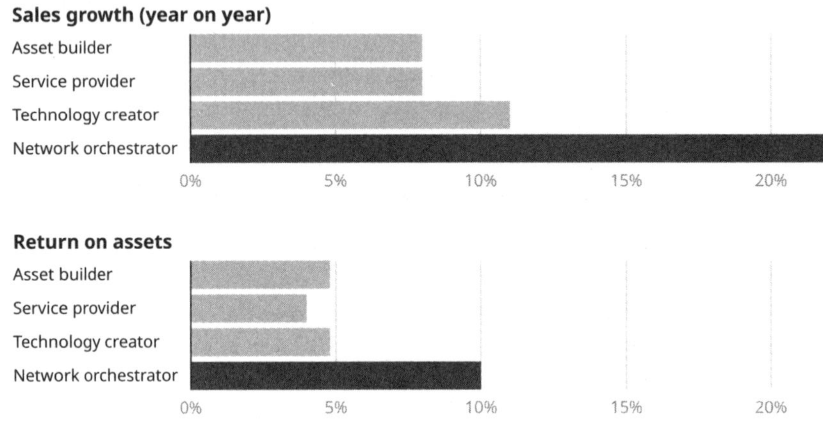

Chart: Igor Pejic • Data from: Wharton (Libert, Beck, and Wind)

creators feed off patents and trademarks. Microsoft has to develop Windows only once, regardless of whether they have a million or a billion users. But the top of the profitability pyramid is the so-called network or platform orchestrators. Their average yearly sales growth rate is double that of technology creators. Their return on assets is at 10% vs. 4–5% for other categories. For platforms, the profit margins are also higher, as are the multipliers of price over revenue. The picture is very clear.

Platform orchestrators are those companies that cater to two different groups of customers. Hence, some people also call them double-sided platforms. They don't necessarily have to be tech companies. Newspapers sell content to readers and readers to advertisers, providing an attractive platform where two groups meet. Yet the number of platforms has exploded in the digital age, and their profitability has gone through the roof thanks to low marginal costs in the software business. PayPal brings together retailers and buyers. Phones and computers create a space where users get access to company services and vice versa. Facebook connects advertisers with people seeking a glimpse into their friends' lives. Video games, dating apps, flight comparison portals—the list could fill an entire chapter of its own.

Platform mechanisms have been one of the reasons tech's corporate valuations have ballooned to sizes unseen in history. But not every technology lends itself to platform models, and there are few successful platform orchestrators. Platforms gobble far more cash than any other model, during buildup and during scaling.

28

Super-Charging Platforms: Metcalfe's Law Meets the Data Flywheel

PLATFORMS MAKE UP ONLY A TINY FRACTION of all companies—2% of all publicly traded ones, to be precise. Partly because of the enormous resources they gobble initially, but partly also because most companies working with a platform model will fail. Usually, platform markets can sustain one or two companies. Google has a de facto monopoly in search. Apple is entrenched with Google in a duopoly for mobile platforms and

CHART 28

Two speeds of network growth

Metcalfe's Law

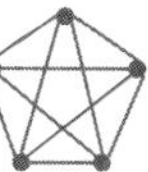

Metcalfe's Law + Data Flywheel Effect

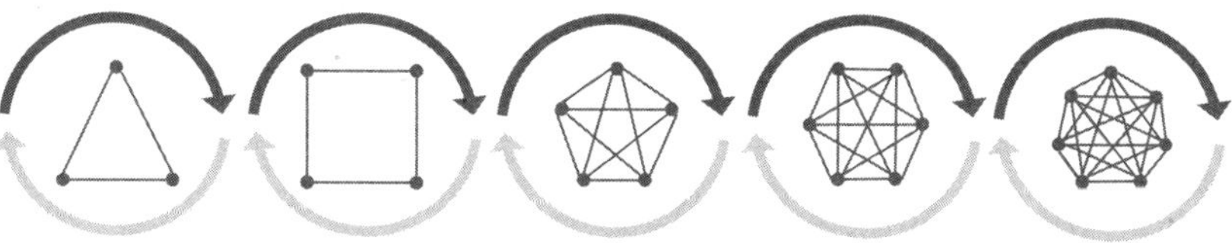

Chart: Igor Pejic • Data from: Flywheel Effect: Concept by Jim Collins. Metcalfe's Law: Concept by Robert Metcalfe

with Microsoft for the desktop space. Coinbase dominates cryptocurrency trading, Uber owns three-fourths of the ride hailing market. Meta and Google make up almost half of the digital ads market. And so on. What makes things even trickier for investors is that the rise of platforms and their orchestrators is stellar and the opportunities difficult to catch.

This speed is explained by a phenomenon observed as Metcalfe's Law. In essence, what it says is that a network gets more attractive the more users are on it. Think of it like this: Would you buy the first telephone? Or would you ditch X for Bluesky? With every new user, the platform offers more value and thus grows quicker. It is a spiral set in motion. The growth trajectory becomes exponential. Or as Metcalfe's Law puts it mathematically: A network's impact is proportional *to the square* of the number of nodes in the network. While Bob Metcalfe, founder of the Ethernet, initially described the mechanism for the connection of physical communication devices, George Gilder later observed that it also applied to users in a network.

Tech platforms have another spiral driving their growth in parallel: The flywheel effect as popularized by Jim Collins. This phenomenon explains how incremental improvements, continuous over a long time, can build momentum that keeps accelerating. Initially, these improvements seem to have no impact whatsoever. Yet, over time, just as with a mechanical flywheel, it spins faster with less effort. Why? Because each small improvement builds on the previous ones. Compare it to the compound effect we discussed earlier.

The flywheel concept applies to all actions of a corporation. I talk specifically about the *data* flywheel effect, which explains the benefit of collecting and crunching data. For tech companies, big data is their lifeblood. More data means more accurate predictions. From a certain point onward, insights become statistically significant and you can have them for ever more scenarios. This mechanism is a special boon for platforms. The more people are on it, the more data the company gathers. This makes the services become better, which brings in more users. More users create more data. The flywheel spins.

Both Metcalfe's Law and the flywheel effect are powerful in and of themselves, but combined they can catapult individual platforms as well as the underlying technology to global scale so quickly that investors have an extremely short time frame to jump onto the bandwagon.

Betting your chips on a promising technology gives you a wider time frame than betting them on a single platform. That doesn't mean, however, that investors can close their eyes to the companies applying the technology. In order to figure out whether a tech lends itself to Metcalfe's Law or the flywheel effect in the first place, they must understand in which way it will be used and what underlying business models will be viable. They must understand which branches of the tech will be most profitable. And they must understand what features to expect further down the road.

29

Platforms Locking the Market

SO PLATFORMS GROW RAPIDLY. And they grow profitably. But there is even more to them. They are sticky. Once on top, it is almost impossible to dethrone them. Nothing locks the market better than a successful platform. This chapter's chart shows the market share of a leading network orchestrator and how it develops over time: Google's search engine. The only other search engines that even register are Yahoo! and Microsoft's Bing. Keep in mind that Bing is primarily used because it is preinstalled on Windows PCs. In fact, the most searched term in Bing is "Google." YouTube and Gmail, two other Google services, also make the top four search terms. Despite this domination, for years the market shares have looked as flat as the heart signal of a dead patient.

Even as Microsoft announced and introduced an AI-powered version of Bing, the patient showed not the tiniest movement. If a powerful GPT like AI cannot move the needle, is there anything that can?

Why is it that platform businesses hardly ever face serious competition? Because once established, users don't really have an option to go for another provider. Sure, you could switch from WhatsApp to Signal,

Search engine market search

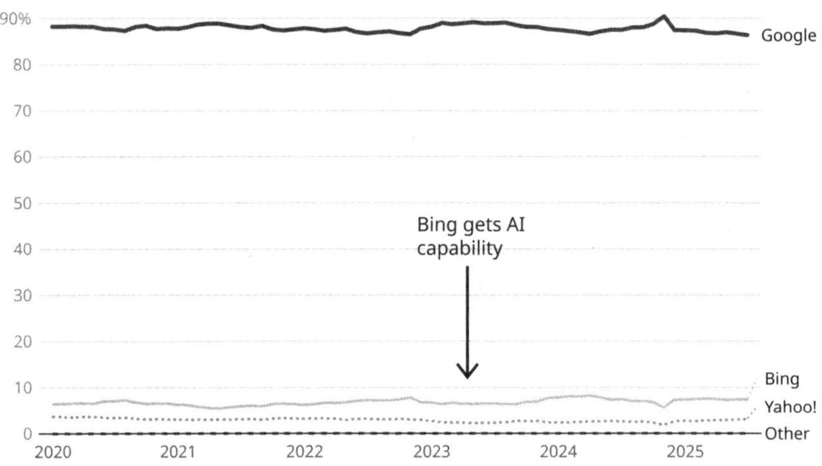

Includes all platforms (desktop, mobile, tablet). US market shares.

Chart: Igor Pejic • Data from: Statcounter, Microsoft

but can you really? Your contacts and your communication history will likely not be on the new app. So, de facto, you have to stay. When Elon Musk acquired Twitter in 2022, my Twitter feed overflowed with posts vowing to leave the platform. Users with political viewpoints opposed to Musk's insulted him and announced they would migrate to competitors like Mastodon. Today these people are still tweeting. The only thing that has changed is the platform's name. As for Mastodon: It is as relevant today as its eponymous elephantine mammal.

When Musk's involvement with the Trump presidency in 2025 drew even more anger, Twitter users (by that time called X users) didn't even bother to threaten boycotts. Instead, the ire turned to Tesla cars. This time, cybertrucks burned and market shares across the world took a nosedive. Musk might think of a Tesla as a "sophisticated computer on wheels." He is probably right, but it is certainly not a platform of the same magnitude as X.

Another lock-in can be found in crypto assets. Take Ethereum as an example. It is the second largest cryptocurrency and the largest one with smart contract capability. This means that, unlike Bitcoin, it can do all types of actions, not just transferring a currency-like token. Developers can build new applications and tokens on the Ethereum blockchain. But when they do so, they are bound to Ethereum. And for every operation performed on their application, they must use Ethereum's underlying Ether tokens. The lock-in is permanent.

The cleverest companies manage to widen this lock-in to their entire ecosystem. Let's say you decide to replace your old iPhone with a new Samsung Galaxy. You will have everything but a seamless transfer. You won't be able to use iMessage anymore, nor will you be able to keep your communication history. If you have made Apple Pay the center of your financial life, bad luck. No way to access it anymore. Your Apple credit card? Can't be used without Apple Pay. Your Apple savings account? Not usable without Apple's credit card. You get the point. Leaving the ecosystem lets large parts of your digital life collapse.

The picture is the same for all platforms: Users, as well as partners, are bound to them. Hence, new challengers are almost certain to fail. As a result, the pricing power in the hands of successful platforms is enormous. Good for shareholders.

30

Spotting Platform Tech

SO PLATFORMS ARE DIGITAL GOLD MINES. Naturally, the million-dollar question (in a literal sense) is *how to find those gold mines before others have taken most of the gold*. There is good and bad news. First, the good: There is a way to be ahead of the curve by looking at entire technologies rather than individual companies. The bad news: The number of targets is highly limited.

Before we look at future platforms, we must be clear what exactly we are looking for. Because of its unique profitability, the term *platform* is en vogue. Everything these days is called a platform, but the platforms of interest to us must display three characteristics: First, they must be

Platform-enabling technologies of tomorrow

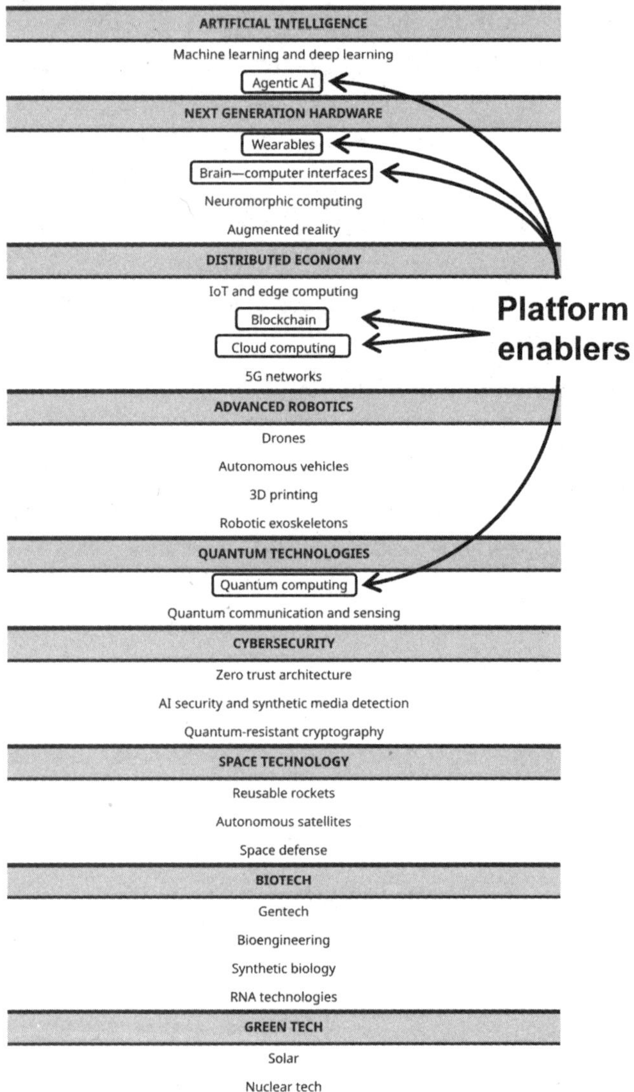

The list covers the most important tech sectors and technologies at the time of writing. It is neither exhaustive nor constant, but it allows us to pinpoint which tech is likely to create markets that work on platform-principles.

Table: Igor Pejic

double-sided, meaning that they are linking two groups. Whether those are users, advertisers, developers, sellers, buyers—it doesn't matter. Second, the platform's success must be determined by network effects. Third, the marginal costs of adding new users must be negligible.

Trying to apply these criteria to a future technology rather than a company is tricky. You don't know how the technology's capabilities will evolve, nor which business models will prevail, nor how many users will adopt it. At a time when we were carrying around BlackBerrys and Nokias, nobody thought of mobile as a platform-enabling technology. It took the iPhone to think of cell phones as having operating systems and apps. You will have to live with some of your predictions being wrong. Yet, despite the difficulty, looking at your technology canvas and pinpointing those areas where you can imagine platforms being built should be essential in every investment decision.

If we apply the three criteria to our list of emerging technologies, only six of those are platform-prone. Wearables and brain–computer interfaces are the natural evolution of desktops and mobile phones. It is easy to imagine how they can be the next place where users encounter software. So could quantum computers, in case they ever manage to advance the tech's stability and the cost base to make them affordable for the broad public. Cloud computing, blockchain, and even agentic AI resemble the traditional software business. You have foundational systems (operating systems, layer one blockchains, LLMs), applications, and users. Maybe other groups like advertisers will join in too. To balance and link these groups, you need a network orchestrator. Blockchain is basically an overhaul of one of humanity's oldest platforms: Money. It brings together issuers and users. Of course, you can also argue that 3D printers or satellites have software running on them and that they might become a platform too. They might indeed, but so far purchase decisions are made primarily on hardware. This is why their platform potential is limited from today's perspective.

As I mentioned earlier, the technology canvas is a list continuously in flux. Christian Busch, business professor at the University of Southern California, has reached global renown with his serendipity mindset concept. Business leaders refer to it to push the odds of positive serendipitous encounters. In order to find a promising new technology earlier than others, he told me that the key is to institutionalize curiosity. "In my experience, investors who consistently step outside their bubble—talking to unlikely people, inviting outsiders (or even their kids!) into meetings—start to see weak signals much earlier." He says a critical habit is to notice and actively reflect on what has surprised you recently. "When you treat surprises as data, not noise, and create deliberate 'serendipity triggers' such as random cross-team pairings or unstructured time at conferences, you dramatically increase your odds of spotting the next wave before it breaks."

If you look closely at the chart, you will also notice that there is some, but not complete, overlap of platform-prone technologies and GPTs. In previous times, that overlap was much smaller. GPTs like electricity, the conveyor belt, and the steam engine made an impact because they revolutionized the cost structure of the economy. But some historic GPTs did foster platforms too. What most of those had in common is that they revolutionized communication. Writing systems, the printing press, the internet. The platform GPTs of tomorrow follow in their footsteps.

Identifying a tech as platform-prone does not mean it has better chances of success than others. But if it does succeed, it will be the one driving exponential gains. So, building a tech portfolio overweight with emerging GPTs and upcoming platform tech can be a powerful strategy for achieving exponential technology alpha, even without waging bets on individual companies.

IV

GETTING THE TIMING RIGHT

LET'S SAY A COMPANY DECIDES TO SPLURGE on the latest AI software, a VC fund throws a lifeline to a startup, or your neighbor buys stocks for his retirement fund—all of these can be splendid but at the same time horrible investment choices. The difference between the two is timing. The *when* in investing is second only to the decision about *which* technology to put money into. But make no mistake about it: Those trying to time the market will almost certainly be disappointed. Rather, technology alpha comes from spotting long-term tech trends before others and committing to a long-term investment strategy. Everybody has their interpretation of long-term. For this book, it means holding an asset across multiple market cycles, which translates into decades, not years.

The major question thus becomes how to find a successful emerging technology before the mainstream investor does. Once the press hypes up a technology, the biggest profits have already been made. What usually follows after a short uptick is disillusionment. Successful technologies will survive this downturn and come back, riding a more solid upward trend. Not as stellar, but sustainable. And still, if you missed to get in before the initial hype broke out, it might be a long time until you see returns even from a steadily growing technology.

Savvy investors thus earn their tech dollars by catching waves across the hype cycle and the technology life cycle earlier than others. This part of the book teaches readers about the subtle early trend indicators of emerging technologies for both cycles. It looks at growth metrics like the CAGR or the funding going into a technology. Yet, above all, it puts a special emphasis on those early signals you will not find on balance sheets or earnings calls, things that most other investors will miss. Job vacancies and hiring practices. Research papers and patent applications. Google searches. These are just some indicators that illustrate the diversity of metrics you can use. But there are probably dozens of others that you can include in your own dashboard, many of which will even be specific to a certain technology. Are you tracking blockchain? Then you will examine things like transactions per second, and the total value locked in an ecosystem. Is AI your thing? In this case you will certainly keep an eye on FLOPs, a metric that shows the total amount of computational power used to train a single, large-scale AI model.

Building a radar for new technologies with such metrics will let you pinpoint the life cycle phase of a technology. This means better anticipating stellar growth periods. The subsequent sharp decline that is triggered by disillusionment is very hard to foretell, but the dashboard can help you prepare for the saturation stage. It can also help you understand the difference between overhyped technologies and those driving real productivity gains.

Finally, this part exposes some of the dangers at taking expert assessment at fair value. While they certainly know a lot about the technology, they don't know about the future. We know for a fact that their forecasts are no more accurate than those of nonexperts. So, instead of blindly following experts, there are ways you can use their assessments as a complement to your own analyses.

31

Detecting Long-Term Trends Is the Winning Feat

TECHNOLOGY ALPHA IS WON BY SPOTTING long-term trends, not by day trading. Even if you are an exceptionally good—or rather lucky—trader, you are unlikely to be more successful than somebody not even trying to time the market. How come?

Most people don't realize that the key to high returns is to avoid missing any of the particularly strong days. Let's say you invested $10,000 into the S&P 500 for a period of 20 years. If you didn't touch your investment, its value would have been close to $65,000 at the end. But if you missed only the 10 best days over a period of two decades, you would have ended up with less than half of that. Every further strong day you miss massively slashes your wealth. Eventually, after missing the best 40 days, you end up with a net worth lower than what you invested 20 years earlier. Studies have proved this effect over and over again. It holds true for the

CHART 31

Value of $10,000 invested over 20 years

Based on an investment into the S&P 500 from January 2003 to December 2022

	$10,000
Invested all days	$64,844
Missed 10 best days	$29,708
Missed 20 best days	$17,826
Missed 30 best days	$11,701
Missed 40 best days	$8,048
Missed 50 best days	$5,746
Missed 60 best days	$4,205

past 20 years, but also for the past 90. The aggregated S&P 500 returns between 1930 and 2020 stood at 17,715%. But if you exclude the 10 best days in each decade, you get a meager 28%. That is a difference of having $1.7 million or $10,280.

It is a simple matter of probability that you will miss some of those positive outliers if you are not invested the entire time. After all, there are no reliable predictors that help anticipate outperforming days. Many investors try to limit risk by avoiding periods of pessimism and decline altogether. They trade only in bull markets. This is a terrible mistake. Out of the 10 best days, seven happened very shortly (within two weeks) of the 10 worst days.

Understanding the cost of trying to time the market is essential for every investor, but for those trying to make money with tech, the effect is even more pronounced. The volatile nature of technology assets makes these up- and downswings heftier. For example, NVIDIA added $277 billion in market value in a single day in February 2024, a 16.4% increase. In the period displayed in chart 31, the best day was a plus of 12%.

That does not mean that timing is irrelevant. It does play a crucial role, but you have to extricate yourself from the classic dimensions in which you think about timing. It is not the daily or even yearly performance of a company that matters, but in which phase of the adoption life cycle the technology is. This is easier said than done. All figures, all news reports, and all commentary are based on the way the calendar slices our time, whether that is quarterly earnings calls or a listicle bringing you the hottest stocks of the past week. But the mindset of a long-term tech investor should defy this thinking. He or she should aim to navigate the waves of tech adoption, to spot trends early, and to understand the ripple effects these trends will cause.

A common mistake is to focus exclusively on first-order effects. Consider the following example. Investors convinced that consumers will soon flock to wearables can buy companies that produce smart glasses and watches, but they can also conclude that this abundance of newly generated data will result in a higher demand for data storage and more precise AI algorithms. This is quite challenging even for professional investors, as Elizabeth Yin, founder of the Hustle Fund, admits: "We

VCs try to make guesses based on second- and third-order effects of trends, which means thinking through implications of which tech trends and new problems and opportunities are created. Of course, where this fails is if a trend stops or tapers." Either way, thinking in terms of trajectories instead of monthly returns is the best way to stay committed to an investment and not be swayed by the regular news cycle.

32

Tech Hype and Real Productivity Growth

IN CHAPTER 16 WE DISCUSSED THE TECH adoption life cycle and concluded that the best time to get into a technology is when you see it catching on with the pragmatist segment. From there, sticking with your investment is what matters most. This is easier said than done. It almost certainly will seem that your chosen technology is falling back. Asset values will fall, sometimes plummet. The media enthusiasm will subside and turn into commentaries soaked in disenchantment and pessimism. Analysts will trash the technology as overhyped and useless. Many industry darlings will go bankrupt and high-profile initiatives will be abandoned. Large corporations will often jump off the bandwagon and channel their investment capital into the new big thing. I felt it firsthand. I was giving one blockchain keynote after the other. Then ChatGPT sucked up all the oxygen. Demand for any tech knowledge besides AI fell precipitously.

Though hard to believe, this is a normal step after the new tech sugar rush is over. In fact, the phases a new technology goes through is so predictable that the IT research firm Gartner has perpetuated them in the "Technology Hype Cycle." A new tech triggers mass interest among companies and entrepreneurs, sometimes even a media hysteria. This is necessary to propel the technology beyond the chasm and into the mainstream. However, once users beyond the early adopters get in, the

CHART 32

Emerging GPTs and their position on the hype cycle

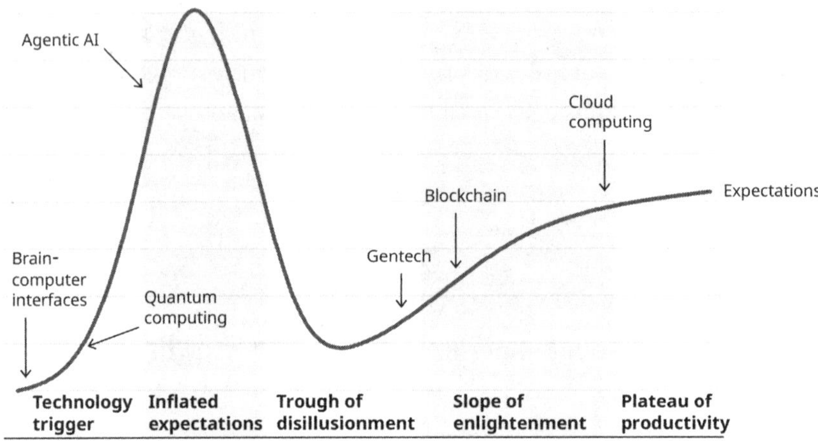

Chart: Igor Pejic • Data from: Based on the Gartner Hype Cycle

hype peak is passed and disillusionment sets in. The realization dawns that pundits and startups have oversold the technology. And, unlike early enthusiasts, mass users are merciless in speaking about the shortcomings and challenges.

At the same time, some valuable market consolidation sets in. Weak and bad actors are weeded out. What remains are the most promising use cases and the best solutions. Those lead the second wave of the technology's hype, providing better products and collecting venture capital that is now starting to return. Optimism swirls again around the technology, though with more realism and less excitement. This phase is called the slope of enlightenment. It is not as steep as that of inflated expectations, but the trend goes up.

This second wave is not driven by overblown promises, but by proven productivity. Gains and savings for companies can be more accurately quantified. Consumer gadgets are bought in increasing quantities. Eventually, the plateau of productivity is hit. Advances and improvements still occur, but they are small and steady. So how long until we reach the plateau? As with all cycles presented in this book, there are no generally valid timelines. It can be years, but more often it is decades.

In chapter 25, we identified some likely general-purpose technologies of tomorrow. This chapter's chart lays them over the hype cycle. It is a bird's-eye view that each tech investor should build and consult every time when making decisions. But remember that this is a snapshot in time. The positioning changes constantly. Perhaps by the time you read this, you will place some technologies more to the right than I did in my chart. So update it constantly. And remember that this is not a precise science. Yet the mere exercise of mapping technologies on the hype cycle will make you ask many critical questions. It is not about getting the point on the curve right, but about thinking through the trajectory.

So what do successful tech investors do with such a map? They understand the hype but decide based on productivity growth. It is crucial to keep an eye on the hype cycle so that you don't buy into a technology at the peak of expectations. You can spot the peak when there is a stark mismatch between promises and productivity. Consider what the creator of the Gartner Hype Cycle told me about the two sweet spots of getting into a new technology:

"Like investing, the hype cycle is about human attitudes to and belief in a technology (or other innovation). Understanding the hype cycle lets investors take advantage of the initial enthusiasm, inevitable disillusionment, and ultimate maturity of the technology by anticipating adoption patterns that result in purchasing and market shifts.

But unlike companies, where the goal is to dampen the peaks of expectation and troughs of disillusionment to make sure that adoption is fueled by real value rather than trends, investors need to anticipate the ups and downs and act on them. For example, good investment opportunities include catching a technology on the rise to the peak, or just as it escapes the trough to rise up the slope of enlightenment."

—JACKIE FENN, creator of the Gartner Hype Cycle

33

Digital Assets Defy the Hype Cycle

THE HYPE CYCLE WORKS FOR MOST TECHNOLOGIES. At least roughly. It does not, however, work for Bitcoin and other digital currencies. Or not anymore. Initially, the Bitcoin market cap and the hype cycle moved in lockstep, but in 2020 and 2021, Bitcoin's success stopped following what the theory suggested. If you think about it, that makes perfect sense: While digital assets are an application of the underlying technology called blockchain, they are an asset class and thus they behave like one. For the blockchain, on the other hand, the hype phases are just as predictable as for mobile technology or cloud computing.

In the early 2010s when Bitcoin and blockchain were used synonymously, it appeared that the hype cycle worked for cryptocurrencies too. At one point in time, however, investors started separating the two, resulting in two different discourses. The one about blockchain became confined to bankers, supply chain managers, and executives charged with corporate innovation. The applications they were discussing couldn't be farther away from cryptocurrencies. Bitcoin, on the other hand, was about issuing and transferring money without central or commercial banks, or any institutions of trust. Speculation, grift, bubble—this is how the media framed it for a long time. And yet Bitcoin and its peers eventually made their way onto Bloomberg screens and into ETFs issued by asset management behemoths. Banks started selling them and governments started buying them. Every boom was followed by a bust. And then by a bigger boom. No slope of enlightenment. No plateau of productivity. Just new all-time highs.

When the media reports heavily on Bitcoin, its price usually surges. Just like for any technology. Bitcoin's value shoots up, the more people hold it. That is also true for users of any technology. So why doesn't the hype cycle apply to Bitcoin like it does to blockchain? As an asset class,

Bitcoin performance vs. hype cycle theory

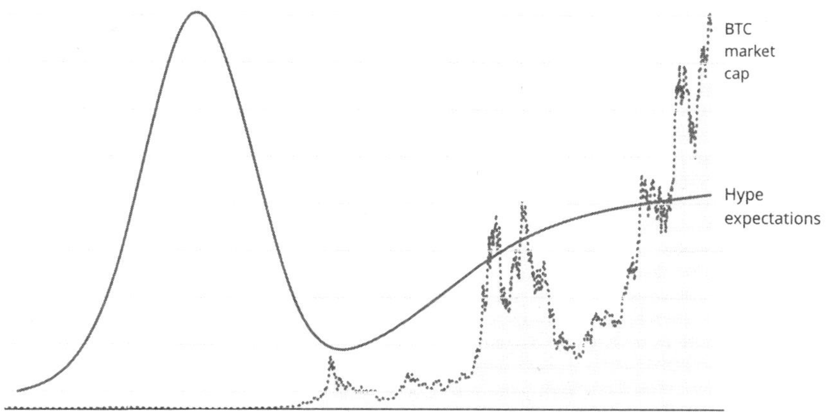

Chart: Igor Pejic · Data from: Based on the Gartner Hype Cycle, BTC data from CoinGecko

Bitcoin's value is not determined by whether it can solve problems. It is also not determined by improvement and evolution. If it were a currency, the value of Bitcoin would go up if, say, a protocol update made transfers more efficient. But cryptocurrencies are first and foremost an asset class. Ergo, it does not matter how good the technology gets. Just as it does not matter to the price of gold if a new tool is invented to press the material into jewelry more quickly or more cheaply. People are holding it for one reason only: Value appreciation over time, driven by scarcity.

The lesson for investors is this: Make sure you are applying the tools presented in this book to a technology. That is not to say that you should keep away from crypto assets. Those can be extremely valuable to your portfolio, but they work by different rules. Check part 7 for those.

"Bitcoin does not follow the Gartner Hype Cycle. Its volatility is at the lowest level it has ever been historically. The Gartner Hype Cycle is not a law of nature. It is not like gravity. Things don't have to follow some chart. I think it is a really useful heuristic, but technologies can go through the cycle multiple times. You can make the case that the internet went through a Gartner Hype Cycle in the early 1990s but then went through a much

larger hype cycle in the late '90s. And did it reach a plateau of productivity?"

—ALEX TAPSCOTT, CEO of CMCC Global Capital Markets and the co-founder of the Blockchain Research Institute

34

The Acceleration of Tech Adoption

CATCHING THE ADOPTION TREND OF A TECHNOLOGY becomes continuously trickier. This chapter's chart illustrates why. In most cases, adoption today is simply too quick to catch up with it. Transformative technologies in the last century took decades to reach 50 million customers: 68 years for airplanes, 62 years for cars, 46 years for electricity. The closer to the millennium and to the digital age, the shorter it took products to spread: 14 years for the computer, 7 years for the internet.

Yet adoption really started to happen in the blink of an eye only once smartphones proliferated. They were affordable even to people in the global South, and they allowed users to leapfrog over entire generations of technology, catching up rapidly. A street vendor in Kinshasa suddenly had access to the same apps with the same underlying technology as a stockbroker in Manhattan. ChatGPT brought AI into the pocket of 100 million users within only two months, most of whom had previously only read about AI in science fiction novels. Meta's Threads, a competitor to Twitter, passed the 100 million mark in five days. Investors cannot catch a trend anymore by solely monitoring adoption. Thus, monitoring the capabilities of a technology and its cost structure are more crucial than ever to get the timing right.

We all know that technological breakthroughs are accelerating exponentially. It is impressive that the spread of new products based on these technologies is accelerating too. People are adopting multiple technologies and products at the same time. And since many of them

CHART 34

How long it took to reach 100 million users (in months)

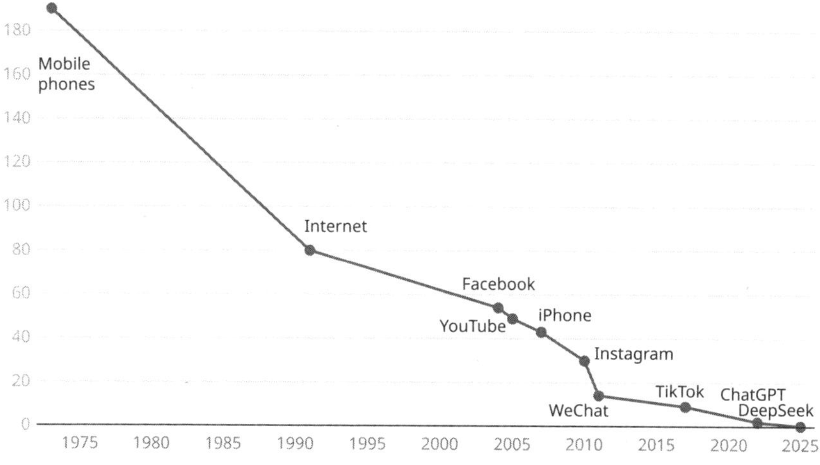

Chart: Igor Pejic • Data from: PwC, Vox, Ebert/Louridas

are usable at the tap of a button, and often for free, it means users might drop the product very quickly if there is no added value or if a better alternative arises.

One important thing that all investors should understand is that inventions and adoption don't go hand in hand. It can take years before a technology is ready to enter the adoption life cycle, even if the adoption itself can then happen in a blitz. The impulse is often a breakthrough in a seemingly unrelated field, which is why a broad awareness of technological progress is key. Consider the cases of the metaverse and generative AI. "Success comes from observing the many parallel, or otherwise disparate, technological progressions that begin to intersect, converge, or combine in powerful new ways," says Matthew Ball, the CEO at Epyllion, an investment advisory behind the largest and first metaverse ETF. By the end of the 2010s, he and his co-founders had concluded that this century-old concept was finally about to become a practical opportunity due to advances in multiple technologies such as GPUs, blockchains, rendering engines, CDNs, and wearable computers. "AI advances are not dissimilar—today's wave stems not just from novel architectures (e.g., the transformer model, first proposed in 2017), but unrelated advances in GPUs and, to a lesser extent, the deployment of CUDA across scores of industries, and so on." Range is the make-or-break characteristic in tech investing. The best investors have the clearest understanding of how similarly timed innovations can build off one another and how new advances outside of the field might unlock old theories. In other words, since adoption is continuously speeding up, they are moving their attention to an earlier level: impacts on a technology's productivity promise.

35

Adoption Driver #1: Productivity Growth

FOR TECHNOLOGY INVESTORS, it is critical to distinguish between hype and adoption. The two are inextricably linked. Adoption is often preceded by hype, but not every hype ends up boosting adoption. This is where a third variable comes in: productivity growth.

If the new technology offers superior productivity at the point, it becomes a hype, adoption takes off. ChatGPT is such an example. Less than a year after it hit the markets, 60% of companies had implemented GenAI or were actively looking to do so. The algorithms were by far not perfect, but even at that early stage they could slash costs substantially. Coders or translators could bolster their output multiple times, only equipped with free test versions and one-hour YouTube tutorials. Serial tech entrepreneur Harald Trautsch puts it like this: "It comes down to two things: First, does the technology or feature solve an important problem for users? Second, with which frequency will they use it?" If a tech boosts a company's or person's productivity, it usually fulfills both criteria. The investment case tends to be good. The best counterexample is the metaverse. The hype was triggered by a dream sold skillfully, not backed by any productivity or functional boost.

Of course, to keep the trajectory going, productivity boosts have to keep coming. Sooner or later, they won't. This is the point where the

CHART 35

The technology adoption triangle

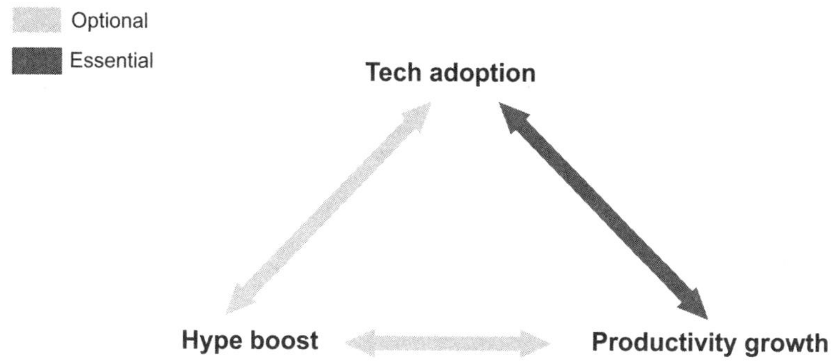

Chart: Igor Pejic

technology boards the hype cycle roller coaster. There is one caveat, though: Only truly disruptive technologies are allowed on the ride. Most innovation is sustaining. Improvements to its predecessor are straightforward, as is the case with new generations of microprocessors or larger hard drives. Disruptive innovation is different. It changes how things are done and what things are done. That is why new tech suffers from substandard performance for years or decades, which is where disillusion sets in. Researchers have named this phenomenon the "productivity paradox." The electric motor ended the age of steam and sounded the bell for a new techno economic era. But it only did so 30 years after it had powered the first factory. Technological leaps helped, but the real game changer was when managers realized they needed a different layout of production plants. Instead of equipping the factory with one giant machine as with steam, the electric motor allowed for decentralization. Each workstation had its own small motor. Productivity exploded.

The triangle of adoption, hype, and productivity growth will never be in perfect balance. Usually it is the productivity that is lagging behind. This is nothing that should make you discount an emerging technology as long as it is somewhere on the horizon. Hype is a powerful booster for the two other factors, but it is optional. Productivity growth is not. Transistors caused few media headlines and even less excitement. They became hyper-efficient and made their way to everything from calculators to portable radios before the public even took notice. If productivity surges, so does adoption. Thus, the only red flag for investors should be if there are no productivity gains in sight.

36

Adoption Driver #2: Falling Costs

THERE IS ANOTHER ADOPTION DRIVER and thus another variable for savvy investors to track: The cost base of a technology. When you see the costs for applying a technology being slashed significantly, look closer. Adoption might be about to take off soon. Low costs make the business case work out for a much broader user segment. Some companies need an innovation urgently, so they will splurge on it anyway. Yet the majority of enterprises that might benefit from it will only look into it after costs are down. For end-customers, high pricing is an even bigger barrier.

Sinking costs trigger a virtuous circle. They stimulate demand, which in turn pushes the supply side. New competitors enter, which is good for the wallets of technology consumers, regardless of whether they are corporations or individuals. Plotted on a graph, the relationship between costs and adoption looks like the letter X. As costs are falling continuously, adoption is increasing at roughly the same pace.

A splendid example of this relationship can be found in biotechnology. The cost of editing a genome sequence fell from around $100 million in 2002 to under $1,000 within just 18 years. Three years later, sequencing giant Illumina claimed to have brought down the price to as little as $200. Needless to say, more genomes were sequenced. But DNA sequencing is also a great illustration of how a significant cost drop enables completely new application fields. It went from a purely research-oriented tool that was used to decode the human genome and garner general knowledge to practical testing for individual patients. Personalized genetic profiles are

CHART 36

DNA sequencing costs and their impact on adoption

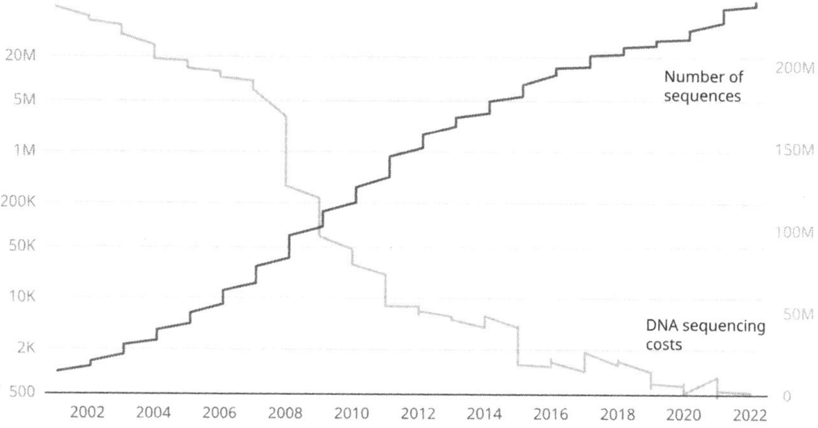

The sequencing costs are presented on a logarithmic scale to fit in one graph. Log scales compress large values, so the physical distance on the chart does not correspond to absolute changes, meaning that the cost reduction is exponentially times higher than what appears in the chart.

Chart: Igor Pejic • Data from: National Human Genome Research Institute, National Library of Medicine

created to tailor drug treatments. Genetic screening can tell a patient about dormant disease early on. And during the Covid-19 pandemic, genomic sequencing was used to track the spread of the virus and identify new variants in near real time. Think also of the internet from the skies. Without SpaceX pioneering reusable launch systems, it would have stayed an idea confined to the pages of sci-fi novels. These new application possibilities also come with new business models and radically change the way an industry works.

What the chart also demonstrates is that costs usually don't fall in a linear fashion. There is one point where they plummet and go from punishingly high to affordable for the mainstream market. This is the moment to look out for. While adoption before that point might also be growing, it will probably stop at the early adopters if prices don't drop further in due time. Productivity growth and cost considerations work in tandem for corporations. For private consumers it is usually the costs that make or break a technology. Had ChatGPT been priced at $1,000 per month, neither hype nor adoption would have happened.

"Dramatically falling costs are a huge enabler. Consider a classic example of disruptive innovation: Steel minimills. Bethlehem Steel built the last integrated steel mill in the United States in Burns Harbor, Indiana, in 1962. It took two years and cost $4 billion in today's terms. Steel minimills involve using an electric arc furnace to melt scrap steel and turn it into finished product. Nucor's first minimill, built in 1968, cost $40 million in today's terms. Of course, its capacity was much lower, but per ton it was sharply cheaper. Low costs enable new business models, and new business models are the special sauce of disruptive change."

—SCOTT D. ANTHONY, professor at Tuck School of Business at Dartmouth and author of *Epic Disruptions*

37

Beating the Technology Life Cycle

IN BUSINESS SCHOOL, EVERY MANAGER is equipped with hundreds of tools and models. Only a handful of those stick with them for life. Porter's five forces. The 4Ps of marketing. The Ansoff matrix. And the technology life cycle. This simple curve shapes how decision-makers think about technologies, regardless of how much else they learn in their careers.

The technology life cycle is the direct result of the trends in productivity and cost structure. It sketches how a new technology passes through different phases until it gets replaced by a newer one. While the length of a technology's life cycle and that of its individual phases can vary significantly, the pattern is predictable. After the introduction of a new tech at a slow pace, it catches on rapidly in the growth phase. Then it slopes into a longer maturity phase, before starting to slowly decline. It is in this final period that a nascent technology in its growth stage outmatches its old counterpart. Though parts of the curve resemble the hype cycle, the trends do not necessarily occur simultaneously.

CHART 37

Early indicators in the technology life cycle

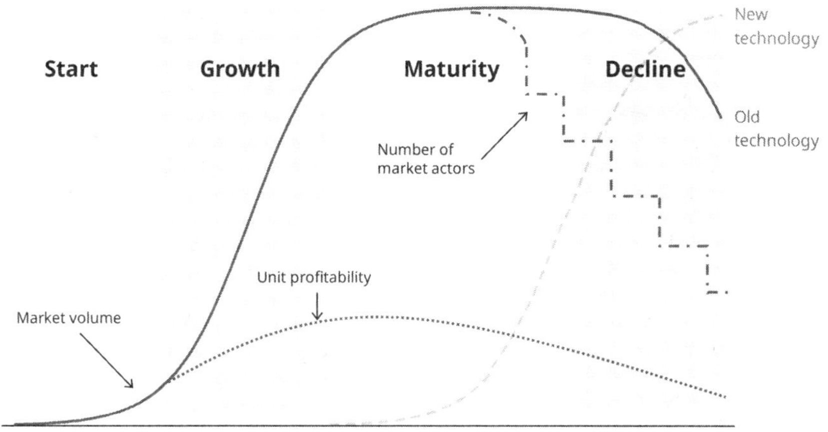

Chart: Igor Pejic · Data from: Cyclical concept based on Anderson and Tushman

Market volume is the prime metric that defines the stage of a technology. How does market volume differ from what we discussed previously—namely, customer adoption? Indeed, those are two sides of the same token. But they are not the same. Adoption tells you how many people or companies have tried out a technology. Market volume tells you how much money they are spending on it. Trends in adoption precede market volume. So, to anticipate the growth of market volume, track adoption rates very closely.

But getting in on time is just half of the story. Getting out before the decline is the other. Luckily, there is one very telling indicator that foreshadows decline: The number of market players. As economies of scale unfold, consolidation sets in among suppliers of a tech segment. The first companies now start focusing on the next technology. Once the rise in market volume grinds to a halt, the number of suppliers drops precipitously and leaves the most successful companies to salvage a slightly declining, but still large and profitable market. The good thing: The number of market actors drops much more sharply than the market volume. A strong sign to get out on time.

So, to beat the technology life cycle, pay close attention to market volumes and the number of market players even in the maturity stage.

And there are many other indicators to watch out for. Take the example of decentralized autonomous organizations (DAOs). DAOs are blockchain-based protocols that create enterprise-like entities by code only. No humans or incorporation needed. Kevin Owocki, founder of multiple companies in the space, says that for DAOs, as for any other tech, steep growth is triggered by a number of factors such as the proliferation of different use cases, easy accessibility, and legal clarity. "Mainstream happens when a technology becomes the standard. For DAOs, mainstream will happen when they stop feeling like 'crypto' and just feel like a better way to organize, like Slack or Discord with a treasury." There are many other such early trend indicators that are ahead of market volume growth. But before we discuss those, the question is how best to measure the critical variable market volume.

38

Keeping Track of Growth

JUST AS RETURNS COMPOUND, so does market growth. If you want to know how a technology has done over the past three, five, or ten years, simply adding the annual growth rates is not enough. Assume, for example, that the cloud computing market grows by 10% two years in a row. In absolute numbers, that second-year 10% would be a larger increase than the 10% in the first year, because year two applies to 110% of the initial market volume. So, the combined yearly growth rates would be 20%, while the compound annual growth rate (CAGR) stands at 21%. In other words: The CAGR better visualizes the total growth. It is also more convenient, as it requires less data. You don't need to know every year's performance. Two values—starting point and end point—are enough. The CAGR is a powerful metric that is used to calculate everything: Investments, returns, users and customers, revenue growth and market volume.

In tech investing it has become a generally accepted means of determining how well a technology is gaining traction. Rightly so. Yet on

CHART 38

Would you invest in this technology?

Based on CAGR and absolute market size, perhaps yes:

CAGR 90%	**Absolute market size** $249B

But the YoY growth shows another picture:

Year 1	Year 2	Year 3	Year 4	Year 5	Year 6
$ 10B	$ 20B	$ 50B	$ 200B	$240B	$249B
	+100%	+150%	+300%	+20%	+4%

Fictional scenario depicting the shortcomings of the CAGR when assessing a technology's growth trajectory.
Chart: Igor Pejic

its own the CAGR is insufficient to even determine the phase on the technology life cycle. Two other variables you will certainly need are absolute market size and total addressable market. Most technologies will have impressive CAGRs when their user base is still miniscule. And they might continue to be high while conquering the pioneers and early adopters. The CAGR only really becomes telling when it has crossed the chasm to the early mainstream. That's when volumes become meaningful. And that's also where you get a glimpse of the real total addressable markets. Who will really use the technology and how often? The total addressable market tells you how long this growth will last.

Sam Rahman points out that the addressable market is particularly important for dominant companies and technologies. "It defines the multiples of these stocks. But it is a harder one to analyze. You must understand the evolution of an entire industry. You have to make some educated guesses, especially in an early-stage industry like AI." Take VR glasses as another example. You can guess what the addressable market might be, but what about the adoption rate? Is it just going to be people that wear glasses anyway? Is it going to be seen as an accessory? How frequently will they use it?

A critical distinction is between past and anticipated CAGRs. The tech investment world brims with CAGR forecasts, which are the result of guesses on the total addressable market—whether that is for new technologies, industries, or individual enterprises. Usually research institutes, consulting companies, and self-proclaimed experts all seek to outdo each other. The most bombastic claims often win media attention. So, while these figures give you a sense of how technology growth trajectories compare to each other (in analysts' minds), there is little more to them. I dare you to pick up this challenge: Find a popular forecast that foretells a negative or insignificant CAGR.

Finally, even understanding the market potential is not enough, as chart 38 shows. CAGR is a powerful shortcut, but single-year growth tells you more about the trends within the trend. This is critical for the volatile and exponential world of emerging tech. For example, two super-strong years in the beginning and the CAGR looks strong, which might blindside you to recent challenges to growth. Whenever available, you should also give single-year growth a look.

39

Early Trend Indicator #1: Direction of Funding

FOLLOW THE MONEY. THIS IS NOT JUST A USEFUL motto for investigative journalists, but also for trend hunters. Money doesn't lie. Executives and professional investors might not always be honest in press releases and interviews. But when they invest significant sums into something, you can bet they truly believe in it. Second, money itself often moves the needle. You need it to turn scientific research into innovative products. And you need money to scale every technology, company, or product. A lot of it. So big dollars spent on a tech easily become a self-fulfilling prophecy. And if they don't immediately, funding usually continues

CHART 39

Blockchain market volume vs. VC investment

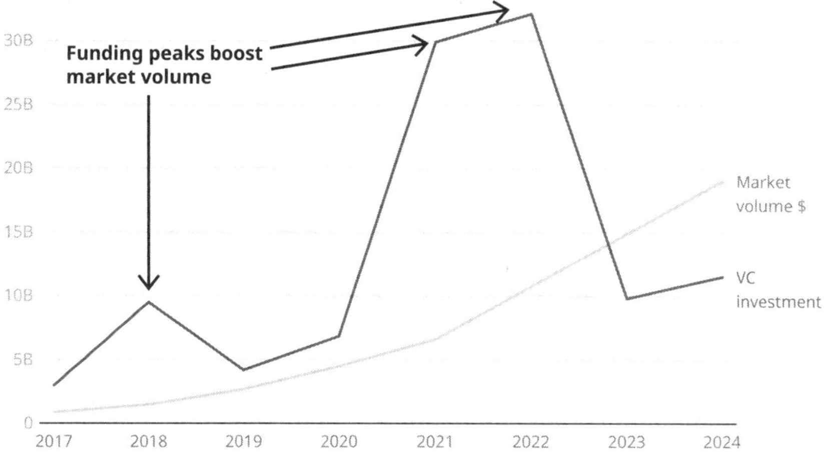

Yearly Google trend scores from January.

Chart: Igor Pejic • Data from: Galaxy, ElectroIQ

to flow for some time. Thanks to the sunk-cost fallacy, managers are unwilling to pull the plug before they can show their investment decision has led to an outcome. They will rather throw good money after bad than admit they backed the wrong horse.

Consequently, growth in investment volumes precedes growth in market volumes. And while private companies are reclusive about where they are betting their chips, annual reports of major public companies speak volumes and are available to everyone. As for venture capital trends, you can easily keep track with tools like PitchBook.

This chapter's chart illustrates the relation of capital inflow and market volume using blockchain technology as an example. Blockchain in this case of course excludes the value of cryptocurrencies and other digital assets because they work by different rules. We are talking mainly about corporate adoption. In every year that funding reached a new peak (2018, 2021, 2022), market volume growth accelerated in the following year. Once put on a solid growth path, VC dollars were not even needed anymore to keep the momentum going.

Tracking corporate capital is crucial to catch a technology before its steep growth. Following venture capital even more so. VCs are pouring much of their budgets into Pre-Seed, Seed, and Series A investments—i.e., the early stages of a startup. They need to bet on nascent technologies far earlier than the stewards of corporate behemoths. Those can easily catch up with their market power. Also, the farther you get to the right (i.e., more mature) side of the technology life cycle, the less likely it is that a new player will emerge to successfully monetize the technology. So VCs are by nature a good pointer toward things to come.

It is not just important to look at the overall venture capital flowing into a new tech, but also to the median investment size. While the total volume over time shows you the trajectory, the sizes of investment rounds give you an idea of the maturity. In the beginning, VCs are spreading their investments to learn and try out different use cases. After that, fewer, but larger investments show clarity in terms of direction. They also show that there are fewer investment targets as the market shakeout has passed.

While it is good to chase the money flows, you should also understand what money chases—namely, past returns. If previous investments into a technology have yielded a good return, checks will continue to roll in. This means that while investment volumes into a technology are helpful to anticipate growth, they are useless to anticipate saturation. Often, money will flow in past a technology's prime, even after the best ideas have already been taken. There is something else that investment flows cannot reveal: Whether the technology will be sustainably relevant. To find this out, you will have to wait and see how the adoption turns out. How many customers are really using it and paying for it?

> *"Silicon Valley has turned into a big grift. Starting with the cheap money after 2009, there was too much capital chasing opportunities. And when you have mega VCs with huge amounts of capital to deploy, they can fund companies to do what Reid Hoffman called 'blitzscaling': grabbing market share by underpricing their product and spending tons of money on marketing. This is what happened with Uber and Lyft. Instead of there being real experimentation on product, pricing, and business model, with the market picking the winners, the VCs picked the winners at the beginning. Effectively we now have a centrally planned tech economy in many ways. And in so*

many ways, what Silicon Valley is creating today are financial instruments rather than real companies. It's a bit like what happened with the banks leading up to the 2007 mortgage crisis."

—TIM O'REILLY, founder of O'Reilly Media & AlphaTech Ventures

40

Early Trend Indicator #2: Research Papers

FUNDING VOLUMES ARE CLOSELY CORRELATED with market volume. They yield a small edge in timing, but don't really help to catch rapidly emerging (let alone exploding) tech. Yet precisely this type of early technology often makes for splendid asymmetric investments. Sure, the failure rates

CHART 40

Blockchain market volume vs. research papers

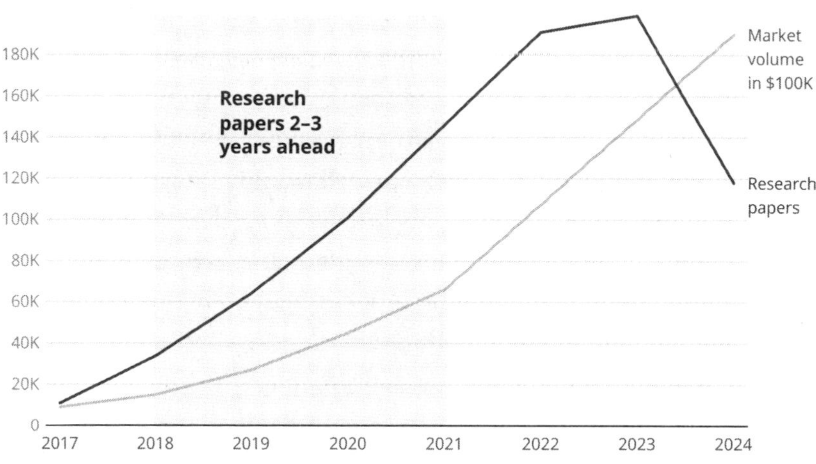

Chart: Igor Pejic · Data from: Google Scholar, Electrolq

are high, but one successful bet can make up for multiple failures. So, how to find technologies that will have their prime time in the next one, two, or three years?

The good news first: There is an early telltale sign of nascent technologies. It is a quantifiable indicator with a lot of knowledge attached. The bad news: It involves delving into complex and often bleak academic prose. I am talking about the study of research publications. While tedious, it should be part of the foundation of your radar for new technologies.

To understand why, look at the visualization in this chapter. As before, I look at the ascent of blockchain, though the principle applies to most new tech. What you see is that trends in research activity foretell which way market volume will go. In the case of blockchain, this strategy helped investors to get a clear time advantage over those who shunned the world of academia. The biggest increase in research papers percentagewise was in 2018. Market volume saw the strongest growth one year later. Then research activity fizzled out and even started declining in 2024. The money companies kept spending on blockchain still kept growing but slowed from year to year. So, again, publication rates served as a solid weather vane of trends to come.

The chart also illustrates the common phenomenon that research activity drops at one point precipitously, while business activity plateaus. Technological breakthroughs become rarer. In other words, innovations mature more quickly than markets. So, while the number of research papers should be on your dashboard to identify upcoming tech trends, it doesn't tell you much about when decline will kick in. And as with everything in investing, it is not a law of nature that research activity will *always* precede growth trends. You always have to analyze it against the backdrop of other indicators such as those we discuss in the following chapters.

Keep in mind that scientific research is more than another quantitative signpost. Academic writing doesn't exactly make for enjoyable evening reading, but if you want to beat the market on timing, you will have to bite that bullet. Buying Bitcoins before reading Satoshi's white paper is more akin to gambling than investing. If you don't understand how mRNA vaccines are different to live-attenuated ones, you probably shouldn't buy shares of pharma companies that pioneer mRNA technology. There is no shortcut around a lot of reading and critical reflection.

Warren Buffett has been finding alpha buried under mountains of annual reports for decades. Just how important this approach is in tech is succinctly summed up by Chris Wake: "If you are looking at capitalizing on cutting-edge tech, diving into research papers and scientific journals is a great way to stay ahead of the curve. You have to be a nerd."

Luckily, academic papers have succinctly written abstracts, none of which is hiding behind a paywall. There is no excuse to stop your research with the number of papers published.

41

Early Trend Indicator #3: Patent Applications

JUST LIKE RESEARCH PAPERS, patent activity is a harbinger of trends to come. You will notice that this chapter's chart looks much like the previous one. I illustrate the early advantage of following patent applications with the familiar blockchain example. Just like papers, patent application trends were about two years ahead of market volumes.

The two indicators are not interchangeable, though. Patents naturally follow basic research with a small lag of time, so the time advantage you get over the market is smaller. But unlike research, patent applications prove that companies believe in the commercial viability of a technology. A flurry of patents only happens when the theoretical results can be cast into real-world applications. Sometimes patents are filed for defensive reasons, sometimes even to grab headlines and position a company as cutting-edge. So filings are not always evidence that a company sees a huge profit potential in the technology. But its total number is a solid signpost. The less hype is buzzing around a technology, the more reliable is the metric. And often upward and downward trends are more pronounced for patents than for research papers, so they are more easily detectable. You can see that in the chart. Research builds on other research and thus grows organically. Private applications of

Blockchain market volume vs. patents

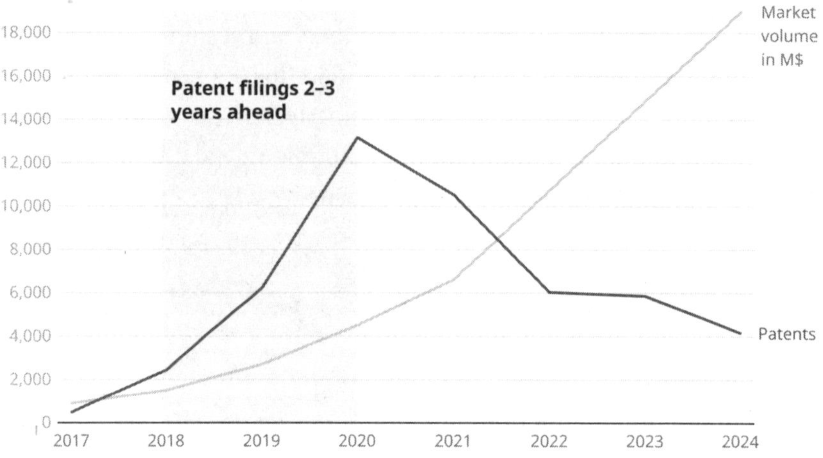

The number of patents granted keeps changing even for previous years as patents can be added years after filing, but the trend displayed above still remains.

Chart: Igor Pejic • Data from: WIPO, ElectroIQ

those results do not. Companies unleash a torrent of activities after a breakthrough but are also quicker to pull the plug.

Tracking patents allows you to drill down and pinpoint where the activity is happening. Is there a particular industry that is more active? Which companies are filing the most patents? Are those startups or incumbents? Is there a country or region with more filings than others? And just as with academic papers, patent filings can be read. Again, very technical, but very helpful too. Research papers teach you a technology's basics, but patent filings are one of the best resources for learning about the use cases.

There is one caveat, though. In many countries, including the US and Europe, patents take 18 months between initial filings and publication. This blocking period refers to the entire text. Thus, the fact that a company applied for, say, an AI patent becomes public quickly. Be aware, however, that while patents can cover a large chunk of innovation activity, they occasionally leave a large blind spot. "A big part of innovation happens outside of the patent system, simply because it takes so much time and so many resources to file and defend them," explains

Harald Trautsch. The other reason why many companies choose not to file for a patent is that they don't want to give away to their competitors what they are working on. And then there are segments like software, in which innovation is very difficult to patent. How should Google or Amazon file their ranking algorithms when they change constantly?

Media outlets occasionally also report on the numbers of patents granted. These statistics provide very little value to investors. Patents take years to be granted. Those footed on novel technology take even longer. So, stick to the immediate patent applications and follow them in tandem with research activity.

42

Early Trend Indicator #4: Talent Trends

WHEN COMPANIES SECURE FUNDING to enter a new technology, the money goes to infrastructure investments, to acquisitions, but also to people who are supposed to build the solutions. Tech staff falls into two categories: Generalists and domain experts. Usually the generalists outnumber the technology experts. Project managers or developers can often transition from one product or technology to another, and for most positions deep tech expertise is not needed. So, the hiring of experts for a new technology is actually not the costliest position. The important lesson

CHART 42

AI PhDs hiring by sector pre-ChatGPT

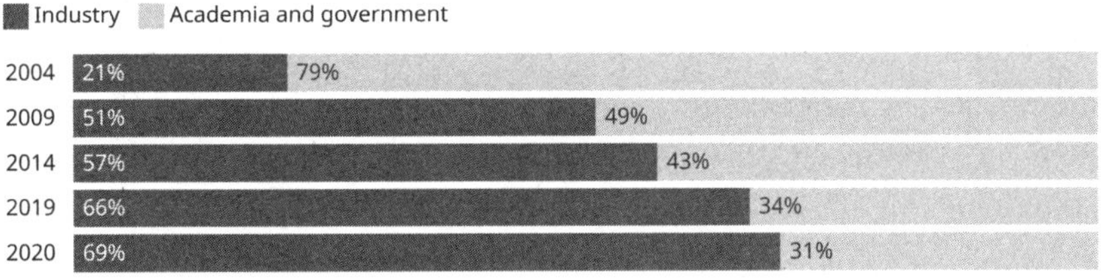

Chart: Igor Pejic • Data from: Ahmed/Wahed/Thompson

for investors is thus that funding does not necessarily precede the hiring of new experts. On the contrary. Studying hiring practices can give you an edge even against investors looking at the money going into a technology.

There are many metrics to look for in the staffing practices of a company or an industry in general. Did major players announce new departments or even business units focusing on a novel tech? Is the number of job ads increasing in an area? What about the actual hiring numbers? Have they gone up? And a look at some of the open job ads not only gives you a valuable glimpse about the strategy of a company, but also at which hierarchical level the new tech will be located.

One particular type of transition is particularly telling: The switch from academia to the private sector. You see an example at the top of this chapter. AI has been around since the middle of the 20th century, and for most of that time, AI research happened primarily in universities and similar research institutions. Only between 2004 and 2009 did the picture start to change. And it changed dramatically. The number of AI PhDs working in the private sector leaped from 21% to 51%. And from there it only continued to grow. This was a very long time before the AI funding hike, let alone before the media buzz around generative AI took hold.

So why is the ratio between research and industry so critical to watch? Because it is an indicator that a technology has transgressed the stage of pure foundational research and is on its way to real-world applications and industrialization. In this phase, companies have a huge need for experts in a novel technology but there aren't enough of them to poach from their competitors. Academia thus becomes the number one talent pool.

Talent migration is not only an early indicator that monetization of a new technology might soon occur, but it is a driver of the change itself. Another self-fulfilling prophecy. In the previous case: More AI PhDs in the private sector means that more of them will work on transforming theoretical knowledge to usable applications. This will accelerate the tipping point.

43

Early Trend Indicator #5: Public Interest

THERE IS NO SUCH THING AS BAD PUBLICITY. No PR consultant would question that rule. But does this logic also apply to investing? Enron shareholders will probably say no. But putting scandal stories aside, there is actually evidence that technologies benefit tremendously from high publicity. Hikes in public exposure precede hikes in market volumes. Sticking with the blockchain example, in this chapter's chart you can see how the relative interest of everyday people evolved. It shows how the Google Trends score for the term "blockchain" went up or down per year, meaning how often people searched for it historically. The interest exploded in 2017, foreshadowing the increased market size in 2018. For the next two years people googled "blockchain" less often, before showing renewed

CHART 43

Blockchain market volume vs. Google Trends score

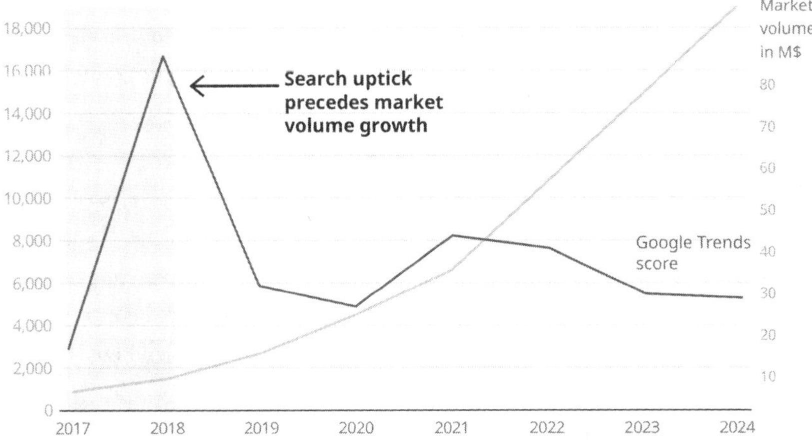

Yearly Google Trends scores from January.

Chart: Igor Pejic • Data from: Google, ElectroIQ

interest in 2021. Again, a harbinger of things to come. The next year, the money spent on the tech started accelerating once again.

Public interest is probably the trickiest early indicator to catch. It can skyrocket from one moment to the next, remain steady for years, or plunge overnight. Many technologies might never leap into collective consciousness at all. And for those that do, public attention might be snapped away by unexpected crises. Also, the exuberant mood around a technology can sour quickly. Unlike patents or research papers, babbling about a technology or googling it requires no long-term commitment, so it is rather a snapshot in time. But if public interest reaches a certain threshold and manages to stay in the news cycle for more than a couple of days, it starts impacting companies' plans. Investors who pay close attention are then ahead of the technology's growth curve.

The important thing with public interest is not to focus solely on media coverage, but also to track whether people are actively looking for it. It is crucial to survey the broad population. If your Twitter or LinkedIn bubble hypes up a tech, that is a good start. But it offers no insight on whether it will eventually rake in money for the companies behind it. This is why tools such as Google Trends should be an essential part of your toolbox. They give you the quantitative backbone to the hype cycle. Jackie Fenn, the analyst who has come up with the hype cycle concept, explains how each stage of the cycle has its own indicators: "The first part of the hype cycle is driven by human sentiment, particularly our natural attraction to novelty. So investors can use sentiment analysis to watch for a rising tide of articles and social media activity speculating about the transformative power and impact of the technology."

Of course, search activity is not as telling as the number of buyers of an actual product or even of an app's users. Yet, in the early stages of a technology, there might not be any viable products. Ergo, search volume is one of the best clues at your disposal.

This kind of monitoring is not an exact science. None of the early trend indicators is. And none of those indicators should be the sole basis of an investment decision. Sometimes those metrics might even contradict each other. However, if you see multiple metrics pointing in the same direction, something is going on. Having a dashboard of those early barometers is the best way to jump on the right bandwagon at the right time.

44

Why Expert Forecasts Should Be Viewed with Caution

KEEPING TRACK OF ALL THOSE EARLY TREND indicators is a real grind. Where to get the data? Is it reliable? Is it up to date? What are the thresholds to define for buying or selling? Are other technologies moving in the same direction? Are the growth rates adequate for the technology's capabilities or are they hype-driven? It is no wonder, then, that many—if not most—investors rely on a shortcut: Expert forecasts.

And why shouldn't they? Experts spend most of their time reading about a technology, talking to other experts, and many of them even work in the field. They know the companies, the regulators, customers' pain points and needs. Your knowledge will never parallel theirs.

That all might be true, but if experts could predict the future better than the market, they would be the richest people in the world. They are not. In fact, it turns out their predictions are no more accurate than those of nonexperts. This has been proven time and again, some studies even stretching over two decades and evaluating close to 82,000 expert opinions.

Chart 44 confirms that you should be skeptical of experts. In the years before ChatGPT, most indicators we discussed in the previous chapters were surging. Funding, patents, scientific papers, industry hiring of researchers. And still experts were caught flat-footed by OpenAI's new product. They revised their forecasts of how long it will take GenAI to perform at the level of a human specialist in basically all major capabilities. Heavily. Creativity or natural language understanding, for example, are now supposed to be reached more than 20 years earlier than initially thought. I don't know any investor that would have gotten into GenAI before ChatGPT's breakthrough based on these forecasts.

There are many reasons why experts don't get it right despite their knowledge. First of all, their super-expertise in one field often causes

CHART 44

Expert forecasts on when GenAI will reach the level of a human specialist

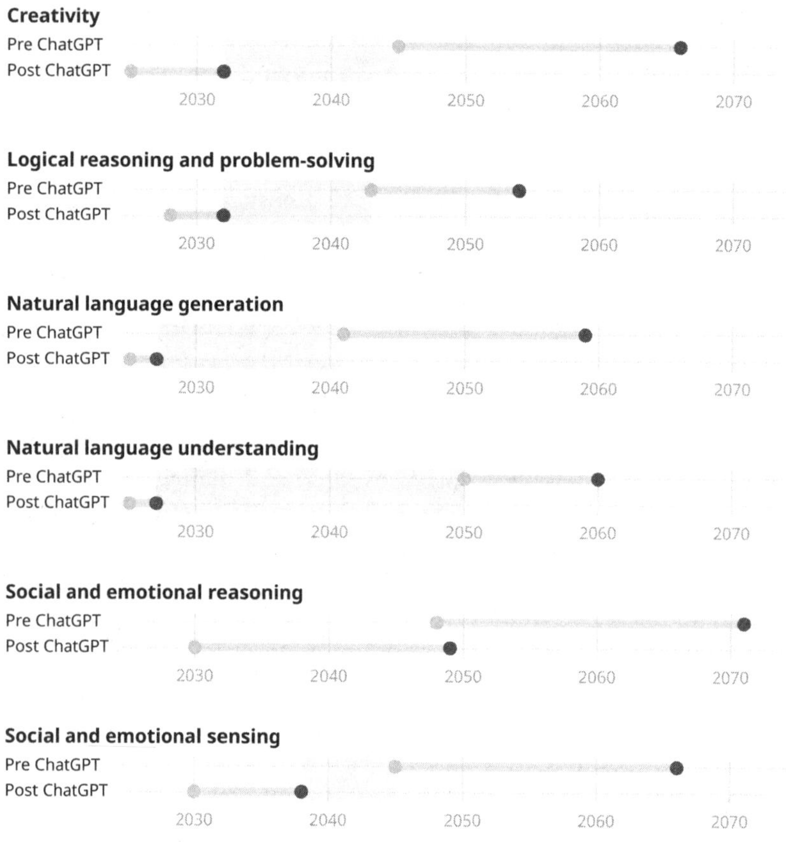

Specialists are defined as the top quartile. Experts were asked in 2017 and 2023. The lines represent the ranges of responses.

Chart: Igor Pejic • Data from: McKinsey

tunnel vision. Second, they are prone to groupthink. Dissent in the community usually comes at a cost, whether that means lower chances of getting published in academic journals or being invited to interviews. This fosters unanimity and thus overconfidence. There are many experts that break this mold, but many do not.

Third, experts have particular interests too. If you have dedicated your entire career to studying gene therapy, there is no way you will ever argue its potential is anything but revolutionary. Others blare out grandiose forecasts just to grab headlines. Or they own companies in the field. So obviously they won't make any forecasts that are bad for their business. And even with the best-intentioned experts, I have never heard them even off record as much as mumble a silent "I don't know." Experts are paid to know—so, just like an AI tool, they would rather say something wrong than admit it.

That is not to say that you should ignore experts. Independent experts tell you what the market thinks. Corporate expert commentary lets you glimpse into their strategy around the new tech. What use cases are highlighted? What risks are stressed? What topics are avoided? Experts are another important jigsaw piece but unfortunately not the shortcut we (want) to see in them.

> *"As an investor, the ultimate thing is to go with the truth and not be trapped in the Potemkin village that is often created. A lot of people do not know how to decode the news. What's the motivation behind why people say and post things? That's always the question you have to get down to. How do I decode the news? It's map theory. Once you understand where you don't want to go, that is just as valuable to know as where you want to go. I was a CEO of NBC Internet. I've seen from the inside how the media functions. If you receive information that is probably not true, that's actually valuable information. And this is the thing most people don't take into account. Why did they say that? There is a reason. So, what you are really doing is you're moving yourself up a level. It is the difference between walking on the street or having a map."*

—CHRIS KITZE, chairman at Alphabit Digital Currency Fund, former CEO of NBC Internet

V

———

GETTING THE
COMPANY RIGHT

MOST STOCKS WILL SHED VALUE, even when viewed through the prism of long-term investing. Many of those that do go up will still underperform the S&P 500 benchmark. The reason: What drives the stock market are a few outsized successes. But how do you identify those top performers? The vast majority of these exceptional performers are tech companies. So, as a tech investor, you already have a natural advantage, but this is not enough. Luckily, top performers share other crucial characteristics. If you are able to identify these, you will dramatically increase the odds of finding the next Amazon or Microsoft. Many of those traits go against the grain of what mavens and common investment wisdom teach you.

Important lessons can be learned from metrics like the P/E ratio or the correlation of past performance and market cap. Perhaps you have read about those and perhaps you remember what conclusions to draw from them. In case you do remember, forget them. Most of these lessons don't apply to the tech sector. In fact, the tech sector defies the entire paradigm of value investing. Many core tenets of the methodology simply do not work. Try comparing Walmart and Boeing to Palantir or

Coinbase and you will understand why. In the models of Ben Graham and Warren Buffett, tech stocks always look expensive and overpriced. Asset-based analysis does not work because they don't have tangible assets defining their value. Historical averages are of no use either because tech valuations just keep soaring into ever giddier heights. Ergo, reversion to the mean does not apply either. Above all, it is software stocks that cause this kind of headache, but also other technologies that work with similar logic—say, double-sided platforms.

It is no coincidence Buffett has never actually touched tech stocks. He bought Apple because, to him, it is more akin to a consumer goods company in which the iPhone hardware drives most of the sales. That doesn't mean you should steer clear from them. Viewed realistically, you will fail in your search for the next tech shooting star. Most of the time. But not all of the time. And these lonely success stories make a difference in the world of tech investing more than anywhere else. Due to their stellar rise, tech winners are a prime example of asymmetric investments. Even if you lose on 10 bets, the 11th might deliver returns that are so disproportionally high that they more than make up for many complete losses. For that strategy to work out, you have to make sure to be backing the eventual winner, while at the same time eliminating as many likely non-winners as possible from your portfolio. The first question is to know where to start looking.

Technology pioneers are revered by pundits, but history shows that investors that seek out mass-scalers rather than first-movers are better off. A type of particularly valuable company is the "diversifying entrant" that easily outpaces even blitzscaling newcomers. These are giants from one industry breaking into another. I am not saying startups cannot disrupt an industry. Michael Dell and Jeff Bezos did so single-handedly to mega-industries like computing and retail. But I am saying it is less likely than another behemoth claiming the top spot.

Furthermore, the layer at which a company competes determines your success chances. Bets on infrastructure providers are, per default, more likely to succeed than wagers into the highly competitive application layer. Given, of course, that you have rightly identified what a new technology requires. You don't truly understand a technology until you understand its supply chain. So let's start with that.

45

Understanding the Technology
and Its Supply Chain

IMAGINE IT IS NOVEMBER 2022. You are given a crystal ball that tells you about a new GenAI tool called ChatGPT that will be launched by the end of the month. One of the largest tech hysterias in recent history will be kicked off. A bull run will lift valuations of entire stock indices. You have $10,000 to invest. What do you do?

All the possible use cases run through your head. The obvious thing to do is to look for companies churning out lines of AI code. But there are thousands of them. And most of those aren't even public. So the grand realization strikes you that if AI companies turn out to be successful,

CHART 45

Chipmakers (not) capitalizing on the AI revolution

Share price development

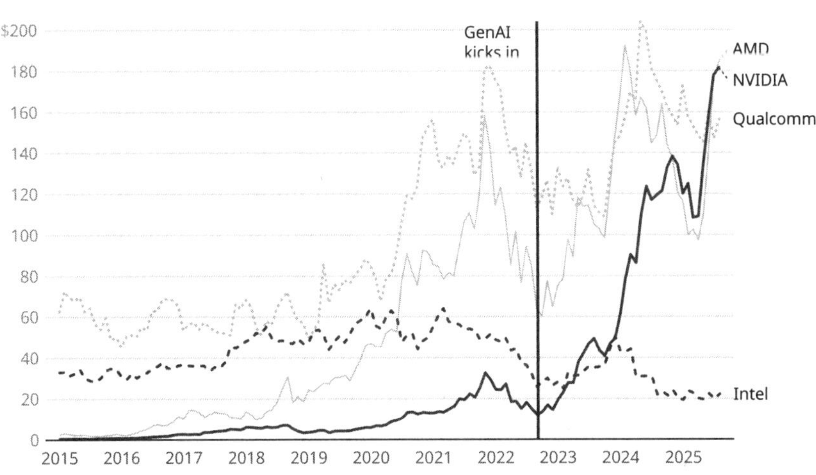

Chart: Igor Pejic • Data from: Investing.com

this will fuel the rise of their suppliers too. And those suppliers sell their services to many similar companies. Hence, less competition. Hence, they scale faster and fail less often. AI companies will need a lot of server space, even more data to train their algorithms, but most of all they will need better computer chips to build and enhance their large language models.

Moving up that supply chain is already an extremely valuable step that boosts rewards and shrinks the risk. The higher up you climb the supply chain, the less crowded it becomes. But the question now is which semiconductor company to choose. Intel, AMD, NVIDIA, Texas Instruments? All of them should benefit from the AI wave, right? Not quite. As the chart on the previous page illustrates, NVIDIA was most successful in riding the AI wave. By far.

The reason for NVIDIA's outperformance lies in the type of chips they manufacture. Coming from the gaming world, NVIDIA has always been strong with chips that have powerful graphic capabilities. It primarily produced GPUs (graphic processing units), whereas the other manufacturers were more focused on CPUs (central processing units). Think of the CPU as a CEO and the GPU as an accountant. The CPU is very good in coordinating processes in the computer, orchestrating all components. The GPU, on the other hand, is a highly qualified expert. It can do only a small number of tasks but is unmatched in speed and skill. It turns out that training AI algorithms requires extreme performance in only a few processes. GPUs, not CPUs, are the backbone of AI progress.

It is easy to post-rationalize this distinction now. But before NVIDIA kicked in its stellar growth, it would have been impossible to tell the difference for anybody without having dug deep into the supply chain, the requirements of AI training, and without knowing how many CPU vs. GPU chips each semiconductor company was manufacturing.

"Our strategy is looking for the right layer of abstraction. This often means understanding the supply chain and going one layer deeper. We were looking into frontier nuclear companies some four to five years ago. We realized that all of the things we were seeing exist at an application layer. However, if you go a layer deeper, you realize the fuel is a massive bottleneck. And so even companies that are trying to do things that have a clear

and present demand are hindered by the lack of supply. So, we invested in a company trying to crack that supply constraint. And you have the immediate demand from all of those application layer companies."

—CHRIS WAKE, founding partner at Atypical Ventures

46

The Odds of Picking Winners and What They Mean for Your Portfolio Strategy

THE ODDS ARE NOT ON YOUR SIDE. Roughly two out of three companies in the S&P 500 have historically performed below the average. And only roughly one out of ten investments will outperform the average tech sector. Not discouraged yet? Then consider this: In June 2025, the *Financial Times* reported that the S&P 500 even beat private equity. Yes, those

CHART 46

How many individual stocks are outperforming the index?

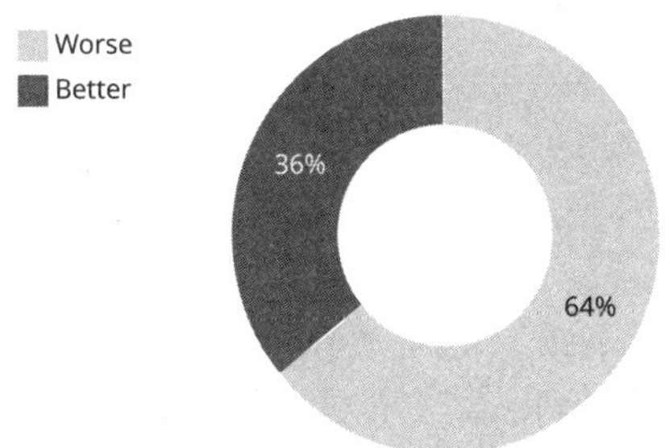

Performance vs. S&P 500 average

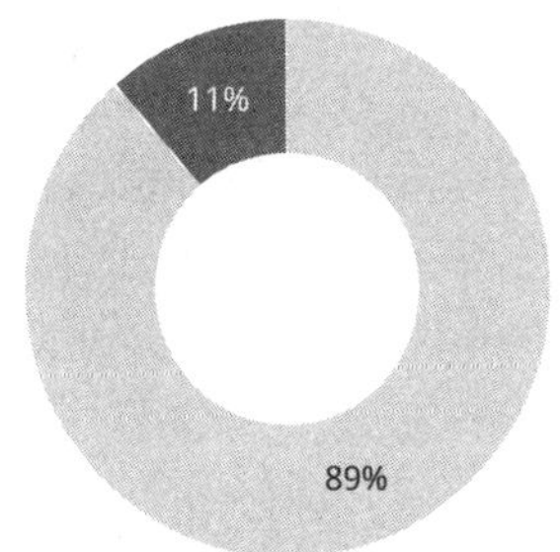

Performance vs. S&P 500 tech segment average

Five-year cumulative returns as of April 2025. Including dividends. Tech sector performance measured by the Technology Select Sector SPRD Fund (XLK).

are the guys whose full-time job it is to hunt for gems hidden from the public eye. For the first time since the year 2000, the State Street Private Equity Index (SSPEI) lagged behind the S&P 500 over a three-month, one-year, three-year, five-year, and ten-year period.

So what happened since the year 2000? In one sentence: Tech giants took over Wall Street. And they are not loosening their grip. More specifically, it is the performance of a few large-cap tech companies that has been driving the profitability of the entire index. And with each new tech wave, more of them have made it to the pinnacle. EVs catapulted Tesla into the market cap top 10. AI did the same for NVIDIA and TSMC. Before that, Apple and Facebook rode the wave of mobile. But unlike previous generations of market-beating companies, Big Tech proved very sticky. They have built adaptive capabilities.

Is this all a trend or are we witnessing a lasting shift away from how stocks and stock markets used to behave in the 20th century? If it really is a fundamental shift, then tech stock pickers shouldn't be scared by this chapter's chart. All they have to do is throw their money behind the tech goliaths and turn the odds in their favor. While there are many reasons to believe this dominance will continue into the future, nobody knows for certain. And the argument that I am making is not that investing in Big Tech is a bulletproof strategy. I am arguing, however, that it has a higher probability of succeeding. The likes of Microsoft or Amazon have proven their genius time and again. It is hard to imagine Jeff Bezos committing a strategic blunder or Satya Nadella losing the preeminence of Windows and MS Office. They are reliable, just like a person who has been diligently paying off the mortgage for 25 years. He is less likely to miss the next payment than a person who has yet to pay the first rate. I am convinced that these companies have a higher than one-in-three chance to end up above the market benchmark.

All these likelihoods should be factored into your portfolio creation. You can still decide to go with a newcomer instead of a tech incumbent, but you have to have strong reasons for doing so. It is a very high bar they have to clear.

"I always try to consider the contrarian viewpoint and consider what others may be missing. I call this 'looking at the B-Side of

the record.' If the whole world is chasing AI, I try to consider those tailwinds, and what secondary or tertiary effects it may have. For example, if the speed of AI increases potential threats, I'll look at cybersecurity. We also mitigate concentration risk by making a lot of bets. In some ways we index the market around our perspective or worldview. Venture capital is driven by outliers, and power law returns. To find those outliers, I think you can rely on proprietary access, systematic process, or by indexing around a core belief and making a lot of portfolio bets. With those bets we are buying information access, and as we uncover what we think is asymmetric advantage, we'll try to dial up positions. This is a strategy that could work in both public as well as private markets."

—SCOTT HARTLEY, co-founder of Everywhere Ventures
and author of *The Fuzzy and the Techie*

47

Long-Term Alpha of
Top-Performing Companies

"WINNERS KEEP WINNING." This is the simple, yet powerful truth shared by this chapter's expert. The greatest athletes are those that win titles at age 20, at age 40, and in between. The greatest musicians are those that produce number one hits on every album. And the greatest companies are those that outperform their rivals year after year after year. Consistency is greatness. You can be the best sprinter at the Olympics or the best stock of the year, and you will capture headlines, but if you don't manage to repeat that for a very long time, you will never be among the best. Success compounds.

Big Tech has collectively beaten the S&P 500 benchmark and the average tech benchmark not only for the past five years, but for the past

CHART 47

Cumulative returns of Big Tech winners

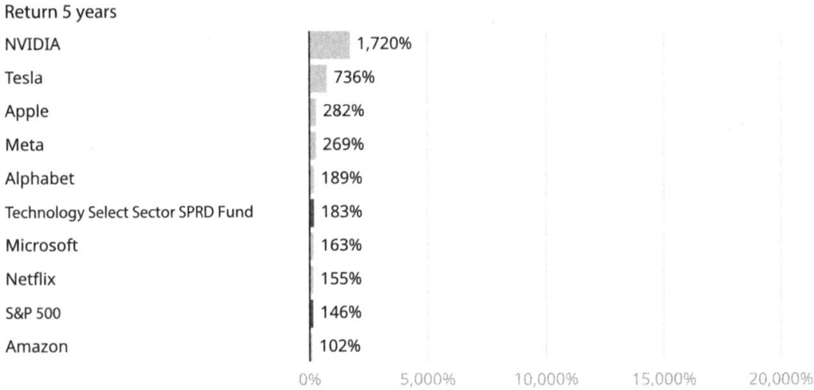

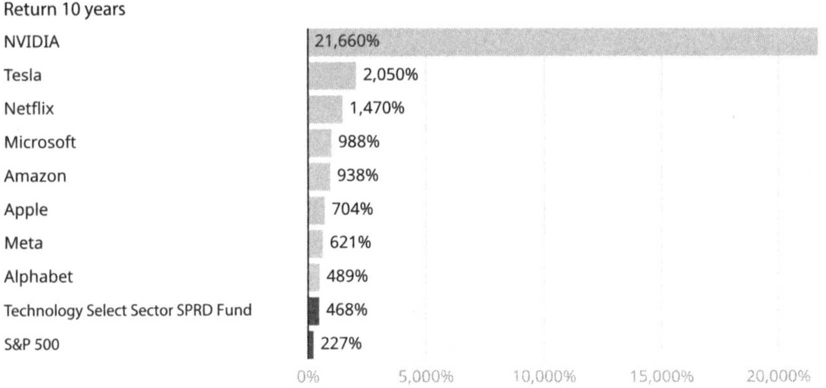

Cumulative returns as of April 2025. Including dividends. Tech sector performance measured by the Technology Select Sector SPRD Fund (XLK).

Chart: Igor Pejic • Data from: YCharts

ten. In doing so, America's tech titans invalidated the argument that massive companies might be stable but have limited growth potential. NVIDIA alone delivered a return north of 21,000% if held for 10 years. And though Tesla is a distant second, it is still beating the S&P 500 by a factor of nine. For the past 15 years I have been hearing how tech giants are overvalued and how they have reached their limits. Yet they have been consistently finding new room to grow and thereby consistently boosting shareholder value.

David Gardner actually views it is an asset that companies like NVIDIA grow bigger and stronger. "They have more assets. They have more resources. They have more possibilities." He highlights Amazon as an example for successfully using size and clout to fuel growth rather than inhibit it. "Amazon has never struck me as complacent or destroying its own assets or resources. It has been expanding and helping the world all the way through, now in its fourth decade of doing so."

Another notable thing in the chart is that Big Tech actually performs better against the market the longer the time horizon. You would assume that individual stocks are more volatile than the market to new disruptions, pandemics, interest rate changes, and the like. Not so the top performers. Though they had short setbacks, overall they have been marching in one direction only over the last 10 years.

This consistency has compounded into incredible returns, and this is exactly why—despite the poor odds presented in the last chapter—it does pay to search for winners. Not just because you might be hitting an NVIDIA. But because, once you have found a consistent top performer, you will benefit from it not only in the next year, but in the next 10 or 20. That is also why it is so critical to hold on to them. Because if you have chosen to take the risk of any individual company over just indexing the market or the tech sector, you must have had strong reasons to do so. Perhaps because they are best positioned to ride the next tech wave. Perhaps their product is superior and hard to copy. Or perhaps because you believe in their founder and his vision. In any event, those are reasons that don't just vanish. They persist over a couple of years. So let your winners win and don't sell them.

"What do winners do? They keep winning. But many people, they don't believe that or act off that conviction. They think about the stock market as a parabola. They think what goes up must come down. The stock market is actually a hyperbola. It goes up over time. It's Newton's first law of motion, which is that an object at rest tends to stay at rest, and an object in motion tends to stay in motion. And so an object that's winning tends to keep winning. For this reason, momentum is real and it really does

propel. And even if sometimes winners lose—because we know that sometimes they do—if you hold the ones that keep winning, they will wipe out all of your losers."

—DAVID GARDNER, co-founder of the Motley Fool and
author of *Rule Breaker Investing*

48

Where Did All the Trillion-Dollar Companies Come From?

WHEN WINNERS KEEP WINNING FOR A LONG TIME, they don't just become great; they become big. In 2018, Apple became the first company ever to break the one-trillion-dollar barrier. A new era of mega-sized companies was ushered in. Ten other companies followed at rapid pace, eight of which were tech companies. The burning question that thus arises: Have Big Tech stocks become too expensive?

For those seeking to pick "cheap" stocks, one metric stands above all others: P/E ratios. Popularized by Benjamin Graham and Warren Buffett, this metric is at the foundation of the value investing school of thought. You get the P/E ratio when dividing the company's stock price by its earnings per share. A low P/E value suggests that a stock is undervalued and vice versa. The P/E ratio goes up when the market is willing to overpay because of expectations of future growth. In the next chapter, we will look at whether low P/E ratios really correlate with better performance. But before we do, let's determine how the new titans compare to the market.

Reportedly, Warren Buffett looks for P/E ratios below 15. Each of the companies presented in chart 48 is far away from that threshold. Even Buffett's Berkshire Hathaway itself couldn't reach that value. So, Big Tech certainly isn't cheap. But is it expensive? The S&P 500 market average stands at 28. Hence, less than half of the trillion-dollar mega-caps are in the average territory and the rest is utterly expensive by that measure. What is more, the newest members of the $1 trillion market-cap club tend to have higher

CHART 48

Year and P/E ratio when hitting a 1T$ market cap

Company	Year	P/E ratio (trailing)
Apple	2018	19
Amazon	2018	162
Microsoft	2019	29
Saudi Aramco	*2019*	*23*
Alphabet	2020	27
Meta	2021	26
Tesla	2021	330
NVIDIA	2023	214
Berkshire Hathaway	*2024*	*22*
TSMC	2024	31
Broadcom	2024	87

Non-tech companies in italics. P/E ratios rounded.

Table: Igor Pejic • Data from: YCharts, CompaniesMarketcap.com, Macrotrends, CNBC, Brookings, *The Guardian*, BankRate

ratios when hitting the one trillion mark than the earlier ones. Amazon can be disregarded. Its ratio was not meaningful due to its reinvestment strategy and low reported earnings at the time. The same cannot be said about the later giants when they broke the sound barrier. Also, tech companies on paper seem more expensive even than the two non-tech trillion-dollar giants. Growth is baked into tech because even disruptive technology often ends up being additive. Tech companies continue to rake in profits with the old generations of technology while they grow in the new.

"We have had big companies before, but the tech world is continuously expanding because it is adding layers while still feeding off the existing ones. It all comes down to the cycles of technology," says Ronit Ghose, who heads Citibank's Future of Finance division. He told me to think about it in the lens of hardware. "First you have mainframes, then you have desktops, then laptops, then mobile. And then some sort of more integrated and immersive experiences. The phone will still be in our pocket as our computer, but we might be interacting with the world through smart glasses or other wearables."

In the chart, two companies tower above all others: Tesla and NVIDIA. Valuations are ballooning because investors are expecting massive future growth in multiple mega-industries. No company captures that speculative drive better than Tesla. The optimists are talking up its soon-to-come autonomous-driving robo-taxis and robotics. They stress its position as a potential mega-collector of torrents of data, which then will be crunched by the powerful algorithms of xAI. If one of those materializes, it might indeed change the picture (and the ratios), but we have been hearing about those ambitions for years. Buzzy initiatives are started, R&D budgets are ratcheted up, and tweets are sent out. And the potential is there. Just as with the computing example, those new forays would be additive. Tesla would still make money with the vehicles on top to the newly added services. It would even sell more of those if the autonomous driving module got good enough or if better robots make the production cheaper. There is little evidence of new profits as of yet, but as long as investors haven't given up hope, the P/E ratios will stay high and stocks will look overrated.

49

Do *High* P/E Ratios Herald a Good Performance?

VALUE INVESTORS DON'T BUY THE STRATEGY of excessive growth. They argue that eventually even tech stocks will revert to the mean. And they point to history. Stocks with strong fundamentals, they say, have eventually always outperformed growth stocks. And research proves them right. Value stocks indeed performed better for the largest part of the 20th century, especially for large caps. On average, high P/E ratios

CHART 49

Price and growth of Big Tech

Company	P/E ratios	Revenue annual growth	Gross profit annual growth
Alphabet	19	14%	17%
Amazon	31	11%	15%
Apple	**31**	**2%**	**7%**
Meta	21	22%	23%
Microsoft	30	16%	17%
Netflix	46	16%	28%
NVIDIA	35	114%	121%
Palantir	367	29%	28%
Tesla	**118**	**1%**	**–1%**
S&P 500	28		
Technology Select Sector SPDR Fund	37		

Ratios justified?

P/E ratios trailing.

Table: Igor Pejic · Data from: YCharts, Macrotrends, GuruFocus

correlate with a weaker performance. There is, however, one industry that defies this pattern. You might have guessed it: Technology.

Traditionally, P/E ratios of tech companies are significantly higher than the S&P 500 average, with many outliers boasting even much higher multiples. At the time of composing the above chart, Tesla's P/E ratio was four times higher than the market average. Palantir's was an incredible 13 times higher. Yet, those are exactly the kind of companies that have driven the surge of American stock markets more than anything else. The chart in chapter 47 paints a crystal-clear picture.

As I described in the introduction of this section, many of the traditional value investing frameworks don't fit to tech businesses. They fail to prize in innovative breakthroughs, winner-take-all markets, and the expansion to ever more industries. Tech companies are an extreme version of growth stocks. And if you want to know just how much more extreme it gets, look to digital assets. It makes almost zero difference whether the blockchain behind a coin generates tons of fees or whether there is a business case at all. Investments are driven solely by expectations of value appreciation.

So, should investors simply disregard P/E ratios when it comes to tech? The short answer is no. While they are often useless for comparing tech to non-tech stocks, they do reveal a lot when you compare tech stocks to each other. They are even more telling when interpreted along other indicators—say, growth trends for revenues and profits. This is what I did in chart 49, and I was able to spot two Big Tech companies that don't quite live up to their growth stories: Tesla and Apple.

Tesla is a wild card. They put all their chips in disruptive tech, which will take them either to the moon or to the grave. Apple is a more solid company with the problem that it can't be clearly put in the value or the growth basket. Most of its revenues come from hardware that is often bought with religious-like brand loyalty. And just in case this isn't enough, Apple forces a golden handcuff approach upon them. Plus, Apple is steadily boosting its highly profitable Apple Services business. But it lacks the innovative gravitas of an Amazon or a Microsoft. It's R&D budget is sunk into projects like Apple Car, Apple Pay Later, or the VR headset. To no avail. AI? Blockchain? Cloud computing? Not even the slightest attempt. Amazon has a similar P/E ratio but more than five times the growth. It successfully attacks industry after industry and reinvests most of its earnings. Hence, the question is whether Apple really deserves to be viewed from the prism of a growing tech stock. Or will it simply continue to churn out iPhones and monetize the platform in a mature mobile market? If that turns out to be so, a correction of the stock price is imminent. The key for investors is to find out whether the growth trajectory is realistic or whether it is just feel-good corporate storytelling.

"P/E ratios are important because they tell you how expensive and hyped up the stock is. It's like buying a Ferrari. It's expensive, and you should understand that. And therefore, it's

in a different risk category than a railroad company. Think of Cisco. It was really run up back in 2000, went way down, and then stayed flat for decades. That's the danger if you get hyped up on a company where it turns out the fundamentals are not there to support a high price. Another thing that can justify high P/E ratios is when there is a growth perspective thanks to a new technology. Look at Tesla's robo-taxi possibilities. I see a way that Tesla is going to really disrupt Uber and Lyft, and transportation in a new way."

—ROBERT SCOBLE, publisher of *Unaligned* and *Scobleizer* and former Microsoft strategist

50

Identifying Mass-Scalers, Not Pioneers

ONE REASON WHY TECH GIANTS are much stickier at the top of corporate valuation lists is because of the nature of technological revolutions. Those are happening and spreading ever more quickly. Above all, however, they are more recursive. This means that they more strongly rely on predecessor technologies and thus require somewhat related core competencies. If you were good at producing typewriters, that know-how wouldn't have helped you to produce a computer, let alone write the software for it. Computers and smartphones—that's a different relation. Sure, building an app for iOS or Android is different from building one for Windows, but in the end it is still programming. Setting up cloud data centers requires knowledge about computers and networks. Training AI algorithms requires such data centers and it requires data. A lot of it. Setting up a blockchain is easier when you are an expert on databases. You get the point.

The chart on the next page shows from where the dominant forces in each new technology age came from. Most of them are diversifiers, giants from another field that threw their entire weight into a new arena and

CHART 50

Where winners of technological revolutions come from

Technology	Newcomers	Diversifiers
(Personal) computing	Microsoft, Apple	
Internet	Amazon, Google	Microsoft (late-stage)
Mobile	Facebook	Apple, Google, Samsung
Cloud computing		Microsoft, Amazon, Google
Fintech	PayPal	Apple, Google, Alibaba
Generative AI		Microsoft (OpenAI), Google, NVIDIA, TSMC
Digital assets	Coinbase, Circle	JPMorgan Chase, BlackRock
Blockchain	Consensys	Google, Amazon, IBM
Satellites and new space		SpaceX*, BlueOrigin*
mRNA vaccines	Moderna, BioNTech	Pfizer

*This is not an exhaustive list of beneficiaries of new technologies, but a list of the most prominent and often most relevant examples. *While SpaceX and BlueOrigin are newcomers on paper, they are de facto an extension of Tesla and Amazon, led by the same founder and paying into the same big strategy.*

Table: Igor Pejic

outpaced the pioneers. Alex Lazarow also points out that a lot of newcomers are too early, and it's actually about getting the timing right and getting the packaging right. "Apple does this probably better than anyone else. They take things that work, repackage them, and then sell them through their incredible brand and distribution machine." This is why his company, Fluent Ventures, like many other VCs, looks for models where the problem is massive, but where there's some amount of de-risking, where people have proven the product-market fit and they have proven that there is scale. Being on time, getting the packaging right, and scaling quickly at the same time is extremely hard to accomplish. This I why a lot of the biggest winners are not necessarily the pioneers.

But on the left side you can also see some successful de novo entrants. That's management lingo for newcomers. These startups did manage to translate their tech edge into a market edge. This usually happened when more foundational technologies upended the market, as in the case of the computer replacing the typewriter. And only when really exceptional companies like Amazon or Microsoft led those disruptions. That's why these successful newcomers even went on to become diversifiers themselves in future tech revolutions. No truly great company is a one-trick pony.

A highly interesting distinction is that between blockchain and digital assets. Digital assets are an application of the underlying blockchain technology, yet both groups behaved in a completely different way. Tech giants like Amazon and Google conquered the blockchain-as-a-service space by offering managed blockchains to other corporations. Digital currencies, on the other hand, are dominated by a new breed of companies like Coinbase, the largest US crytpo exchange. Hence, in the end, it is the use cases that are disruptive rather than the technology itself.

So what does all of this mean for investors? Quite simply, that new tech territory is more likely to be occupied by a current tech titan than by a newcomer. There is an even stronger mathematical argument to place your bets on incumbents: It is more likely that you pick the winning one. There are only five to ten real IT supertankers, which means you have a 10–20% chance your bet will work out. Compare that to the thousands of crypto-brokers, cryptocurrencies, fintechs, or messaging apps. What is the likelihood you would have picked Coinbase, Circle, PayPal, or Facebook before they rose to the top of their industry and not one of their many failed competitors?

Often we also see collaboration between large incumbents and shooting stars. In the list presented in chart 50, I included mRNA vaccination. This novelty was distant enough from what pharmaceutical companies do traditionally, so it was young biotech companies that were first to have the breakthroughs. Yet to grab market share quickly enough, the upstart BioNTech had to partner with pharma giant Pfizer. This is a frequent pattern. In such a scenario, the likelihood to get one part of the winning duo right is much higher when picking one of the few established players than one of the hundreds of challengers.

51

Incumbent Stickiness Factor #1: R&D Spend

INCUMBENT SIZE MATTERS. The financial muscle, loved brands, and hordes of lobbyists help in every industry. Tech supertankers have yet another trump card, which in their case is more important than all of the above: Humongous R&D budgets. Innovation is really the heart of every technology company, often the main purpose of its existence. That is why companies like Meta are spending up to 27% of their entire revenues on R&D. Some Big Tech companies are listed in a non-tech area. Meta is categorized as an advertising company, Amazon as a retailer. Their R&D spending is excessively higher than that of their peers. Others like Microsoft or Alphabet are measured against other tech companies and are actually lagging behind in relative figures. Yet, due to their size, there is still no way they will ever be outspent in absolute terms. Currently, Amazon alone spends $96 billion on R&D per year. And the trend is just going up. That is a 12% increase over the previous year. There are only 35 companies in the S&P 500 that make even this much revenue. And most of these investments come directly out of their pockets. They require no loans. Tech giants are sitting on unmatched piles of cash.

So how is any upstart supposed to compete with Big Tech? Sure, a dollar spent at Amazon or Meta gets you far less than one spent at a startup. After all, they are behemoths whose bureaucracy alone swallows amounts a startup can only dream of. But still, we are talking about dimensions where, no matter how efficiently you work as a smaller corporation, chances are you will be out-innovated by the incumbents. That is why so many investors are flocking to Big Tech. Valuations swell. Innovation budgets balloon even more.

Sam Rahman, who launched a growth ETF focused on large caps and tech, describes how R&D muscle helps to entrench Big Tech's position: "CapEx in and of itself is a competitive advantage because if you

CHART 51

R&D to revenue ratios as compared to industry average

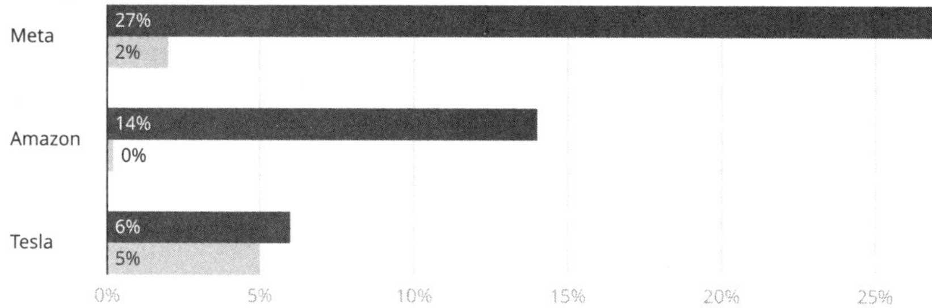

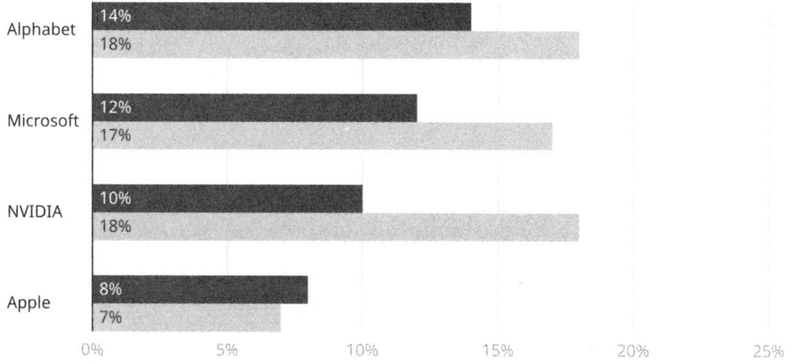

Ratios as of April/June 2025. Meta categorized as advertising, Amazon as retail, Tesla as auto and truck, Apple as health and information systems, Alphabet and Microsoft as software, and NVIDIA as semiconductor

Chart: Igor Pejic • Data from: YCharts, Aswath Damodaran

can generate that much cash and spend that much CapEx, there's very few companies that can compete with you." And this is truer for AI than any other recent technology. In the case of AI data center expansion, we've seen a massive spending increase over the last few years. "There's only four or five companies that are able to have seriously competitive LLMs. And I think that number will only shrink over time. It certainly won't go up. So scale and CapEx are a moat in and of themselves."

And yet a large R&D budget does not assure that a company will not get run over by a new tech wave. Nokia, Kodak, IBM. They all spent heavily to catch tech trends, smartphones, digital photography, and personal computing, respectively. Kodak even had the first patent for digital photography. Yet we all know their fates. New technologies arrive in ever shorter circles, and every time they deal the cards anew. Hence, while investors do have to keep an eye on the size of R&D budgets, it is even more critical to be aware of *how* these budgets are spent. As the next chapter demonstrates, savvy investors pick corporations that use their budgets to wage parallel and competing bets. This is an expensive approach, but a highly efficient one.

52

Parallel Bets—The Reason Large R&D Budgets Matter

AS WE HAVE SEEN IN THE LAST CHAPTER, each tech giant boasts a tremendous R&D budget. Yet one giant has been more successful in betting on new technologies than anybody else: Microsoft. It has been a force for decades, claiming the title of the world's most valuable company at the end of the 1990s as well as in the 2020s. Time and again Microsoft hit new technologies spot on. Driving its success: Parallel bets.

The Windows-maker has made many smart investments, but its valuation had been catapulted first and foremost by the numerous outsized successes it had. Its computer operating system dwarfs any other. Microsoft Office is the undisputed number one in productivity software. The Xbox gaming console and its cloud suite Azure are among the top three in their segment. And its partnership with OpenAI elevated GenAI to a global phenomenon. None of those triumphs happened because of a clever gamble, but because of clever risk management. Microsoft always waged many bets in parallel. It bet on competing technologies, competing standards, and competing players. Not just parallel but *competing*. It's not schizophrenia. It's a strategy.

In chart 52, every bet in bold is contradictory to at least one other bet. In its early days, Microsoft developed and marketed both MS-DOS

CHART 52

Microsoft's parallel bet strategy

Technology	Parallel bets	Outsized success
Operating systems (1980s—'90s)	MS-DOS vs. Xenix (Unix)*, OS/2 (with IBM) vs. Windows*, stake in Santa Cruz Operation	Windows
Productivity software (1980s—'90s)	Office for Windows vs. Office for Mac vs. Cross-Platform MS Office*	Cross-Platform MS Office
Mobile (2010s)	Windows Phone (inc. Nokia-acquisition) vs. Surface devices*	-
Gaming (2000s—'20s)	Xbox vs. Xbox Cloud Gaming (xCloud)*, Game Pass Ultimate	Xbox
Cloud computing (2010—'20s)	MS Azure in different formats (single vs. multi-platform, broad market vs. niche*)	Azure in multi-platform, broad market variant
Blockchain (2015—2021)	Azure Blockchain-as-a-Service on Ethereum vs. Ripple vs. Hyperledger*	-
Artificial intelligence (1990s—'20s)	OpenAI partnership vs. in-house AI development (e.g., MAI, Phi)*, third-party AI models (e.g., Anthropic, DeepSeek) vs. Azure AI*, Copilot	OpenAI, Copilot

Directly competing bets

Table: Igor Pejic

and Xenix, two opposing operating systems. In 1985, it jointly developed the OS/2 with IBM, while simultaneously continuing to develop Windows. Today, Microsoft markets Xbox cloud gaming and at the same time pushes the Xbox console. In AI, Microsoft has taken technological diversification onto a new level. It has worked on in-house initiatives for years, but it also pumped more than $10B into OpenAI and became its main partner. When the ChatGPT maker turned out to have a better

LLM, Microsoft had no qualms to let its internal LLM projects take the back seat. And still, it is not putting ChatGPT on a pedestal, but challenging it by testing models such as Meta's Llama, Anthropic, and DeepSeek, even integrating them in its Copilot AI engine. Artificial intelligence, so much seems clear, is a must-win battlefield.

Other times, when Microsoft waged too little or placed bets that were too narrow, it failed. Take blockchain. When the Azure cloud offered Blockchain-as-a-Service on multiple platforms, including the big ones such as Ethereum, Ripple, and Hyperledger, it turned out to be too narrow. Microsoft could have offered its own stablecoin, a powerful wallet, or its own smart contracts. Instead, it was too certain that providing blockchain infrastructure from the cloud would be the best business case. The effort was discontinued in 2021. Mobile was a similar story. Microsoft focused on the Windows phone and the surface device. While those were competing bets, they left a huge blind spot. It allowed Android and iOS to shoot up and build an unbreakable duopoly on mobile operating systems. Windows was first and foremost built for PCs, not mobile devices. Only later did Microsoft at least open its software like Office for iOS and Android, but it never became a mobile colossus like its Big Tech rivals.

Parallel bets are a powerful strategy in fast-moving, uncertain tech markets. Even more so with general-purpose technologies, which are tech arenas where failure is not an option. Parallel bets allow companies to hedge against backing a wrong technology or player, to combat tunnel vision and the sunken-cost fallacy, as well as to quickly pivot when the landscape changes. But is there more proof than just the anecdotal evidence from Microsoft? There is. Researchers confirmed it in multiple large-scale studies. One critical limitation applies, though: The relationship between technological diversification and firm performance is generally an *inverted U-shape*. While diversification enhances the chances of backing the right horse up to a point, excessive diversification can make a company spread so thin that it lacks the gravitas to turn successful bets into market dominance.

In the first part of the book, we discussed scenario planning as a key tool to understand the possible and likely directions in which the tech world could be headed to. Investors should also ask themselves whether a company's R&D spending is based on scenario planning. Is there a strategy that coordinates parallel bets and ensures that all scenarios are covered? Or do the investments seem redundant, opportunistic, and driven by corporate politics more than an overarching complementary strategy?

> *"Technology markets are uncertainty-dense and power-law distributed. A handful of moonshots make all the difference. You simply can't forecast every disruption, so the advantage comes from structuring your habits to be alert and adaptive. A serendipity mindset gives you more shots at upside by surfacing unusual ideas early, while a disciplined evaluation process limits the blowups that come with hype cycles, helping you 'filter.'"*

—CHRISTIAN BUSCH, business professor at the University of Southern California and author of *The Serendipity Mindset*

53

Incumbent Stickiness Factor #2: Deep Pockets and the Kill Zone

UNSURPRISINGLY, LARGE CORPORATIONS have large war chests to fend off newcomers. Turn up ad volumes for the product under attack, cross-subsidize it, or simply hire more staff to make it better. Deep pockets explain much of incumbent stickiness across industries even in the face of technological disruption. Big Tech has come up with another savvy way to use excess capital to wall off its business. Enter the kill zone.

This is a territory dreaded by tech startups that work on services even remotely interesting to tech giants. As soon as a startup grows to a scale that one of the technology juggernauts perceives as a threat, it gets snapped up by one of the incumbents. The alternative is being driven out of business by force. Since the latter option usually costs more

10-year returns based on acquisition frequency

2000—2010

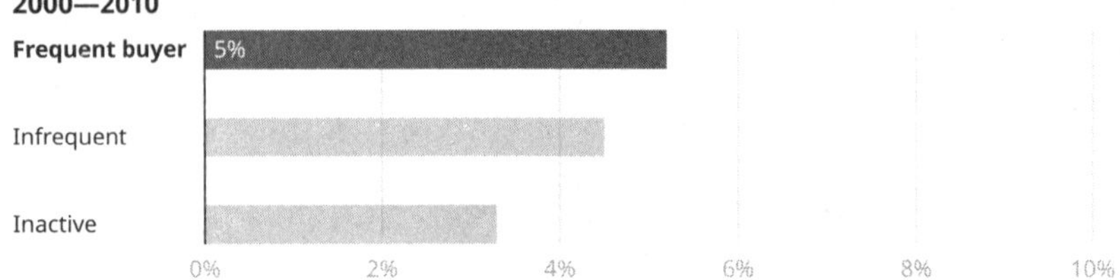

2010—2020

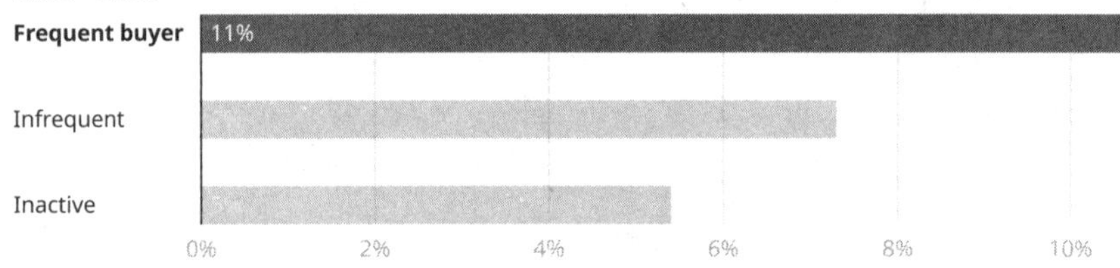

2012—2022

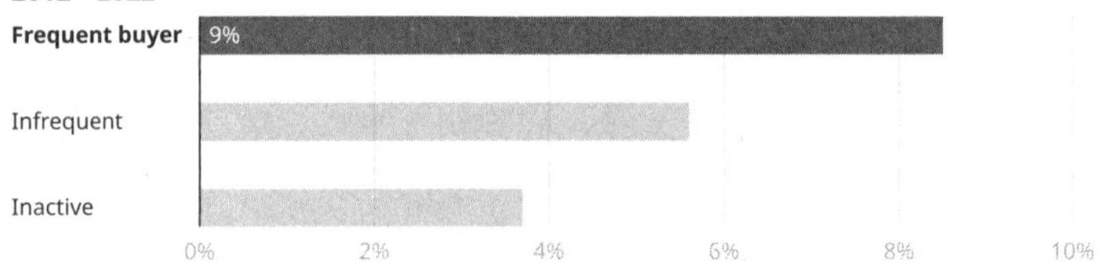

Assuming dividends are reinvested.

Chart: Igor Pejic • Data from: Bain & Company, Capital IQ, Dealogic

for everybody, Big Tech frequently overpays for acquisitions and still adds value for its shareholders. Just think of Facebook's 2012 purchase of Instagram—13 employees with no revenue were deemed worth $1B. And yet it was one of the best deals Facebook ever made.

What lessons can investors draw from that? That companies with much cash on hand will automatically perform better than others because they can buy up competition? It is not that simple. While on average companies that do an occasional acquisition here and there fare better than their peers, serial acquirers handily beat both groups. Whether you look at enterprise value, total shareholder returns, or return on invested capital over a period of three years—the picture is always the same. Infrequent buyers outperform non-buyers, while frequent buyers always outperform both other groups by a lot. Studies confirm that serial acquirers delivering better returns is not just a recent trend. They have always delivered superior results. Even more, the performance gap is increasing. And it makes perfect sense. Just like everything else, buying and integrating a company is a skill that needs to be learned and honed. And it fosters a culture of permanent change. This comes in handy when you are competing in an arena that is constantly reshaped by new technologies. Finally, frequent acquisitions help to drive parallel bet strategies. Nothing challenges tunnel vision like fresh blood in the enterprise.

For frequent acquirers, the CAGR in enterprise value is more than double that of occasional buyers and more than triple that of non-buyers. Does this also hold true for total shareholder returns? Yes. While those are only slightly better for infrequent buyers (6.4%) than non-buyers (5.2%), frequent buyers leave both other groups in the dust. Shareholders of those companies see average returns above 10%. Ergo, seeking out companies with strong and consistent M&A activity increases your odds of beating the industry average. And it narrows the field of potential investment targets because for every frequent buyer, there are five infrequent buyers and ten non-buyers.

54

Incumbent Stickiness Factor #3: Brands and Customer Base

IN JULY 2016, PEOPLE ACROSS THE GLOBE started storming out of their apartments and houses. It was not to enjoy the sunny summer weather, but to hunt. Not with rifles, but with their smartphones. They were not looking for deer or ducks, but virtual monsters only visible in a new app called *Pokémon GO*. The size of this new hunter tribe would swell to a staggering 232M until the end of 2016, outshining even the most successful apps in history. *Pokémon GO* used geolocation services to place

Pokémon GO and the Nintendo brand

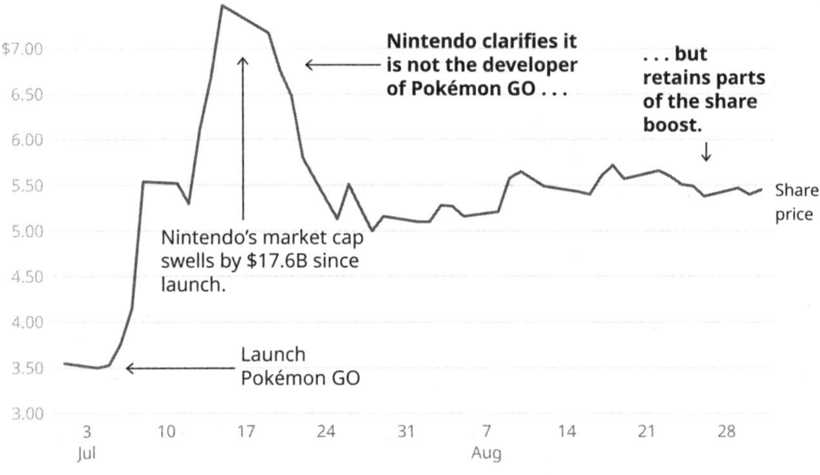

Chart: Igor Pejic • Data from: Investing.com

virtual creatures at certain spots in the physical world. By holding their phones over the spots, users could see and catch the creatures, train them, use them for battling others, or even trade them. Adding a virtual layer to a real-life environment is called augmented reality, a technology that was hyped years earlier but never truly found mass-adoption until *Pokémon GO* came along.

Nintendo, who had released the first Pokémon game for its Game Boy in 1996, saw its share price explode. It shot up by 56% in just one week. Not surprised? You should be. Here is the catch: Nintendo had no active stake in the app whatsoever. While the Japanese game-maker was the inventor of the Pokémon console games and the Pokémon brand, the app was created by The Pokémon Company and distributed by Niantic. Nintendo owned just a partial stake in both. Yet nobody seemed to care, not even seasoned analysts sifting through spreadsheets and data feeds.

The hype had become so frenzied that Nintendo felt compelled to issue a press release some days after launch, clarifying that there would be no significant earnings impact from *Pokémon GO*'s success. This message erased 17.7% of the company's value the very same day. And still this left Nintendo's shares up some 60% as compared to before the launch of a game it didn't release and that had very little effect on its balance sheet. Paradoxically, the app also boosted Nintendo's hardware sales by 19% for the quarter, even though the game was running only on smartphones.

The *Pokémon GO* story powerfully underscores how brands create irrational behavior. Even more, it underscores that brand power tilts the odds toward incumbents. Consumers, investors, and partners alike trust the big names to deliver on a new technology. Here is another example: Apple has been lagging behind in terms of generative AI. Yet when it announced its own LLM called Apple Intelligence, industry specialists as well as retail investors saw Apple's future getting more profitable as a matter of course. Not only did they automatically assume Apple Intelligence would be a formidable LLM (never mind that Apple had no track record in AI), but they saw in it transformative potential for the entire corporation. Siri would be heaved on a new level and alter how people are finding information, they rhapsodized.

Investments, goodwill, and publicity come rolling in to big brands. Often this creates a self-fulfilling prophecy. David Gardner explains how, on paper, companies often seem overvalued, because we are not putting numbers on the things that matter most. There is no entry on the financial statements for brand in most cases. He concludes that "therefore the best brands, by definition, will look overvalued. So another reason why we love strong consumer appeal as investors is because it is unrecognized by people with their algorithms and their valuation ratios."

When it comes to brand power, Big Tech reigns supreme. And just as with corporate valuations, Apple, Microsoft, Google, and Amazon are not just topping the charts, but they do so with a stunning gap. They are not just known in America, but in every single country. Investors should note that brands create an irrationality that benefits recognized and trusted brands.

55

Incumbent Stickiness Factor #4: Lobbying Power

PER DEFINITION, REGULATORS LAG BEHIND INNOVATORS. Recently, however, two trends have tremendously worsened this lag. Technological breakthroughs and their adoption are occurring at ever faster rates, while legislations and bureaucracies are getting more bloated and move slower. As a result, companies are often forced to make far-reaching investment decisions without knowing the rules of the game. Crypto companies in particular have frequently been burned. They actively sought guidance from the SEC on whether certain assets are to be treated as securities. No answer.

At the same time, new technologies require ever more investments. Thus, regulation by enforcement gets more expensive too. As a result,

CHART 55

Lobbying expenses of internet companies in the US

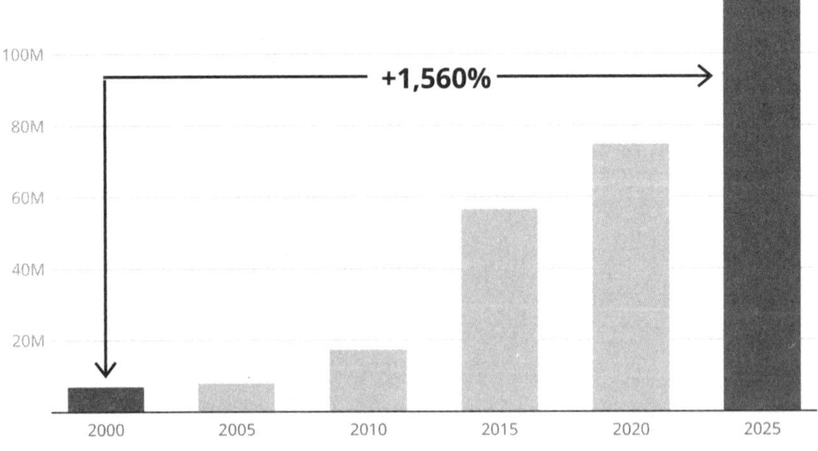

For 2025, figures have been extrapolated based on Q1 + Q2. Amounts in $ and for US government lobbying only.
Chart: Igor Pejic · Data from: OpenSecrets

many tech leaders are flexing their lobbying muscle. The tech industry's spending has spiraled upward continuously. In 2025, it was 17 times higher than it used to be in 2000. It eventually surpassed $120M. Two-thirds of that have been spent by only four companies: Meta, Amazon, ByteDance, and Alphabet. The same trend is visible in the EU. In 2024, Meta alone paid more than €10M to some 14 full-time lobbyists.

Tech wealth is also finding its way to campaign contributions across party lines. In the 2024 election cycle, crypto companies rose to become the largest financial contributors. Big Oil and Big Pharma paled in comparison. The crypto industry poured a collective $119M into federal elections, a whopping 48% of all corporate contributions. Most of the money ended up in nonpartisan Super PACs that supported pro-crypto candidates across the country or attacked crypto skeptics.

UK-based payments infrastructure expert Daniel Jonas knows first-hand how the regulatory environment is a source of significant risk for technology platforms. But having powerful enough investors is a way to mitigate it. "They can help move faster than regulations by definition. And secondly, they can afford to hire lawyers. They give them breathing space. It's the cost of doing business and the big guys can afford it." Many, particularly on the left, flaunt these figures as proof of a corporate takeover in Washington, DC. In reality, they are a sign of weakness. The companies and industries spending the most are not doing so in hope of getting government contracts or eliminating competition. On the contrary, these companies are on the defensive. Tobacco corporations afraid of cigarettes being banned, beverage manufacturers fighting sugar taxes, and oil giants diluting environmental regulations. Social networks are blamed for misinformation, cyber-mobbing, teenage depressions and suicides, feeding user data to the Chinese government, and much more. As an investor, I would prefer lower lobbying budgets and less existential threats. While lobbying has become part of the game to mitigate the risk of adverse regulation, an excessively large budget might be a red flag. Tech companies don't have licenses to operate like banks, but they are regularly forced to pay billions in fines, the access to their products is limited (e.g., social media is increasingly banned from schools to protect kids), and sometimes even the threat of a forced breakup looms over them. By a whisker, Google escaped a court-mandated spinout of its Chrome browser. TikTok was less fortunate. It was forced to sell its US operations or leave the country (though its fate remains in limbo long after Congress passed the ban). Large companies cannot fly under the radar. Especially not those with strong brands.

56

Dominance Is Often Short-Lived

TECHNOLOGICAL PROGRESS IS SO LIGHTNING fast that it does not only catch regulators off guard, but even investor darlings. Shooting stars riding one tech wave can overnight turn to be the losers of the next. Nothing captures this better than two post-pandemic tales. Those of Zoom and ServiceNow.

We all remember how, when the Covid-pandemic broke out, suddenly, instead of toiling away in meeting rooms, we were trapped in

CHART 56

Two post-pandemic tales

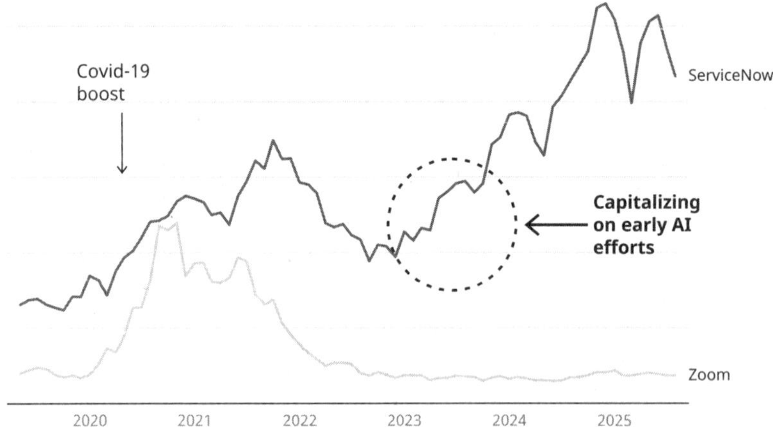

Chart: Igor Pejic • Data from: Investing.com

a seemingly endless loop of video calls. And how after work we didn't grab a beer with friends, but chatted with them in front of our phones. Most of us did so using the products of a company we had never heard of before: Zoom Communications. The majority of digital businesses grew their earnings during the lockdowns, a period when long-overdue digitalization seemed to happen at warp speed. Yet Zoom literally exploded. Everybody knew it. Most people loved it. They even started using it as a verb. It became the synonym for the entire technology of videoconferencing. Despite those skyrocketing user figures, Zoom worked flawlessly without any servers melting or apps crashing. Investors rewarded that. Its stock price shot up fivefold in 2020. Yet fast-forward to the end of the pandemic and it returned to where it was before. It didn't really move since then.

Now let's look at another pandemic winner: ServiceNow. This is a company that specializes in all sorts of digital workflows. Think about writing an IT ticket because the VPN on your iPhone is down. That sort of thing. Their stock soared thanks to Covid, though nowhere near Zoom's explosion. After lockdowns were lifted, it fell again. But not for a long time. ServiceNow rebounded and lived through a similar resurgence, with the difference that it lasted longer than the Covid one. Both Zoom and ServiceNow are forward-thinking tech companies that got the technology and the timing right. And both managed to deliver stable and excellent products when needed. Zoom even had a big breakthrough beyond the B2B world. So what made the difference?

A couple of things. Zoom faced tough competition like that from Microsoft's MS Teams. Zoom's application was far more popular with private users than with enterprises, so it lacked long-term stability. And video calls made up pretty much most of its product portfolio. After grabbing large chunks of the global market within a matter of months, there was simply no more room to grow. Zoom paid heavily for new users, but this slashed margins and scared investors.

What had happened in the market was that a new technological wave was building up. It was hidden behind the Covid-induced digitalization, so it washed across the business world all the more powerfully. ServiceNow was one of the companies riding that wave. They had been working on agentic AI far before Covid or ChatGPT. They understood its ubiquitous nature and how an edge in AI would mean almost limitless growth opportunities. From customer service calls to recruiting processes, AI could enhance every digital workflow.

So imagine you are an investor on the first day of the lockdown. How could you have told those two apart? If you are asking yourself that question, there's already a problem. The pandemic just accelerated trajectories; it didn't change them. The best long-term investment decisions are made regardless of unpredictable events like Covid. What Zoom was focusing on can broadly be described as digitalization. Market adoption for digitalization was not perfect, but maturation was kicking in. Growth potential was limited. ServiceNow, on the other hand, continued reaping rewards from its digital efforts but also leaped on to AI, a technology that was far earlier in its life cycle.

Most companies with a lasting dominance are relentless in squeezing nascent tech into their business models and corporate strategies. Amazon would have lost its top position long ago had it stayed a pure web shop. Google might have shared the fate of most other search engines had it not ventured into cloud computing, AI, or blockchain. When trying to pick specific companies for the long term, make sure they have this tech adaptability. Even better: Watch out for companies that have no qualms cannibalizing themselves. Scott D. Anthony, the professor who has spent his career understanding and managing disruptive innovation, stresses the example of Apple. When it introduced the iPhone in 2007, it did something that most companies hesitate to do: It introduced a product that could cannibalize multiple existing product lines such as computers and portable music players. "What Apple realized is that the growth potential of an easy-to-use computer in your pocket made any potential losses look trivial. That's the power of disruption."

57

Does Joining the Top 10 Stocks Help or Impede Performance?

SIZE IS STABILITY. SIZE IS ALSO *past* growth. We saw in the last chart how Zoom swallowed up most of the videoconferencing market in record time only to fall victim to the limitations of market volumes. It is a phenomenon known to every industry, though the hikes and plunges of tech stocks are more distinct.

Just like technologies, individual companies often pass through years of hyper-growth and years of stability, sometimes even decline. Once a

CHART 57

Returns vs. market average when making the top 10

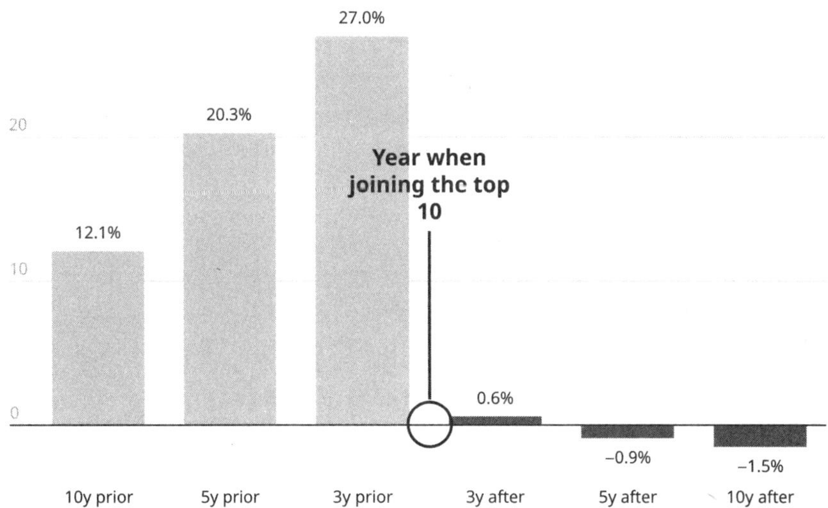

Annualized returns in excess of the US market before and after joining the top 10 largest US stocks according to market capitalization. The market is defined as the Fama/French Total US Market Research Index. Period examined is January 1927—December 2022.

technology has spread across the economy or a company has reached the pinnacle of a stock index, there isn't much room to sustain that pace. This curse is best illustrated by the corporate behemoths at the very top of the roster. In chart 57, you see the returns of corporations that have joined the 10 largest companies as compared to the overall US market. While tremendously beating the market before joining the list, they are even underperforming it after joining it. The "too-big-to-fail" label comes at a cost. In the 1960s, there was a group of too-big-to-fail companies known as the Nifty Fifty, made up of large caps that were solid but still growing well. It included names like Xerox, Coca-Cola, and IBM. They soared in the 1960s and early '70s, creating an aura of invincibility. Yet many collapsed in the bear market that followed. For many, the fate of the Nifty Fifty echoes as a warning sign that there is an end to the winning streak of every company that climbs to the top. It is basically the reversal of "winners keep winning."

As so often happens, however, technology giants have defied this trend. Why? Because they are swallowing ever more industries and monetizing ever more emerging technologies. And while they do so, they continue to squeeze profits out of their well-oiled machines built for established generations of tech. This is what fuels the growth. There was only so much oil that ExxonMobil could produce and only so many cars General Motors could sell. But when Amazon became the number one retailer in the world, it started producing movies and TV shows for its Prime audience. It started to rent out data center space to other companies. And it charged its competitors for using its payment solution at their virtual checkout.

This stickiness of tech giants comes down to the adaptability, which is made possible by all the things we discussed in the previous subchapters. Parallel R&D bets, big acquisition budgets, recognizable brands, and billions of users. This doesn't mean the end of dynamism. New technological breakthroughs will still keep shuffling the cards. Or they will simply produce *additional* tech giants, while the old ones stay strong and profitable. In the last couple of years, the Big Four became the Magnificent Seven. Tesla, TSMC, and NVIDIA didn't rise at the cost of another tech giant. While successful companies usually suffered from new tech in the past, today there is also a big upside. And the new stewards of our global economy have become adept in finding this upside.

> *"I think there is a statistic that seven out of the biggest ten market cap companies fall out of the top ten every decade. In the '70s, it was cars; in the '80s, it was oil; in the '90s, it was hardware and electricity; in the 2000s, it was software, internet, and financial companies; in the 2010s, it was internet technology; in the 2020s, it looks like it will be AI; and in the 2030s, I expect it to be Bitcoin related. Most new technologies begin as decentralizing forces, and then they become oligopolies and more centralized, and they make room for new decentralizing forces."*

—TIM DRAPER, founder of Draper Associates

58

No Corporate Advantage Can Replace Product Quality

IN AUGUST OF 2016, IMAGES OF SMOLDERING smartphones went viral. The Galaxy Note 7, Samsung's new iPhone rival, kept exploding due to faulty batteries. Airlines banned the phones from their planes, while earnings blew up faster than the devices. Samsung issued a global recall, re-released, then recalled again. Its share price tanked, experiencing one of the worst trading days ever.

In 2018 and 2019, 346 people died because faulty software made two Boeing 737 Max planes crash. Luckily, phones and planes going up in flames are a very rare exception. What is not an exception, however, is companies frivolously blowing their prospects for dominating future tech with poor product quality. I am not referring to scrappy startups, but the masters of the tech economy. We already talked about Facebook's legless avatars in the metaverse. We also mentioned Google Glass, an

Reasons for change in tech market leadership

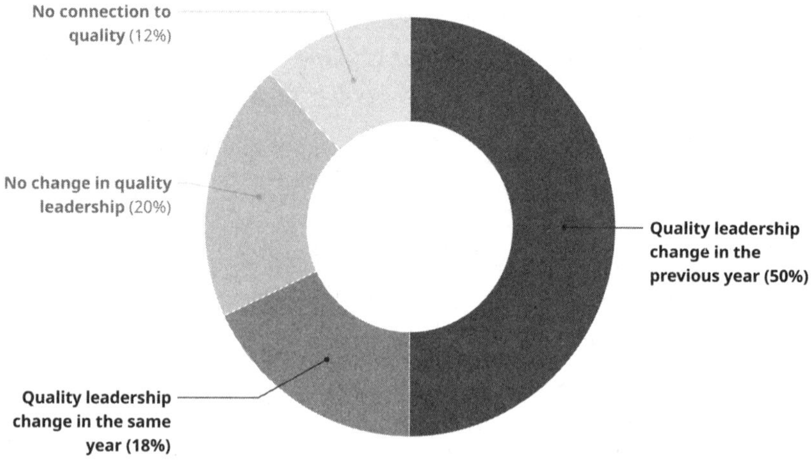

Results for the high-tech sector (hardware, software, and services). Product quality defined as a composite of various brand attributes, including reliability, performance, and convenience.

Chart: Igor Pejic • Data from: MIT Sloan (Tellis/Yin/Nira)

overheating wearable with an abysmal battery life and minuscule functionality. Examples like these abound. Google's AI called Bard gave wrong answers in its first public demonstration, fumbling easily accessible facts about the James Webb Space Telescope. Alphabet's market value dropped by $100B within hours. Bard is now called Gemini. Even Apple, the epitome of superior product quality, had its missteps. Ever heard of Apple Newton or the Butterfly Keyboard?

Sometimes companies get all the big strategic things right: The upcoming technology, the timing, the problems pestering their users. They flood their R&D departments with cash, flaunt their brands, and rapidly scale their product through their giant customer base, only to fail on product execution. A botched rollout does not only let a company bleed red ink; it often ends its sprint to conquer a new technology. Second chances are rare and expensive.

But how come those giants fail to translate this leadership into a stable product? The answer lies in the tech industry's dynamism. The first-mover advantage is the holy grail. Products proliferate at lightning speed. Network effects lock in users. This belief is so deep, it even gave rise to the agile philosophy of product development, which today is universally accepted. Agile means that rather than having big, beautifully crafted products, companies launch with a minimum viable version (MVP) and improve it continuously in iterative loops. Short go-to market times take priority over perfection. The problem is that many companies use timing as an excuse to compromise on product quality.

But does the common wisdom hold true, that quick market share capture is more important than fixing flimsy quality? Perhaps sometimes, but in the vast majority of cases product superiority is a prerequisite to be a market leader. Researchers examined why a product grabs market leadership in high-tech industries—88% of the time, the change in market leadership had been preceded by a change in quality leadership. Things like distribution channels, pricing, and marketing spend were negligible. In other words: Building the best product is more important than being fast.

The study is already dated, but high-profile cases confirm its results over and over again. Remember Friendster? This social media site was launched two years before Facebook and was the first of its kind to gain traction. A year after its founding, three million people were using the platform to connect, post, and date. But this rapid market launch came at a cost: Software glitches, collapsing servers, and identity verification so poor that most people spent their time chatting with fake profiles. Facebook, on the other hand, initially required users to have a .edu email address and didn't spam them with ads. Neither of those applies today, but the cautious approach in the beginning allowed for a controlled rollout. The network was opened college by college, then to high school students with invitations. The growth was carefully planned and sequenced. This is a footnote to Zuckerberg's "Move fast and break things" mantra that rarely gets read. Whether it is Apple's iPod or Microsoft's Word—most categories' dominant products are late entrants with a superior quality.

David Gardner, who has successfully hunted for Rule Breaker companies ever since he co-founded The Motley Fool, puts it like this this: "If you personally love a company or product, it is a strong indicator of product quality. I love Amazon because it's added so much value to my life. How many errands have I been saved from? And these days it's arriving later today. It used to be two or three days." Gardner highlights an important thing: Product quality is fleeting. Amazon has only been so successful because it has been improving relentlessly.

In terms of quality, large companies start out with an advantage. Not only do they have more resources and experience, but researchers found that for high-tech products customers intuitively assume big companies deliver better quality. Investors must do better. They should examine all attributes of product quality: Reliability, performance, and convenience. Companies are not obliged to report quality indicators, and when they do, they should be taken with a dose of skepticism. Investors have to get creative. Look at app store ratings, crawl reviews of users and opinion leaders, search for financial provisions for complaints or recalls. Finally, buy the product. Treat it like an average user, but also like a tester. Make sure to test as many scenarios and edge cases as possible.

VI

GETTING THE INVESTMENT VEHICLE RIGHT

YOU HAVE IDENTIFIED THE NEXT BIG TECH THEMES. You are confident about the timing. You have drafted a shortlist of future winners. And now? You are wondering if you should just get some funds, and perhaps some individual stocks. How many stocks? Diversify or go big on a handful of bets? Stick with public markets or try some of the novel ways that retail investors can tackle private companies? How about seeking out companies between the two worlds—tech IPOs? And by the way, what are these SPACs everybody is raving about?

Even when it comes to the *how* of investing your money, technology is rewriting the rules. In addition to traditional investment vehicles such as stocks or funds, there are many novel ways to tie your fortunes to a company or even an entire technology class. The insane speed with which tech companies grow and churn out products mandates ever faster capital injections. The tech boom has given birth to crowdfunding and has breathed new life into SPACs. But you aren't going to hand your money over to a blank-check company. Or are you? Maybe it is better to check out some of the VCs that are now offering syndicates so that public investors can participate in the hottest startups? The Cambrian explosion of tech segments and companies within them has catapulted thematic ETFs to a global phenomenon. You can now put your chips on trends, technologies, or groups of technologies. Too many options. Retail investors are overwhelmed, and general investing literature is no big help.

But to really realize technology alpha, you have to become aware of the risks inherent in the investment vehicles popular in the tech world, as well as the opportunities. ETFs with their often automatic, no-thrills approach have slashed the costs traditional funds incurred. Investors should understand which new channels can benefit them and from which to steer clear.

Part 6 dissects all the new investment vehicles and highlights how tech alters the rules for traditional ones. IPOs, for example, behave differently in the tech sector. Above all, no other industry accepts founders who exert such outsized control over a public company. But are dual class share structures good for investors? Are *tech IPOs in general* good for investors?

Each vehicle can be viewed through the prism of costs, diversification, and the potential for asymmetric wins. There is no single best way to invest in tech, so your portfolio will likely be made up of some combination of investment vehicles. While every investor should zealously try to cut costs within the investment products they choose, the level and type of diversification will depend on the strategy. Luckily, the plentitude of ways to invest allows you to fine-tune both. You can take the risk on the level of the entire market, a technology, or a single corporation. Whichever way you go, a look at history can reveal what tactics have worked best so far to tilt the odds in your favor. Study them and technology alpha will come a little closer.

59

Ways to Invest in Technology

HOW TO INVEST MONEY INTO TECH largely depends on your overall strategy and risk tolerance. Risk-averse investors will put most of their assets into index funds and sectoral funds. Perhaps they will even venture into some thematic ETFs. Their more daring peers are more likely to pick individual stocks or dabble with crypto assets.

This chapter's illustration sorts the most common investment vehicles from the least to the most volatile (left to right). And it groups them into public (i.e., stocks) and alternative investment opportunities. Being aware of the different risk and volatility levels of categories of securities is important for balancing your portfolio. Investing into vehicles in different groups helps to keep the equilibrium between risk and reward in

CHART 59

Categories of investment vehicles

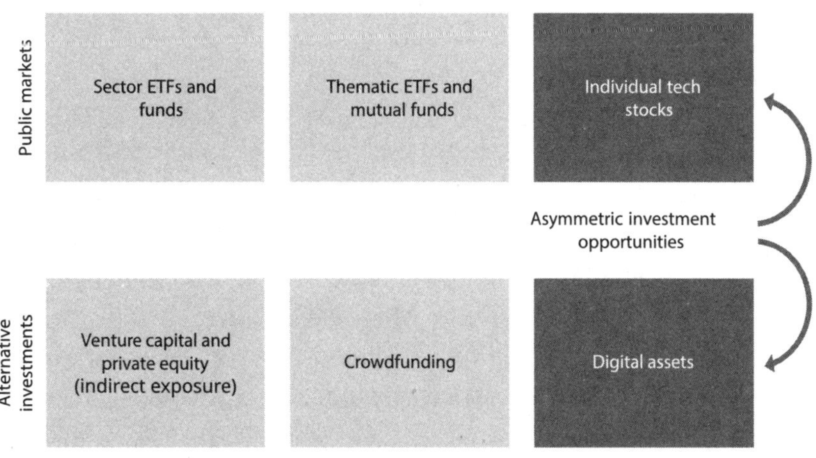

Chart: Igor Pejic

your overall assets. The risk appetite then determines the allocation to the different categories.

For many investors, determining your own risk appetite is a gut decision, but it shouldn't be. "Especially in tech, it is important to consider one's personal risk profile, desired diversification, and investment horizon to select the appropriate vehicle," says Jürgen Kob, who sits on the boards of various Swiss financial companies. And the former Microsoft strategist Robert Scoble cautions never to forget the psychological component. "Ask yourself if you have the mental strength to hold a stock when it is down from 112 to 6 and everything around is going out of business. This is why, for most people, it's better to put their money in an index fund."

Investment vehicles do not simply differ in terms of volatility. Some are demonstrably more expensive than others. Some have been proven to have much lower average returns. And some resemble a donation rather than an investment. We will look at most of them in the next chapters. More volatility does not mean there is symmetric up- and downside potential. In many cases the downside potential is much larger or more likely to materialize. The holy grail of investing is to find the opposite: Asymmetric bets with the possible upside much higher than the downside.

In this chapter's chart, I highlighted where asymmetric bets are most likely to be found. Leaving aside private markets that are only indirectly accessible for public investors, there are basically three bets you can take. You can wager that a specific technology, company, or digital asset will shoot through the roof.

If you are pinning your hopes on a *rising technology*, one of the best ways to do so is to invest in thematic ETFs. These ETFs buy shares in companies that work around a certain theme—say, green tech, semiconductors, or biotech. This can also include companies that are working on the desired technology, but whose major source of revenue is somewhere else. For example, Microsoft's fortunes are tied to the future of AI, but that's not its core business today. Hence, a variant called pure-play ETFs can give you exposure solely to companies that derive a significant, often majority, portion of their revenue directly from the specific technology. More volatility and more possible reward.

Why ETFs and not mutual funds? Because of lower fees, tax efficiency, and trading flexibility. More on that later.

If you are prepared to set aside more time for research and don't shy away from some long shots, then *picking specific tech stocks* is the way to go. Of course, in doing so, you can create your own diversification by spreading your chips to dozens of different asymmetric opportunities.

Finally, *digital assets* are the most complex and dynamic category of tech investing. Digital assets are a completely new asset class with novel risks and a novel logic, but they also hold some of the most potent drivers of technology alpha. Thus, I have dedicated an entire section to them (part 7).

This is not an exhaustive list. There are many other (advanced) financial instruments such as structured products or inverse tech ETFs. But those are usually not suited for long-term investing. So, if your approach to investing is to ride long-term tech waves, more basic investment vehicles will do. Don't forget: Your time has an opportunity cost too. Understanding technologies and their markets is complex enough. Better to use your time studying those than building elaborate financial structures that fall apart if the underlying hypotheses turn out to be wrong. The key priority should be to get the tech trends and their timing right.

60

Fees: A Colossal Drain on Portfolio Value

IMAGINE YOUR ACTIVELY MANAGED PORTFOLIO is performing well for several years in a row, perhaps even slightly beating the market. You are proud. You are celebrating. Somebody is getting rich off of it. The twist: It isn't you.

In 1996, the American financial theorist William Bernstein came up with an intriguing fictional scenario. A 25-year old inherits $100,000. Though retirement is still a long way ahead, he decides to keep it as a buffer for when those days come. Being a cautious, long-term investor,

CHART 60

Growth of investor vs. broker net worth over 40 years

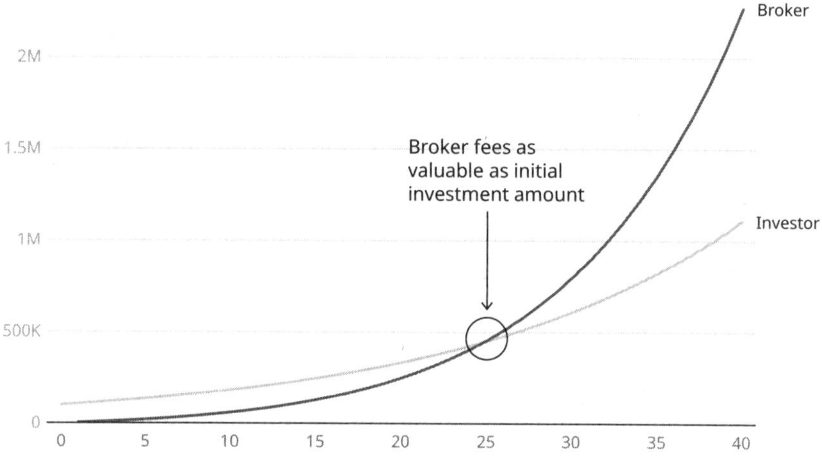

Assumptions: 9.3% total returns and 3% broker fee over a duration of 40 years.

Chart: Igor Pejic • Data from: Adapted and updated from Bernstein

he opts for a 50:50 split of common stocks and bonds and engages a full-service broker. He instructs the broker to hold the assets for 40 years and not turn them around. The broker mourns the lost commissions on the trades but complies. Now fast-forward to retirement. What is his net worth? And what is that of his broker?

I have updated Bernstein's example with recent figures. While we can still assume a 3% fee for full service brokers, the annualized returns for stocks and bonds have grown. Over the last 10 years, a 50/50 mix of common stocks and bonds yielded annualized returns of 9.2% So let's assume the broker in our example was of average skill and returned just that. The young heir would have grown into a millionaire retiree with a net worth of $1.1M. Perhaps more than enough to get him through old age. But the broker is the one that really made a fortune. If he took the 3% commission every year and invested in the same assets, and thus had the same yield, he would have ended up at $2.3M. The fact that the broker wouldn't have to pay the 3% commission had such a tremendous impact on the returns that after 25 years his net worth was higher than that of his client. Never mind that he had zero initial investment. From that point on, the gap simply widens inexorably.

You probably believe in technology alpha, or you wouldn't have come this far in the book. That also means you share my assumption that over the decades a tech-tilted portfolio will yield more than the average return of 9.3%. In this case, you are leaving yet significantly more money on the table due to fees.

In 1996, you might have been forgiven to begrudgingly accept those punishingly high fees. There were very few alternatives. Today, most online brokers are offering completely free trading. Optimizing costs and fees is perhaps the easiest and safest way to fast-track your wealth accumulation. If you are a retail investor, there is another cost bloc you should look to optimize: Fund managers.

61

Actively Managed Funds vs. Index Funds: Costs

REGARDLESS OF TECH OR NON-TECH, every investor must decide on two fundamental questions: How many active choices do I want in my portfolio? And how many active decisions do I want to outsource?

The risc of passive investment philosophy has been a game changer. Jack Bogle of Vanguard launched the first index fund in 1976. It replicated the S&P 500 and for the first time gave retail investors cheap access to a maximally diversified fund. You didn't need expensive analysts and stock pickers. Those, after all, couldn't be smarter than the market. The rationale behind it: Why pay somebody else to find the needle in the haystack if you can buy the entire haystack?

Since then, things on Wall Street have never been the same. Bogle had sounded the bell for an era of low-cost index funds. By 2025, net assets invested in index funds had overtaken those in actively managed ones in America. Most investors seem to conclude that since you can't

CHART 61

Cost differences of mutual and index funds adding up

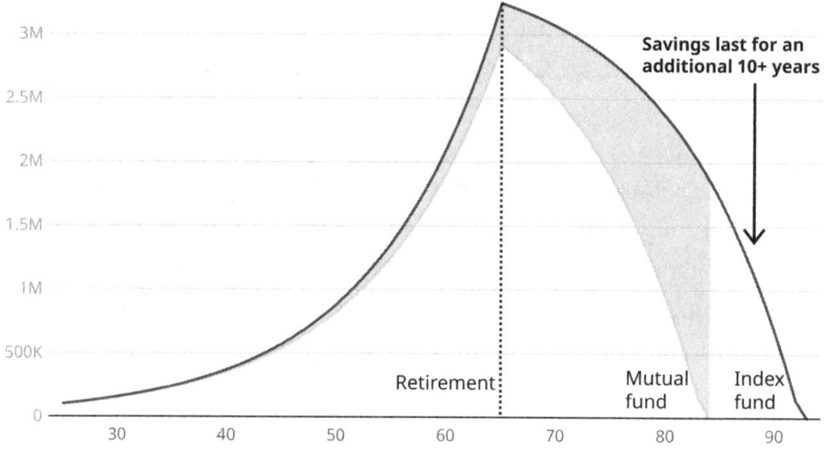

Assumptions: Costs for mutual funds: 0.40%/year. Costs for index funds: 0.11%/year. $50K taken out per year in retirement phase. No difference in performance.

Chart: Igor Pejic • Data from: Own calculations with average cost assumptions from ICI and Morningstar

beat the market, it is better to *be* the market. Index funds mainly come in the shape of ETFs, but those are not the same. ETFs are just a form of financial technology with many benefits, such as the possibility to sell at any time during market hours or to automatically optimize trades for taxes.

ETFs can be actively managed, too, and indeed a growing number of them are. Most actively managed ETFs revolve around a tech theme, so we will look at those in more detail in the next chapters. For the sake of illustration, let's now focus only on the index ones.

So, are index funds worth the hype? The answer to that question comprises two components: First, what is their total return compared to actively managed funds? And second, what is the impact of the cost savings? More about the return perspective in the next chapter. We will look at the fees first.

How much active management fees really cost can only be understood through the prism of time. To illustrate it, I elaborated on our previous scenario of the young heir who deposits $100,000 for his retirement.

This time he doesn't pay a broker. All his expenses are the management fees of the fund. I created two scenarios based on the current fee level in the US market. One in which he invests the money in a managed mutual fund at a 0.40% expense ratio and one where he chooses a passive index fund at 0.11%. For the sake of simplicity, I leave aside optional fees and taxes. Let's assume both variants deliver the average return of 9.2% annually. How do the net returns look once he is ready to retire?

A difference of 0.29% in fees at first sounds insignificant when compared to the 9.2% gross appreciation of the portfolio. Or when compared to the 3% broker fee we saw in the last chapter. Yet, in 40 years, the fee savings snowball into an additional $328,000 in his portfolio. Assuming he takes out $50,000 each year in retirement and leaves the rest invested, he could live off of those saved fees for more than 10 years.

Stephen Foerster, a finance professor at Ivey Business School who has authored numerous books on the pursuit of the perfect portfolio, notes that fees are so fundamental that Jack Bogle even postulated something called the Cost Matters Hypothesis (CMH). In his words: "CMH posits a conclusion that is both trivially obvious and remarkably sweeping: The mathematical expectation of the speculator is a loss equal to the amount of transaction costs incurred." Here is Foerster explaining in more detail why the average active investor will do worse than the passive one precisely because of the costs. "William Sharpe, Nobel Prize winner and creator of the capital asset pricing model, makes a straightforward yet profound argument. Consider two groups: Passive index fund investors and active investors. It is obvious that, before fees, the average return for index fund investors must be the index or market return. But that also implies that before fees the average *active* manager performance must be the market return. It is also clear that passive fees are lower than active fees, often considerably so. Therefore, when we consider returns *net* of fees, *on average* passive investing must do better than active investing. It's simple arithmetic."

62

Actively Managed Funds vs. Index Funds: Performance

THOUGH INDEX FUNDS HACK THE COSTS for selecting assets, that was not the reason they were invented. In the 1950s, the economist Harry Markowitz developed something called MPT, short for modern portfolio theory. Markowitz later went on to win the Nobel Prize for it, while MPT became the philosophical backbone of passive investing. The core tenet is that diversification is the best way to achieve long-term returns because it slashes unsystematic risk—that is, risks inherent in individual companies or industries. The broader the diversification, the better. It is the only way to get to the "efficient frontier," which is the MPT term for the highest possible expected return at a given risk level. In other words: The perfect portfolio. So is Markowitz right?

Study after study suggest he is, including the famous 1962 report for the SEC Committee that became known as the *Wharton School Report*. Over the years many others, including the Nobel laureates Eugene Fama and William Sharpe, continued to strengthen the empirical case for MPT.

In down market years, research did show that active fund managers beat the least active ones in the range of 4.5% to 6.2% per year. Yet this is insufficient to offset their poor results during expansion phases.

There is a powerful scorecard for investors looking at more recent figures: The S&P Indices Versus Active (SPIVA) scorecard. It is an up-to-date benchmarking study that encompasses more than 20 years of comparison data. According to SPIVA research, the record of active investors looks dismal in most years. But here is the kicker: The further you stretch the time horizon, the grimmer the picture. SPIVA tracks dozens of categories—i.e., different regions, corporate sizes, equity classes, etc. After 15 years, there was not a single category in which a majority of active managers outperformed their respective index.

CHART 62

Active funds vs. their passive benchmark

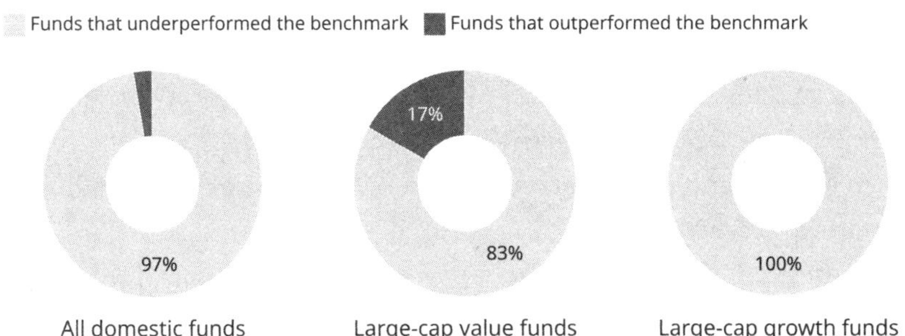

Analysis of US equities over 20 years. Period analyzed: 1/1/2005—12/31/2024. Risk-adjusted returns.
Chart: Igor Pejic · Data from: SPIVA scorecard

From those dozens of categories, I chose to highlight three in the chart. The pie chart to the left underscores how abysmal the results of active managers are across all categories. The other two show that active investors are doing best for value funds (though still poorly) and worst for large-cap growth funds. The latter is where tech-wealth creation happens. Or put differently: If you are trying to pick tech stocks, you are facing particularly bad odds of beating the market.

The case for diversification gets even more mind-boggling. The S&P 500 does not just outpace active fund managers, but also private markets. On all possible time horizons. One year. Five years. Ten years. The State Street private market index, which tracks returns from private equity, private debt, and venture capital funds, delivered 7.08% to investors in 2024. This is less than a third of what S&P 500 index investors got.

Stephen Foerster argues that probably the strongest theoretical motivation for an index fund dates back to William (Bill) Sharpe's 1964 *Journal of Finance* paper that described what is commonly known as the capital asset pricing model (CAPM). The perfect portfolio according to Sharpe's model "would be the 'market portfolio' of all assets, weighted by market values. If we accept Sharpe's model, then all investors would want to buy index funds—not just country-specific or equity-only, but broad global index funds including stocks, bonds, and beyond." Of course, this relies on certain implicit assumptions, such as that "markets are efficient and thus all securities are properly priced. Active managers reject that premise."

Active managers reject that premise for different reasons. Value investors would say that hype is creating inefficiencies. I would argue that while a market can be very efficient in the short term, this is not the case for the long term. But where does this lead the quest for technology alpha? If even the best professional investors can't beat an index ETF, wouldn't it be hubris to believe we can?

The first thing to keep in mind is that financial managers' goals don't necessarily align with yours. To justify their fees, they must be perceived as doing a lot and doing it constantly. Suggested trades or portfolio reshuffles might be worse than holding equities, but they certainly incur more fees and sometimes taxes. A strategy of buying and holding winners for a long time would paint a different picture. Second, while active managers lose to indices, there are some that outperform them. This is more than pure chance, because many of those that performed better share the same approach: Sectoral or thematic ETFs that revolve around either the entire tech segment or individual technologies. We will now dive deep into what they are and what they tell us about tech's unique status.

63

Tech's Grip on Thematic ETFs

FOR PASSIVE INVESTORS, ETFS HAVE BEEN A BOON. So much that they have even outpaced active funds in terms of assets under management. Yet for those seeking technology alpha, index funds won't do. The good news is, other forms of ETFs can help. There is a passive investment vehicle that replicates the entire tech segment of public companies: Sectoral funds. They are very straightforward and the perfect way to go for investors who don't enjoy being buried under research papers and patent filings, or sifting through technology market share reports. Sectoral funds give you the tech sector benchmark for low fees, which will hopefully yield

CHART 63

Thematic funds: Global assets under management in $B

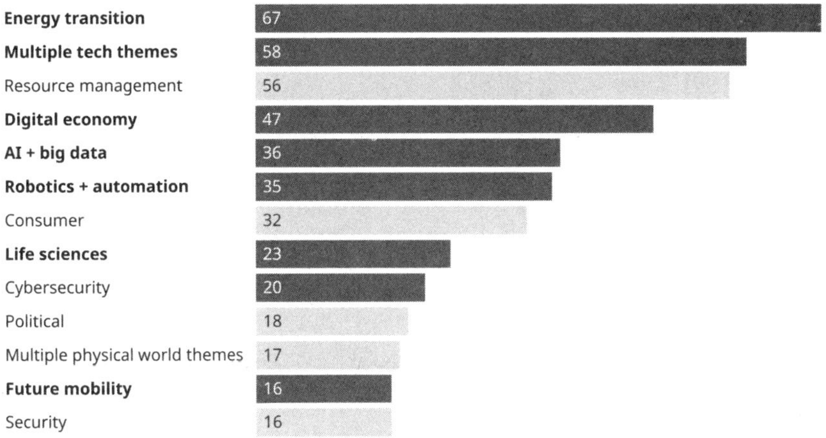

Tech themes in bold. Data as of June 30, 2024. One category called "Broad theme" ($69B) was excluded because it includes tech as well as non-tech equities.

Chart: Igor Pejic • Data from: Morningstar

plenty of technology alpha if you stick to that strategy over multiple tech cycles. But what if you have set your sight on a specific technology? What if you have concluded that quantum computing or space technology will have prime time in the next years? ETFs can help with that too.

The idea to invest in a certain theme is nothing new. In fact, it predates the rise of ETFs. Technology has always been the main driver of thematic investing and continues to do so up to this day. During the dot-com bubble, internet-related thematic funds mushroomed. The total volume of assets under management still remained insignificant for the broader investing landscape. And after the bubble burst, the volumes were reduced even further. At the same time, the variety of themes expanded to topics such as resource management and energy. Thematic funds didn't really take off until the proliferation of ETFs in the second half of the 2000s. New funds popped up as dollars flowed in. Still, it took another 15 years until the potency of thematic ETFs was proven spectacularly by one firm that became the epitome of tech thematics: ARK Innovation ETF. This fund bet on every major disruptive technology—gentech, automation, fintech, blockchain, cybersecurity, and countless others. It is an actively led and concentrated portfolio with a limited number of stocks, which has caused heavy volatility and still impressive returns. ARK had gained such a footprint that founder and CEO Cathie Wood became synonymous with the rise of thematic investing and disruption itself.

By mid-2024, the assets under management in thematic ETFs had swollen to $562B, effectively doubling over five years. Though the volume even used to be much higher at the height of the pandemic, thematics have proven that they are a serious investment vehicle. Most of the assets are invested in tech themes. Tech had so many popular sub-themes that, if you add them up, it accounts for more than half of all dollars invested. And if you only consider the American market, tech is even more dominant.

> *"Due to the concentration of equity returns in 2023, 2024, and 2025 around ultra-cap stocks (i.e., the MAG-7), thematics overall are not in vogue. During times of more diversified growth and/or contraction, they tend to be more popular as investors seek ways to isolate specific sub-themes, categories, or opportunities, whether that's cybersecurity, homebuilding, or sports betting. These can be a better way to invest than individual selection(s) and/or broader indices, though this depends on the timing, the specific index, and the specific theme.*
>
> *Although the "best" pick in a theme will always outperform a basket focused on said theme, any investor with a properly diversified portfolio of social, or mobile, or internet stocks would have had quite the ride over the last few decades."*
>
> —MATTHEW BALL, CEO at Epyllion

64

How Tech Drives Return on Thematic ETFs

SO WE HAVE SEEN THAT TECH'S GRIP on thematics is very firm. The question that remains is: How successful have tech thematic strategies been in the past? The short answer is: Very successful. But it pays to dabble in the details.

If you look at the 10 best performing thematic ETFs over the past 10 years, it is impressive to see that every single one of them is tech-focused. Despite trillions of taxpayer subsidies thrown into energy transition or wars across the globe firing up the defense industry, it has been semiconductors and broad tech themes that ended up on top.

It is critical to understand that, despite diversification within one theme, thematics can fluctuate widely. Tech is a long-term game. Consider this: If you narrow the time frame to one, three, or five years, only

CHART 64

Best performing thematics over 10 years

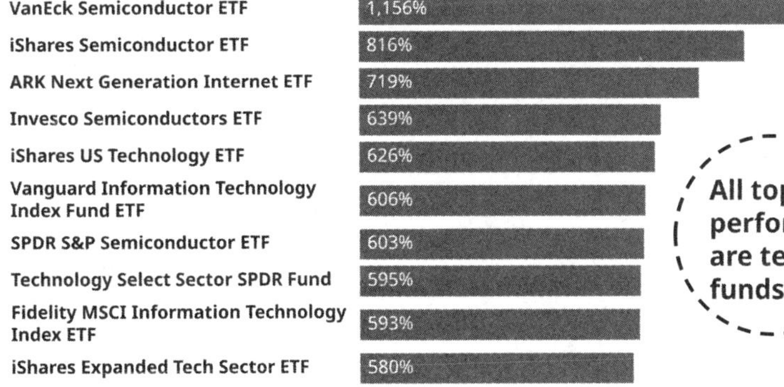

Ten-year total returns (monthly). Top-performing ETFs in terms of total returns (monthly) on an annualized basis between July 31, 2015 and July 31, 2025.

Chart: Igor Pejic • Data from: YCharts

one tech ETF in each year makes it to the top 10. This is due to the cyclical nature of tech. There are years with modest growth and even decline, just as well as years of hyper-growth. And this hyper-growth is caused by the onset of new general-purpose technologies. The internet, robotics, or mobile—all of these can be deployed throughout the economy at large, which means plenty of growth opportunities.

MPT proponents would enjoy the chart too. Nine out of the top 10 performers are passive investment funds. It confirms the results of SPIVA and all the other studies comparing active and passive investing. Sectoral funds even beat those that got a mega hype topic right—say, AI thematics. The one notable exception is the next generation internet fund of aforementioned ARK Innovation. ARK is different to other active managers in that it makes a limited number of very bold bets on cutting-edge technology. Also, unlike most other funds, it tolerates extreme volatility when sticking to its hypotheses. Not exactly an approach all investors can stomach.

MPT dogmatists would caution even against sectoral funds. They might argue that tech is simply on a temporary winning streak that could screech to a halt any time soon. What if the AI craze sours because the technology hits a wall and can't live up to the outlandish expectations? What if the Bitcoin blockchain is hacked? What if one of the tech giants stumbles and implodes? These are all possible scenarios. But my counterargument is this: If the AI engine is choked off overnight, or Google or Amazon go out of business, do you really think that you will be happy owning an S&P 500 or Nasdaq index fund instead? As I have shown throughout the book, Big Tech has reached a historically unique status. Not only because of their size and valuations, but because they have been the reason the US market outperformed all others for decades. Not even to mention the devastation across the economy if, all of a sudden, companies were left without their cloud infrastructure, software kits, marketplaces, advertising platforms, phones, laptops, and so much more.

This is a scenario from which I don't see any plausible path to recovery. Markets have always been driven by a few outsized successes. There is a difference in the tech age, though. The same handful of companies have remained outsized successes for 15 years, some even longer. Thus, they have ballooned to a size unlike anything else in history. If they cease to be the growth engine, there is no other industry that will be able to fill this enormous void. Because every other industry is several magnitudes smaller, and because there is no plausible growth trajectory. If tech collapses permanently, so will the economy.

65

Tech IPOs: Dwindling Opportunity or Overpriced Illusion?

ETFS' MAIN ADVANTAGE IS THEIR AUTOMATIC diversification, yet a more ambitious portfolio also comprises individual stocks. To pick those, you look at the company's fundamentals, the state of its technology, and its outlook. And you assess the historic performance. But what to do if there is no history?

Tech IPOs represent a new source of companies that possibly still have their hyper-growth phases ahead of them. What I like about IPOs is that the lack of trading history forces you to decide on future potential rather than past performance. That's the way it should be for all stock decisions. The IPO offer price is fictional. You can use alternative valuation techniques, but it will not be until the first ring of the bell that you see the market's true valuation and broad public interest. However, tech IPOs have been undergoing a transformation over the past several years.

First, there are fewer tech companies deciding to go public. There was a strong Covid-induced peak in 2021, but their number has been slashed since then. The years 2022 and 2023 saw a decline to single digits. In 2024, there were only 14 new companies to choose from. Whether it is rising interest rates, increased regulatory scrutiny, or the downturn after the digital Covid boom—explanations abound. But there is a factor that makes it a long-term trend—namely, the growth of private equity and venture

CHART 65

Tech IPOs are becoming rarer, bigger, and less profitable

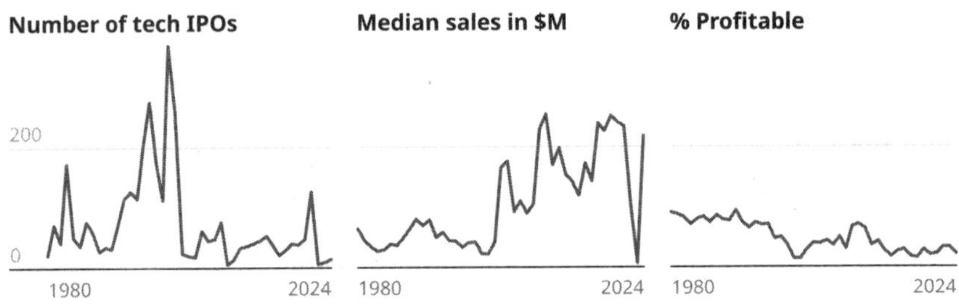

% Profitability indicates if the company was profitable at the time of going public. Median sales in 2024 $ amounts. IPOs including direct listings.

Chart: Igor Pejic · Data from: Jay Ritter

capital firms. This means ample access to capital in the private markets even without the scrutiny and the costs of an IPO. Companies can stay private longer and still raise large rounds from private investors. The AI age has birthed many companies with private valuations of hundreds of billions of dollars. SpaceX, OpenAI, ByteDance, Anthropic, xAI—none of these have to sit through public earnings calls and disclose their strategy to everybody.

Another trend is that ever fewer debuting companies are profitable when they go public. This makes investing in them more a leap of faith than previously. Even if they do rake in profits at some point, it might be a long time coming.

At the same time, companies that are going public are getting bigger and older. In 2024, the typical tech upstart had been founded 13.5 years ago. This is despite the general trend of companies growing more quickly and unicorns being younger than ever. Whereas median sales in the year of going public were close to $60M in 1980, they were just shy of $200M in 2024. This again is a consequence of most of the rapid growth being fueled by private market cash. It is a troubling trend to see retail investors barred from ever more value creation and it pushes them to seek out other opportunities such as those in digital assets or crowdfunding. For this chapter, the question is whether the few IPOs remaining are worth your time. Or are investors overpaying for the hype? Read on to find out how companies are performing post-IPO.

"What's driving the decline of tech IPOs? It's certainly also the availability of the private capital, but it is also the terms to which it is available. Private market investors are increasingly willing to not only fund the company's growth but to engage in buying secondary shares, allowing employees to cash out and even founders to cash out some of their holdings. And then these patterns seem to be going on in lots of countries. They're not unique to the United States."

—JAY RITTER, finance professor at University of Florida

66

Tech IPOs: Characteristics of Winners

WHILE COMPANIES GOING PUBLIC have no trading history, there is plenty of data on how IPOs were performing as a group over the past decades. So, are IPOs a good investment? For IPOs in general, the answer is vague. For tech IPOs, it is clear: They are. And you can even pin down some common success factors. There is a caveat though, that might preclude most investors from benefitting to the full extent.

Professor Jay Ritter from the University of Florida has been collecting and analyzing IPO data going back to 1980 so diligently and consistently that he earned the nickname "Mr. IPO." He told me that, excluding the internet-bubble era, your average return for buying and holding an IPO stock for three years would have been 44.2%, measured from the offer price. "But it is hard to get IPO shares at the offer price. If an investor had bought at the closing market price on the first day of trading, the three-year buy-and-hold return falls from 44.2% to 26.8%." This still

CHART 66

Average three-year buy-and-hold-return

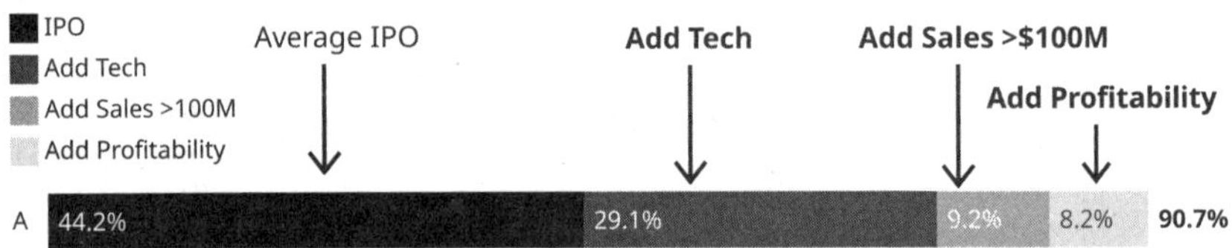

Analysis covers returns of tech IPOs in the US from 1980 to 2024 (based on IPO price).

Chart: Igor Pejic • Data from: Jay Ritter

sounds good at first, but if you adjust it to the market, meaning what you earned relative to the overall stock market performance, then the average IPO underperforms the market by 19.0%, even if one avoided the 1999–2000 IPOs, most of which melted down when the internet bubble burst. Note, however, that one of these was a company called NVIDIA. which went public in January 1999 and went on to become the most valuable company in the world in 2025.

If you had invested only in tech IPOs, the average raw return on the offer price would have gone up to 73.3%, which is significantly positive even when compared to the market. Ritter also calculated the style-adjusted rate to see how well you would have done compared to investors in similar assets. Even here, the return is superb, being 46% higher than that of its peers. So, despite all of the recent trends of IPO candidates being bigger and less profitable, there was still sufficient growth in the past to beat the market.

Another good message is that winning tech IPOs have some characteristics in common. Finding those can increase the likelihood of better performance. Jay Ritter puts it like this: "Of course, you can have a spray and pray approach and indiscriminately invest in all tech IPOs in the hope that at least one of them will shoot through the roof and take your portfolio with it. You can also be more precise. The number one thing I would look for in a tech IPO is high inflation-adjusted sales in the year it goes public." In the past, sales higher than $100M correlated with significantly better returns. Slightly less impactful, but still a crucial booster, was profitability. If a stock had a positive balance sheet when it hit public markets, it magnified the raw earnings by another 8%. Size and profitability worked similarly for non-tech IPOs, but still they performed worse than their technology counterparts.

In a nutshell, tech IPOs of profitable companies with high sales raked in three-year returns of more than 90%, beating similar investment assets by almost 60%. They might be getting rarer, but if history is a benchmark, they are still a good place to look for outperformers. Ritter adds one critically important lesson: "Never forget that not all amazing success stories occur right from scratch. When Apple went public in 1980, it was highly touted. Yet for its first 22 years as a public company, it underperformed."

67

Dual Class Share Structures

WHEN TECH FIRMS GO PUBLIC, the terms on which they do so are different from other companies. The norm on Wall Street used to be that shareholders bought equity to get dividends, capital appreciation, but also voting rights in a company. One share meant one vote in electing a board. After all, transparency and oversight were the cornerstones of retail investor trust. In the '80s and '90s, the vast majority of companies operated that way, yet an alternative shareholding structure slowly began to rise: Dual class shares.

Founders and sometimes influential venture capitalists sought to raise capital, but refused to yield control over the company. That is why they increasingly started to go public with different types of shares. Founders kept privileged shares that have multiple times the voting rights of regular stocks. Interestingly, tech companies initially didn't join the fray. It was only in 2015 that the ratio of tech IPOs with dual class shares soared. It has kept rising ever since, reaching 42.9% in 2024 and by far outpacing their non-tech counterparts.

The trend is not surprising. Tech founders are portrayed as visionaries, and rightly so. To be successful, they do need to see things years

Dual class shares getting hold of the tech sector

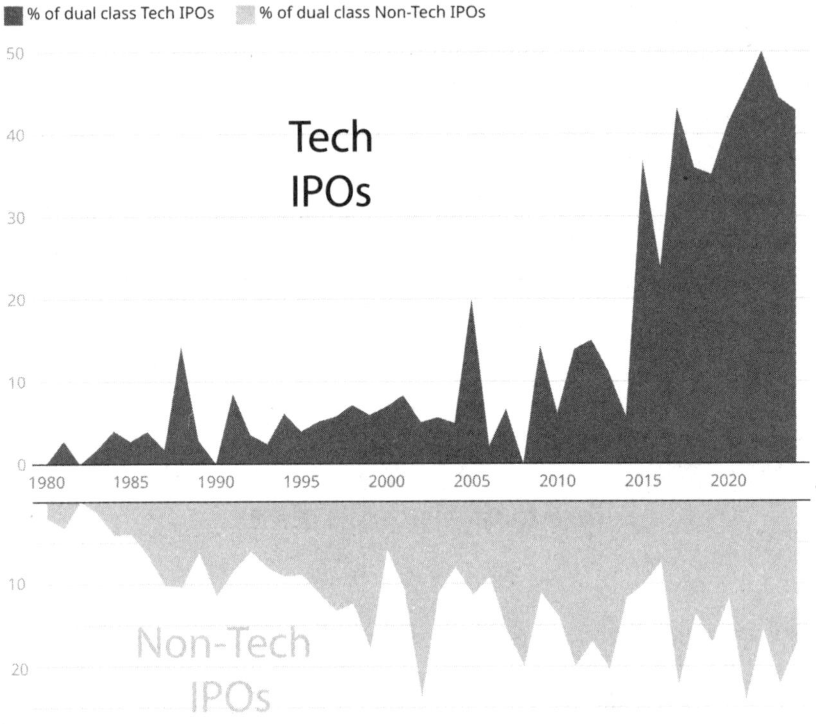

Chart: Igor Pejic • Data from: Jay Ritter

before others. Critics of dual class shares either argue that founders don't make good managers or that they have simply been at the right place at the right time. Their narrative falls apart when you get people like Jeff Bezos or Elon Musk, who has disrupted *multiple* mega-industries. It is hard to imagine Tesla without Musk tweeting Tesla's next moves or Mark Zuckerberg being told by his board what he can or cannot do.

Furthermore, founders that stay in charge have skin in the game. Their interests are aligned with those of the other shareholders. Instead of chasing quarterly returns and making sure to stay on a profitable executive job, they can prioritize long-term growth and escape the gales of creative destruction. And keep in mind that not only the CEO has a lot of equity, but so do key employees. The CEO knows that if his leadership team isn't making money on the stock options, they will have unhappy managers running the show.

So which side is eventually right? Is it better to buy into single or dual share companies? There is only one final arbiter here: Long-term stock performance. Once again, let's consult Jay Ritter's analysis of 43 years of tech IPOs. Let's first look at non-tech stocks. Those yielded slightly better returns when dual class shares were issued. Now let's look at tech. Here the delta explodes. After three years, single class share companies boasted a 19.8% return. Their dual class counterparts stood at 42%. Founder-led companies were more than twice as profitable for investors. There is one caveat, however. A Harvard study found that this dual-class advantage was eroding over time. One-share, one-vote firms were improving their returns faster and catching up.

> *"On the one hand, if you are trying to optimize the price of your stock, you want to get as many potential buyers for your stock as possible. Certain institutional equity holders will not buy stocks that have dual classes or super voting rights for founders. At the same time, you have founders who might take a more meaningful long-term perspective. It also protects you against some of the activists.*
>
> *At Pinterest we gave Ben Silbermann super voting rights. I think that empowered him to be able to make more longer-term decisions. And that is what you want as a shareholder. And it has been proven that founder-led businesses tend to be more successful, not only in terms of delivering product, but also financial results over time."*
>
> —RICK HEITZMANN, founder and managing director at FirstMark Capital and CNBC *Fast Money* commentator

68

Tech IPOs: When Best to Invest in Them?

LIKE ALL INVESTMENTS, IPOS SHOULD NOT BE REGARDED as quick, hype-driven gambles, but as long-term commitments. That doesn't mean, however, that timing doesn't matter at all. Historic patterns can be a useful guide to increase your odds, similar to the common traits of top performing companies that we discussed in the previous subchapters. So what are the most critical points in time for tech IPO stocks?

While tech IPOs have statistically yielded good results when bought and held for three years, their performance usually fluctuates wildly. The good news: It largely fluctuates in patterns. An exhaustive study of all 220 tech IPOs between 2010 and 2019 found regularities in how the share price of a company develops post tech IPO relative to the over-all tech sector. Three crucial findings about the first-year performance stand out.

First, day one matters most. Eighty percent of tech IPOs went up on the first day they started trading. The median pop, as it is known, was a plus 21%. Often underwriters would intentionally underprice the stock to generate some excitement. There is an issue, however, as Sam Rahman points out: "For most investors IPOs are really tricky because, unless you are a big investment firm that has access to the IPO and can get the IPO price, what you get on the first day of trading is completely a gamble."

Second, after day one, the performance of the average IPO histori-cally was lackluster, leading to a poor overall result at the end of the first year. If you exclude the highly profitable first day, the median returns stood at minus 19% when compared to the tech sector at large.

Third, there is a particularly troubling period—namely, months five and six. Is this arbitrary? No. Most VCs and shareholding employees have a lockup period of 180 days. In other words: After six months they are free to sell their shares and flood the market with new supply. They don't

CHART 68

Median returns in the first year after Tech IPOs

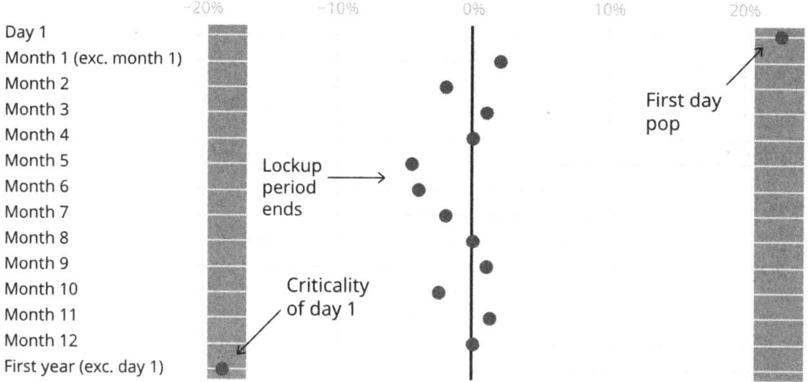

Analysis covers returns of all tech IPOs in the US from 2010—2018. Figures are relative to the overall tech sector.
Chart: Igor Pejic • Data from: Bloomberg and Janus Henderson

actually have to sell for the price to go down. The stock prices often suffer from anticipatory selling. This is why you can see this effect in month five already. Rahman weighs in on this, saying that "the first few days or even weeks of trading are all about trying to establish the equilibrium between supply and demand. Only after a few months when volume and trading has stabilized and the restricted owners can start to sell their stock, it's more about the real value of a company."

Of course, there is no guarantee that future performance will follow past performance. Yet there are no signs of the launch logic, lockup periods, or media buzz changing anytime soon. I wouldn't be surprised if we still see a similar post-IPO pattern in the 2030s.

It is important to consider that the range in tech IPO performances has been extremely broad. Some companies almost collapsed after going public. Others rose in value multiple times. To quantify this: Tech IPOs have three times the variability of the market as a whole. Thus, considering those patterns in your decisions works only if you have a broad portfolio of tech IPOs. Take the first day pop? Get out after a quarter and back in after 12 months? Those are all valid conclusions to draw from historic data, but only as long as you apply them systematically to your entire IPO portfolio.

69

SPACs: The Blank-Check Route to Finding the Next Tech Superstar?

IPOS ARE NOT PERFECT. Their supply has dried up. Those companies that are left are shrouded in ever more hype, infusing irrationality and unpredictability. And companies going public mourn the enormous costs and long lead times. The tech world has answered these with a new—or rather, newly revived—investment vehicle: The Special Purpose Acquisition Company, or SPAC. Imagine a publicly traded company that exists with one goal and one goal only—to find another private company, typically a hot, innovative tech startup, and take it public through a lightning-fast merger.

Institutional investors usually get priority allocation of a SPAC IPO, so retail investors are mostly restricted to secondary markets. But hey, at least they get to share in the bounty of all these world-changing companies, don't they? Not really. As the chart in this chapter illustrates, successfully merged SPACs are unsuccessful investments. On average, they not only fall in value but dramatically underperform the general market after one year. And the longer you hold them, the worse their returns.

CHART 69

Post-merger SPAC returns vs. the market benchmark

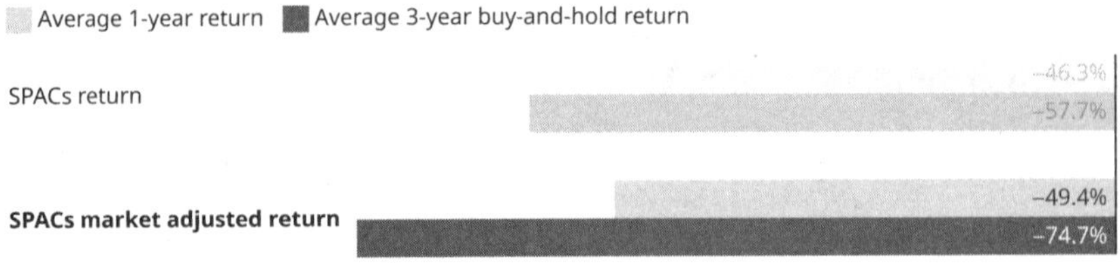

Average 1-year return   Average 3-year buy-and-hold return

SPACs return	−46.3%
	−57.7%
SPACs market adjusted return	−49.4%
	−74.7%

Years analyzed: 2012—2024

Chart: Igor Pejic • Data from: Jay Ritter

After three years, you are 74.7% worse off with the average SPAC than the market average. If you compare that to the performance of the standard tech IPOs we discussed in the previous chapters, the results are even more terrifying. One common problem is share dilution. Sponsors are often given a sizable share of the SPAC to promote it. They only get those shares when a deal is successful. Not exactly a setup that encourages long-term decisions.

These bad results make many good companies shun SPACs and opt for traditional IPOs, which makes it even harder to find the next Google or Amazon in a SPAC. So, SPACs don't yield access to troves of hidden gems. But how about the claim that they streamline the process and slash the costs of going public? Unfortunately, the opposite is the case. Researchers found that the SPAC structure is even more expensive than that of a traditional IPO. A SPAC typically raises $10.00 per share when it goes public. Yet in 2019 and 2020, at the time of the merge, the mean net cash per share was a meager $4.10. The median stood at $5.70. In other words: SPACs are a winning game for their sponsors, but a losing one for their investors.

Despite all of the overwhelming data making the case against SPACs, don't discount them completely just yet. SPACs have a feature called warranties. They give a largely risk-free chance of investing in a company you believe could one day join the ranks of Big Tech, while limiting your downside. The money raised by a SPAC is held in a trust account. If the SPAC fails to find a suitable acquisition target or the shareholders vote against a proposed merger target, investors can redeem their shares for their initial IPO value. The data on redemption rates suggests that most investors do exactly that. In the first quarter of 2025, the average redemption rate stood at 94.5%. Jay Ritter, who was also compiling the SPAC data, points out that "inexplicably high valuations of the acquisition target are frequently the reason why investors pull out. But the public market investors aren't losing a lot because they can redeem their shares. It is rather the shareholders of the operating company that are in trouble." When redemptions are too high, they don't get the money, and their price is put under strong downward pressure.

70

Crowdfunding and Syndicates—A Good Investment Alternative?

DABBLING IN IPOS BRINGS YOU INTO A WORLD in between public and private markets. But what if you could actually hunt for tomorrow's champions when they are in their earliest stages, even before the VCs start to take notice? Enter crowdfunding. Platforms like Kickstarter or GoFundMe had garnered a lot of media attention in the 2010s because they demonstrated how you could quickly and without much bureaucracy raise money from hundreds or thousands of retail investors. The first platforms started with connecting creatives such as film or music makers with backers that wanted to see those projects realized. Fans of a TV show, for example, would chip in to see a movie sequel produced. In return they got movie tickets—crowd rewarding. Soon afterward, platforms for charitable donations sprang up, collecting money for things such as medical emergencies—crowd donations. Following the JOBS Act of 2012, the SEC created legal clarity in 2016 and opened up the space to real investing—crowd lending and equity crowdfunding.

While crowd lending simply means giving a loan to a startup and getting paid back with interest, crowdfunding is where it gets interesting. Nonaccredited investors can buy shares and securities in a small, often innovative business. If they pick one that eventually makes an exit (IPO or acquisition), it's payday. Equity crowdfunding is a way to catch tech companies before their steepest growth. But with so many companies never making it to an exit or failing completely, can the average return for investors really be noteworthy?

This time there is no straightforward answer. Many people regard crowdfunding more as a passion project than an investment case. This chapter's chart looks at the returns in the UK, a mature crowdfunding market with solid data. It illustrates the results of 11 years analyzed by

CHART 70

Crowdfunding in comparison

Annualized returns in the British market

British VC	17.0%
S&P 500	13.8%
Crowdfunding	12.9%
FTSE 100	6.3%

Crowdfunding measured by Seedr, analyzing all 1,038 businesses that were funded since launch. Period analyzed: 2012 to 2022.

Chart: Igor Pejic · Data from: Seedrs, British Venture Capital Association, IG, NYU Stern

the platform Seedr and compares them to other investment approaches. The average crowdfunding returns stood at 12.9%, which was more than double what you would have earned if invested in the FTSE 100, the weathervane for the British public markets. Yet if you compare it to the British private markets, VCs had a 17% annualized return.

The Seedr results include all crowdfunding projects. The more tech-heavy categories like "Finance and Payments" or "Software-as-a-Service" boast much higher return rates.

There are several issues to flag, though. First, there is a wide variance between markets and study results. One Belgian analysis, for instance, found that crowd-funded companies have a worse return on asset than non-crowd-funded. Second, because of the high failure rate, the returns come with a much higher danger of complete loss. And indeed, there is a strong correlation with the number of companies a person is invested in and the results. The more active an investor, the better the average return. More than 50 deals would give you the best pretax annualized returns. Third, investors are much more heavily dependent on a successful exit. Shares are difficult to trade. There is no real and efficient secondary market. Free float is small and investor protection is not on par with public markets.

There are other ways to go for private companies without getting an accreditation. Elizabeth Yin is the founder of Hustle Fund's Angel Squad, which allows individual angel investors to write small checks to startups. She admits that failure rates of investing in startups is high and it takes lots of shots on goal to make any money. "Investments via

Angel Squad can be as low as $1k per startup to stretch a checkbook. This means that an individual could potentially invest in 50–100 companies across a 10-year period with $5k–$10k per year of investment budget." Angel Squad then compiles those checks together to write one larger check to founders. Or you may be able to write a small check into an emerging VC fund that can deploy your check into many companies, diversifying and picking for you.

Furthermore, the proliferation of digital assets has created all kinds of novel, and super-quick, ways to buy tokens, which give you a stake in a project or company. Those are often the least regulated, so you should certainly read parts 7 and 8 before even considering such an investment. For all such private market vehicles, special care is indispensable, as they all share the shortcomings of crowdfunding: Low investor protection and transparency, missing secondary markets, and a wild difference in individual corporate performances.

71

ETFs Reign Supreme Among Advisors

WITH ALL THESE DIFFERENT INVESTMENT VEHICLES, building the perfect portfolio becomes much more complicated than it used to be. More choices are a good thing, and they give you so many more ways to fine-tune your portfolio. But the downside is, you have to dedicate much more time to figure out the best composition. So, the natural question to ask is: What do those people recommend who spend their days doing just that, fine-tuning portfolios? Financial advisors dig deep into different investment vehicles and assets, eventually recommending to their clients not just individual securities but an entire setup of a portfolio. Knowing their approach and the underlying trends lets you identify opportunities for differentiation.

Generally, advisors these days tend to strongly lean toward diversified funds like ETFs and mutual funds, with the former having the clear

CHART 71

Investment vehicles recommended by financial advisors

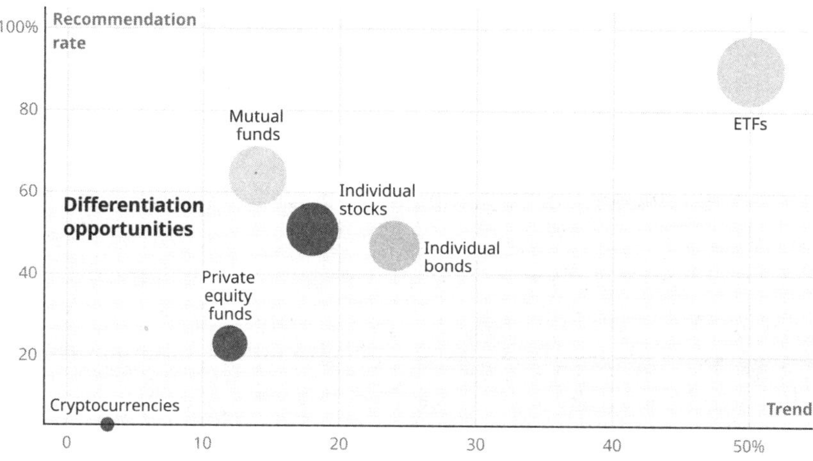

Chart: Igor Pejic · Data from: *Journal of Financial Planning* and FPA

upper hand. The ETF has become the number one tool to build a modern, diversified portfolio. It is the most cost-efficient way to do so, and the track record speaks for itself. The trend is just as clear as their dominance: Every year, more and more advisors include ETFs in their recommendations, so the gap is only becoming bigger, not smaller. Jürgen Kob, who has been a strategic advisor for over 30 years, sums up the rationale like this: "I think to mitigate risk in the volatile tech industry, investors should focus on diversification—both within the tech sector and across different industries. ETFs are a good way to spread risk." Picking individual stocks and bonds has taken the back seat, though they are both growing in popularity quicker than traditional mutual funds.

With the general paradigmatic shift toward ETFs, this trend and dominance among advisors is anything but surprising. But what does it mean to those seeking tech alpha—are there lessons to be learned?

First of all, there is obviously a universally accepted benefit of diversification and an equally universal acceptance of ETF supremacy. And it is only prudent to have a (sizable) part of your portfolio in those index funds. However, only following this path will never let you beat the market. If this is your goal, you will have to go against the dominant opinion and build asymmetric bets into your portfolio. How big that position should be, only you can truly tell. What percentage of your portfolio are you willing to lose? Thematic ETFs are a middle way, but many of those are actively managed too.

The most striking thing to me is that only a negligible portion of advisors suggest their clients should take a look at cryptocurrencies. It does not match the interest on the customer side at all. Crypto ETFs had one big success after the other, and millions of retail investors hold crypto wallets directly. In fact, the very same study of financial advisors reveals that every fourth advisor had been asked about cryptos in the last six months. Where does the gap stem from? Is it the complexity? A lack of knowledge? The outlook? The risks and volatility? We can't tell, but we can answer some critical questions about the risks, volatility, and outlook in the next parts. Because including some cryptocurrency exposure in your portfolio is a differentiator and thus a possible way to lift your portfolio above the market average. At the very least, it shouldn't be discounted right from the beginning.

72

ETFs and the Generational Gap

IT IS AN EXCITING TIME TO BE AN INVESTOR. Countless new possibilities let you get into exciting new startups, buy completely novel assets, or simply bet on a tech colossus that is disrupting the entire economy in front of our eyes. Information and educational content flow more freely and in bigger quantities than ever. Social and mainstream media are whipping up the excitement. With all this, you would think that young people have a much bigger risk appetite and are much more willing to try them out. Yet, according to research, exactly the opposite is true.

As the chart shows, every new generation is more likely than the previous one to diversify their portfolios. While only one in five boomers owns ETFs, it is close to two in five millennials.

CHART 72

Average ETF ratio of portfolio by generation

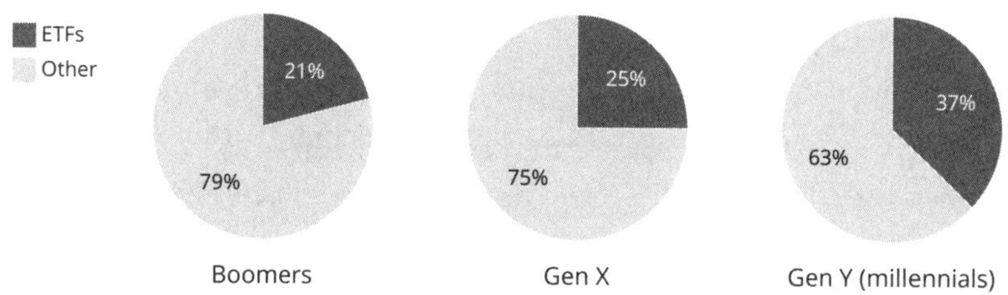

Chart: Igor Pejic • Data from: Charles Schwab

And the gap is continuously widening. Whereas 22% of millennials seek to significantly increase their ETF exposure over the next year, the figure stands at a meager 3% for boomers. This is a trend happening in parallel to the endorsement of ETFs among financial advisors. There is no causality. After all, the younger the person, the less likely he or she is to hire a professional advisor.

Previous generations have been much more comfortable with picking and owning individual stocks. Many put their savings in shares of the Nifty Fifty and similar blue-chip groups. Few millennials opt for stocks of Big Tech, though Microsoft, NVIDIA, and many others boast a multiple times higher market cap than the Nifty Fifty combined. And yet young people don't consider them too big to fail. It seems the idea that you can own a stock until retirement is slowly dying. Younger generations have grown up in a world in which technological disruption is daily business. And it is happening in almost every industry around them. Just think of how everyday life has changed for a millennial. Within some 20 years, almost every aspect of it is different. And so are the companies behind it. Where you get your music from, where you watch your TV series, how you buy your clothes, where you book your vacation, where and how you work—all of these markets have been upended by tech.

Interestingly, instead of seeing opportunities in this disruption, young people see dangers. At least, the majority of them do. Because if you look at the demographics driving new investment vehicles such as robo-advisors, social trading, crowdfunding, or Bitcoin, you will meet young people. But they are the minority of their generation. Most are broad diversifiers. So there is a huge divide along the lines of risk tolerance and the willingness to engage and understand all those new opportunities.

If you project this trend a couple of years and decades into the future, it will actually make companies at the top stickier. ETFs buy shares automatically. Demand is fueled less by the company's outlook or its fundamentals but by its current share of the index. That limits the downward risks of going with Big Tech. The Nifty Fifty did not benefit from automatic capital allocation in such a way. But this trend may also make for good opportunities for active investors. This mechanism rewards companies for simply being at the top, so there might be some market distortion. Blue-chip stocks can more easily become overvalued, while leaving potential disrupters under the radar, often undervalued. Thus, the generational shift might end up boosting the rewards of identifying future tech giants.

> *"Many people think that younger investors have a really high-risk profile. They think about Robinhood. They think about crypto. The truth is that many young investors have a lower risk affinity because they've seen a lot of pillage and plunder over the past few years. They've seen geopolitics. They've seen things happen, more ups and downs. Also, I don't think younger people today are willing to spend the time to get the knowledge to feel comfortable with their own choices of investments. There are so many more investment types, so that just makes it more confusing. Just look at cryptocurrency. Understanding it is a full-time job."*
>
> —APRIL RUDIN, founder and CEO at Rudin Group

VII

———

CAPITALIZING ON
DIGITAL ASSETS

BILL GATES HAS SAID THAT CRYPTOCURRENCIES are "100% based on greater fool theory." The world's most famous banker, Jamie Dimon, called them a "fraud" and a "Ponzi scheme." Yet in eight out of the last eleven years, Bitcoin has outperformed all other assets and indices. Let's get one thing straight: Bitcoin will never replace the financial system. Other digital assets might, but they work by a different logic. Bitcoin will never be an efficient means of payment. But neither is gold, its physical equivalent. Bitcoin might even come crashing down one day like Bill Gates and Jamie Dimon predict. Yet that doesn't mean it has to. Nor that it can't be a good investment opportunity until then. Seems contradictory? Consider this: Even Jamie Dimon now allows customers of JPMorgan Chase to buy Bitcoins. He is still a strong Bitcoin skeptic, but it appears he believes there is an attractive growth trajectory ahead, so why miss the opportunity? Investing is not about dogmas, but probabilities and risk/return ratios.

It is fundamental to distinguish three things: Blockchain vs. Bitcoin vs. other cryptocurrencies. Blockchain is the trust machine powering cryptos, but it has plenty of other use cases. It works by a similar logic as other broad technologies like mobile, AI, or cloud computing. Cryptocurrencies are a specific application of the technology with specific setups. They don't behave like a technology but like an asset class. And, among those, Bitcoin has a very special status. We will see why.

Books and guides about cryptocurrencies can fill entire bookshelves. The technology is hard to grasp. So are the monetary mechanisms. The trickiest part is that they are different for almost every coin. And even once you master these, there is a huge black box, which is called *the market*. Many of these books will prepare elaborate-sounding statistical models, drench them in industry-jargon, and spice them up with a nice narrative of a decentralized world that is inevitable. But if there is one thing the crypto world has taught us, it is that nothing is inevitable. Consider CBDCs. These are blockchain-based fiat currencies issued by central banks. In other words, truly digital dollars. These were regarded as an inevitability too. Yet Congress barred the Fed from issuing a digital dollar. A narrative accepted for years fell apart in days. The metaverse? It didn't even take Congress. The market did the job. And Bitcoin almost shared a similar fate, when in 2014, Mt. Gox was hacked and went bankrupt. Mt. Gox was a crypto exchange that processed 70% of all Bitcoins in circulation. The industry was reeling after the collapse.

So this part highlights what matters most to investors without the ideological and technological side-tracking that is prevalent in most other crypto literature. It dispels myths ranging from decentralization to the drivers of crypto prices. And it offers a fresh vantage point so that even crypto veterans will walk away surprised. In any case, part 7 is a starting point that should prepare you to continue your own learning journey by understanding which facts to look for and how to cut through the buzz and short-termism swirling around the industry. As with many other things, crypto puts the characteristics of the tech sector under a magnifying glass. Above all, it is the dynamism that is in a league of its own. Constantly keeping up to date is the only way to realize the unparalleled potency of crypto assets in any portfolio.

73

Crypto as a Highly Potent Alpha Driver

BITCOIN HAS LIMITED UTILITY VALUE. So whenever its price skyrocketed and crypto enthusiasts paraded their new Lamborghinis, critics were quick to dismiss it as pure speculation and as a bubble in the making. Yet Bitcoin persisted and came back every time a so-called crypto winter eliminated much of its market cap. The same cannot be said about the majority of other digital assets, whether that be alternative coins, pixelated pictures known as NFTs, or land in the virtual metaverse. You could say that Bitcoin has proven to be a volatile, but remarkably resilient, asset. Is it any wonder, then, that Bitcoin over time started to cast a spell over more serious investors?

If you look at this chapter's chart, it becomes clear that Bitcoin has been one of the most powerful asymmetric investments in recent history. And unlike a secretive startup, it is accessible to everybody. In eight of the last eleven years, it has not only outperformed every other asset class, but it has made all other returns look miniscule. It boasted returns ranging from two times higher to more than two hundred times higher than those of the runner-up asset class. In the years when Bitcoin

CHART 73

Bitcoin returns vs.other asset classes

	2013	2014	2015	2016	2017	2018	2019	2020	2021	2022	2023
1	BTC (5,516%)	S&P 500 (12%)	BTC (37%)	BTC (119%)	BTC (1,300%)	HYB (-2%)	BTC (92%)	BTC (302%)	BTC (58%)	Gold (1%)	BTC (156%)
2	S&P 500 (26%)	HYB (2%)	S&P 500 (-1%)	HYB (17%)	S&P 500 (18%)	Gold (-3%)	S&P 500 (29%)	Gold (24%)	S&P 500 (29%)	HYB (-11%)	S&P 500 (25%)
3	HYB (6%)	Gold (-3%)	HYB (-4%)	S&P 500 (11%)	Gold (12%)	S&P 500 (-7%)	Gold (18%)	S&P 500 (15%)	HYB (5%)	S&P 500 (-20%)	HYB (12%)
4	Gold (-29%)	BTC (-58%)	Gold (-11%)	Gold (7%)	HYB (7%)	BTC (-73%)	HYB (14%)	HYB (7%)	Gold (-6%)	BTC (-65%)	Gold (12%)

BTC = Bitcoin; S&P 500 = S&P 500 Total Return Index; HYB = US High Yield Corporate Bond Index

Table: Igor Pejic · Data from: iShares, Visual Capitalist

did not top the chart, it had the worst results of all asset classes by far. Though proof for its volatility, those losses where nowhere near the gains. And they were occurring significantly less often than the gains, roughly one out of four years.

A number of analysts have invoked Metcalfe's Law (see chapter 28) to argue that Bitcoin's value will increase exponentially in the future. Basically, the law stipulates that the more people use a network, the more its appeal grows. It does not just expand linearly but disproportionally. This also applies to credit cards and currencies. Predicting a trend with proven network effects at first sounds more serious than predicting it on gut feeling. Yet if you look at the history of Bitcoin, it is clear that its climbs in value have not accelerated. On the contrary, percentagewise, the appreciation of Bitcoin is slowing. In 2013, for example, the returns were north of 5,000% whereas 2020 and 2023, two very good years, boasted profits of approximately 300% and 150%, respectively. Even 2024, the year Bitcoin broke the $100k sound barrier, did not see an increase above 150%. Still extremely remarkable, but not exactly a trend confirming Metcalfe's Law. Bitcoin is not a payment instrument that rises in popularity the more people use it. Rather it is a store of value that gets its appeal through its scarcity. Sure, when more people invest in it, the price surges, the media buzzes, and more people get in. But not exponentially like in the case of a true network.

Rather, this slowing is indicative of Bitcoin becoming more popular and its price stabilizing. It is still fluctuating more wildly than other asset classes but not as wildly as it used to. Of course, investors must never forget that there are so many developments that could not only kill the historic trend, but the entire crypto industry. Regulation, large-scale thefts, forks—these are just a few of the things that have already occurred in the past. Thus, Bitcoin is best thought of as a catalyst to a portfolio. It might fizzle out, or it might inject stellar growth to your net worth. Like every good catalyst, Bitcoin works best if it is not the main component but only a surrogate in a broader portfolio. How big the surrogate is depends on your risk tolerance and your investment horizons. Some investors might decide that 1% of their total investable assets are the maximum they are prepared to lose, while others are comfortable with 30, 40, or even 50%. And of course it depends on whether you have other possible catalysts that compete for the same allocation of risk budget with Bitcoin.

> *"The famous VC Vinod Khosla once told me on a board call that he looks for asymmetric investments. These are opportunities where he puts in a dollar and gets out $1,000. And that actually is the story of Bitcoin. So, when you're getting into an asymmetric investment, most of your investments will be zero. But if you put in a dollar and you get back $1,000, you don't care that 100 of them failed. That's how you have to view Bitcoin. It does carry unique risks with it, but it can also go through the roof."*

—CHRIS KITZE, chairman at Alphabit Digital Currency Fund, former CEO of NBC Internet

74

Digital Asset Type Overview

BITCOIN IS STABILIZING. Its appreciation, though still impressive, is slowing. That leaves many investors searching for the next stellar crypto coin. And there is certainly no shortage of alternatives. More than 26 million to be precise, with more than a million added per month. The somewhat good news is that very few are traded on exchanges. Coinbase, for example, lists only 150 assets. Yet even this number is overwhelming. The really good news is that the vast majority is pure speculation, and it is pretty easy to filter those out.

Chart 74 breaks down all the possible token categories and highlights those where it pays to start looking. *Digital assets* is the umbrella term for all forms of blockchain-recorded tokens that have some monetary value.

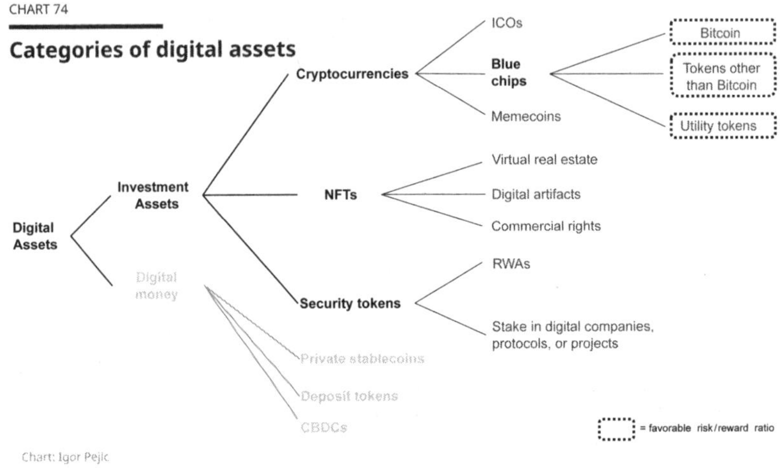

One of the two major groups can be subsumed under the label *digital money*. These are applications that oil the transfer machine. All of them can only exist thanks to the fiat monetary system. These so-called stablecoins peg their value to the dollar, or less frequently to some other fiat currency. They can be distinguished by the issuer: Private stablecoins (any corporation), deposit tokens (licensed banks), or CBDCs (central bank digital currency). Their disruptive potential is enormous, but buying them is no investment. Nik Bhatia, adjunct professor at the USC Marshall School of Business and founder of The Bitcoin Layer, has popularized the concept of layered money, which also explains how Bitcoin is different to CBDCs. He contrasts the dollar credit system to Bitcoin as a commodity. "CBDC, on the other hand, is the digital version of paper currency, which is a liability of the central bank and/or government, however you would like to frame it. So, it cannot be a replacement to Bitcoin. CBDC is simply the digital evolution of central bank layered money."

Apart from this group of digital money tokens, you have a broad variety of coins that can be categorized as "investment assets." Among these, we find security tokens, which are basically blockchain-based representations of an underlying securities contract. You can record shares, bonds, mortgages, or any other real-world asset (RWA) on a blockchain. Again, a great leap for the financial system, but the rules for investors are close to identical to buying these assets off-chain.

Investment tokens can also come in the form of NFTs (non-fungible tokens). NFTs can be used to record assets that cannot be traded on a like-for-like basis—unique digital artifacts, if you will. Previous NFT crazes were ignited by pictures of distorted cats and bored apes, digital art collections, and virtual plots of land in deserted and dull universes. Many business models were somewhere between speculation and conmanship. There are legitimate use cases for NFTs, too, such as representing commercial and exploitation rights. But NFTs are not exactly the place to look for technology alpha.

Finally, there is the cryptocurrency subgroup. The major line to draw here is between blue-chip cryptos and the other 26 million. In stock markets you have a vibrant mid-cap and small-cap segment where you can find plenty of hidden champions. Crypto is different. Even if you only take the exchange-listed cryptocurrencies into account, there is a massive gap to the front-runners. There is no public scrutiny, no proven business model. In most cases, there is no business at all. Memecoins are the symptomatic pinnacle of this. Imagine a coin inspired and named after an internet joke, its popularity spreading like wildfire thanks to social media and celebrity endorsement, with no utility value at all. That is a memecoin.

In summary, the best place to look for asymmetric bets in crypto is among the large caps. The longer they have been at the top, the better. There is yet another important distinction: Bitcoin vs. the other blue chips. Bitcoin is not just the best-known cryptocurrency and the industry's bellwether. It is different in kind. But what implications does this have? Does it mean that other cryptocurrencies can be complementary investments, or are they unnecessarily diverting focus from Bitcoin? The next chapter holds the answer.

75

Is There More to the Cryptocurrency Game Than Bitcoin?

CRYPTO BELIEVERS FALL INTO one of two groups: The first group are Bitcoin purists or maximalists, who view all other coins as mere appendages to the king of crypto. They even group all non-Bitcoin crypto under the label "altcoins." Purists argue that Bitcoin is the ultimate store of value and thus inflation hedge, because it is the strongest in terms of decentralization. It has the largest network of all cryptocurrencies and is thus most difficult to attack. Bitcoin believers also take issue with other cryptocurrencies having other consensus mechanisms. Consensus is the way a network agrees on which transactions are legitimate. Bitcoin uses the

CHART 75

Share of cryptocurrency market cap

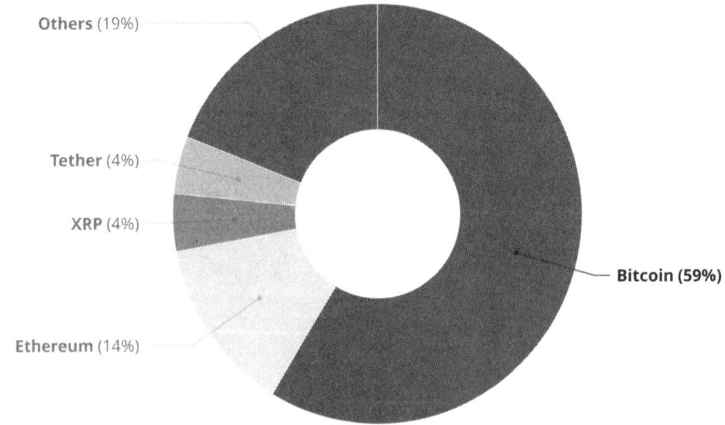

Market capitalization figures as of August 22, 2025.
Chart: Igor Pejic • Data from: CoinMarketCap

inefficient proof-of-work mechanism, while most other competitors like Ethereum agree with proof-of-stake. Instead of burning massive electricity and cutting-edge hardware like in the Bitcoin network, voting power in proof-of-stake is based on how many coins you own.

Opposed to the purists are the pluralists. Their belief is that multiple blockchains and cryptocurrencies can coexist as they offer unique technical capabilities and can handle different use cases. Some allow for programing rules on a blockchain (e.g., Ethereum), others enable much faster and cheaper transactions (e.g., XRP), and still others leverage the strengths of fiat money (e.g., USDC). And the security argument? They don't buy it. Whether you invest money in mining chips and electricity or you buy coins, it doesn't matter. Both are a pay-to-play scheme. You put up an initial investment and it is in your self-interest to keep the network legitimate. Otherwise, you are shooting yourself in the foot. Your up-front investment is gone.

Crypto pluralists have a strong point. But while it sounds reasonable on paper, it is not reflected in the market. As you can see from the chart, Bitcoin captures 59% of the total crypto market cap. It is akin to the US dollar in global trade, the backbone without which nothing moves. Bitcoin's dominance has decreased over the past few years, but only marginally. Despite other coins improving rapidly and widening the functional gap, crypto purists keep the upper hand.

The smartest investors are never ideological. Even if you are convinced that Bitcoin has a special place among all cryptocurrencies, it doesn't mean you have to dismiss the others. Tim Draper is one of America's most important venture capitalists and an ardent Bitcoin proponent. He explained to me why he believes altcoins can even be beneficial to Bitcoin: "Other cryptocurrencies are making Bitcoin more valuable by challenging its hegemony as the currency and financial system of the world. Bitcoin is the Microsoft. The other currencies are the Lotus 123, the WordPerfect, and the Relational Technologies." Draper sees the main benefit when other coins are not competing with Bitcoin but integrating with it, when they bring new innovative power to the ecosystem. Eventually it will strengthen Bitcoin, but they might benefit too. "Some may be very successful, but the features, when incorporated into Bitcoin, will make most of them temporary wins. Still, we hold some of the more important cryptocurrencies at Draper. We know there is growth and value there."

So if Bitcoin is still growing in double or triple digits and its downside potential is significantly lower than in smaller coins, why bother with anything else? Some say that diversification will keep the risk down. Yet this doesn't really apply to the crypto world. If Bitcoin tanks, so do the other coins. There is no cryptocurrency with an inverse correlation to Bitcoin. A stronger argument is the utility one. Some blockchains like Ethereum have powerful use cases and a growing corporate adoption. Whether it is logistics giants or banking goliaths, they are all building corporate applications on top of Ethereum. These don't just drive up the price of the ETH token but also bring in ever more fees. It is critical to understand this kind of business model, as well as the organizational structure behind the blockchain. Ethereum has made major updates that changed the very heart of the protocol. Though being truly decentralized, the multi-year updates went down without even the slightest hiccup. Ethereum is unlike any other blockchain. Just like Bitcoin, it has a special position in the crypto economy, but with a very different proposition.

So Ethereum is worth a look, too, but what about all those other coins? If you have Bitcoin as the ultimate store of value and Ethereum as the machine for the crypto economy, why invest in other coins? Historically, there has been one phenomenon that justifies the purchase of other coins: Altcoin season. It is a recurring period in which altcoins significantly outperform Bitcoin. Altcoin season usually follows a very strong performance of Bitcoin. Profits that are made during Bitcoin rallies are reallocated to smaller market caps in the search for higher returns. Investment volumes go up and drive the price surge. Altcoin season typically starts with Ethereum and other blue chips and trickles down to smaller coins. This is why a broader crypto portfolio might deliver somewhat higher returns. But for that to happen, a lot more things have to fall in the right place than simply holding Bitcoin and Ethereum as catalysts in your portfolio.

76

Stability of Crypto Blue Chips

BUYING A COIN AND SIMPLY HOPING for altcoin season appreciation is speculation. You have to understand and believe in the coin's utility value and the blockchain's business model just the way you should understand a business before buying stocks. The list of the 10 largest coins shows just how diverse the coin cosmos can be.

We have already discussed the two front-runners, Bitcoin and Ethereum, and how their value is driven by completely different factors. There are smaller coins that work with a similar logic. Litecoin or Bitcoin Cash, for example, derive their value from their scarcity, just like Bitcoin. Their

CHART 76

Top 10 crypto coins according to market cap

Companies in bold remained in the top 10.

Position	2021	2025
1	**Bitcoin**	**Bitcoin**
2	**Ethereum**	**Ethereum**
3	Cardano	**Tether USDT**
4	**Binance Coin (BNB)**	XRP
5	**Tether USDT**	**Binance Coin (BNB)**
6	XRP	Solana
7	**Solana**	USDC
8	Polkadot	Tron
9	**USDC**	**Dogecoin**
10	**Dogecoin**	**Cardano**

Data from October 2021 and October 2025.

Table: Igor Pejic • Data from: CoinMarketCap

blockchains can't handle other assets, nor smart contracts. They attempted to be more efficient Bitcoin alternatives, by offering quicker block generation (and thus more transactions per second). But this type of coin fell out of favor as more fundamental innovations dramatically alleviated Bitcoin's limitations. Layer-2 blockchains are one of them. These are more efficient networks built on top of Bitcoin.

Ethereum challengers have been more successful. Solana and Cardano have both been among the top 10 blockchains for the past couple of years. Tron joined them more recently. Those Ethereum clones are younger and more efficient than Ethereum, but they never really lived up to their moniker "Ethereum-killers," mostly because they didn't enjoy the same trust among institutional blockchain users. The trust issues have to do with the governance of the blockchains but also with the tremendous size of Ethereum. Network effects at work.

Binance Coin started on Ethereum as the native coin to the Binance ecosystem and grew into another kind of challenger. Binance is one of the world's largest crypto exchanges and thus had the weight to build the scale quickly. It tries to take on both Ethereum and Bitcoin. While Binance Coin offers a fee-based smart contract machine, it also continuously burns coins to fire up price appreciation.

Another popular group is made up of stablecoins, which are coins without their own exchange rate. Instead, their price is linked to that of another stable asset like the dollar. USDC and Tether USDT are the most successful representatives. They don't live off price appreciations, nor do they earn much on fees. They rise and fall with the interest on their reserves. They also come with very specific risks, as we will see later.

Then there is XRP, the token of the Ripple network. Unlike most other coins, it is managed by a traditional corporation out of San Francisco—Ripple Labs. And while other coins seek to *replace* the traditional financial system, Ripple was conceived to *help* it by making (cross-border) transactions significantly cheaper, while respecting regulatory requirements.

We even see one memecoin on the list. Elon Musk's Dogecoin is the epitome of all memecoins as it lives off community and attention rather than utility value.

The chart tells us two things. First, the crypto universe is extremely diverse. Things like crypto market cycles or altcoin season can give you a hint as to the best timing for increasing your exposure to a coin, but thinking that all blue chips will behave similarly is too simplistic.

Second, it shows us that there is stability. Bitcoin, Ethereum, and XRP have been at the top of valuation lists since the beginning. Otherwise, the top 10 initially saw a lot of rotation. This changed at the start of the 2020s. Within four years, only one coin—Polkadot—dropped out and was replaced by Tron. In that regard, there is even less movement in crypto than in the stock market. It indicates on the one hand that the industry has grown up. New inventions are not any more radical to a point where they can easily upend the market. On the other hand, it shows that there has been significant market consolidation and that network effects make it hard to challenge that consolidation. At the same time, there is significant growth even among those established players. Hence, if you are looking for asymmetric investment opportunities, it is incumbent to understand each of the big blockchains.

77

The Crypto Market Cycle

TECHNOLOGIES AND MARKETS MOVE IN CYCLES. And, surprise, surprise, so does the crypto sphere. As chart 77 shows, the Bitcoin price moves through four successive stages over and over again.

The cycle is kicked in with the accumulation phase, whereby the first crypto bulls jump-start demand. Prices start to rise but do not yet reach previous highs. The traded volumes are low. Slowly, the appreciation is accelerated. Bitcoin enters the growth phase. More people reach the conclusion that the bottom is behind us and another growth path has started. The number of investors rises. As does the price. Once this solid growth phase catches on for some time, Bitcoin starts entering bubble territory. Growth becomes stellar and the price soon eclipses past all-time-highs. Actually,

CHART 77

The Bitcoin/crypto market cycle

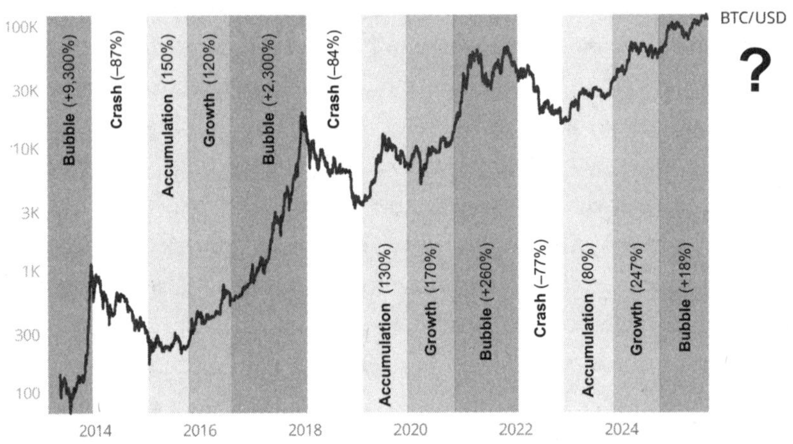

Attention: The BTC price development is presented on a logarithmic scale.

Chart: Igor Pejic • Data from: Caleb and Brown, CoinGecko

it shoots past it by a lot. There are fluctuations, though. On the one hand a hype unfolds and draws in more mainstream investors, but on the other many investors lock in profits and sell. Anticipation of a crash spreads.

Each bubble in the past was ended by a crash. Prices fell precipitously. Minus 87%. Minus 84%. Minus 77%. The losses for anybody who doesn't sell early are dramatic. What causes crashes? Many different things, which makes it difficult to foresee them. Hacks of major exchanges. Collapses of big players. Regulatory crackdowns. Macroeconomic downturns and insecurity. Central bank policies.

But the good thing about cycles is that they start all over again. After the crash, Bitcoin again goes through accumulation, growth, and bubble. And so far, that has more than made up for the losses in the crash. Long-term holders of crypto had excellent overall returns despite the multiple devastating crashes.

One more thing stands out from the chart: The phases of the cycles are getting less distinct. Volatility is decreasing. Both the crashes and the bubbles are becoming less dramatic with every cycle. The number of investors and the value locked in have been going up. The more people hold Bitcoins or crypto, the better shocks can be absorbed.

There are a number of indicators that can presumably help anticipate certain phases. If, say, the ratio of coins held in wallets rather than in centralized exchanges is high, it indicates that fewer people are in anticipation to sell. A sell-off is unlikely to happen. However, these metrics don't work as they used to because ever more of the assets under management are held by broad retail investors that don't tinker with private wallets.

It usually works better to track the macroeconomic environment and other asset classes. Interestingly, though Bitcoin shares many characteristics with physical gold, the price movements of these two asset classes have often diverged. Gold performs well in times of uncertainty. Bitcoin does not. This refutes the safe haven argument. But the Bitcoin price usually moves in lockstep with the S&P 500. Many of the phases are heavily impacted by general market sentiment. Interest rate environments, tariff threats, elections.

Bitcoin enthusiasts downplay this correlation. They want to see crypto as an alternative system, not an extension of the traditional one. They will tell you in one voice that the heartbeat of the crypto market cycle is the Bitcoin halving event, which slows down fresh Bitcoin supply. They're wrong. Many factors feed investors' appetites. Bitcoin supply is not one of them. Read the next chapter to find out what really kickstarted previous bull runs.

"Bitcoin always has a way of surprising us. I don't think anyone could have predicted that in May 2021 China would ban Bitcoin mining, causing the hash rate to suddenly collapse, which then made the price drop. But that was temporary. And then all of a sudden by November 2021, we were at a new all-time high. As Bitcoin continues to be assimilated into the greater financial system and continues to be impacted by geopolitical moves, I think that some of these prediction factors that may have guided people in previous cycles may not be as accurate."

—NATALIE BRUNELL, host of *Coin Stories* and author of
Bitcoin Is for Everyone

78

What Really Makes Crypto Prices Surge and Slump?

THERE IS HARDLY AN AREA OF BUSINESS in which myths swirl around so stubbornly as in the cryptosphere. Some of them we have already dismantled in this part. Here is another one that investors must know about: Bitcoin prices surge regularly because of Bitcoin's infamous halving event, a process by which roughly every four years the amount of newly minted Bitcoins drops by 50%.

The protocol defines only one way Bitcoins can be created—namely, through an automatic mechanism by which new coins are created every time a new block of transactions is added to the Bitcoin blockchain. This happens on average every 10 minutes, a constant throughout Bitcoin's

Crypto bull runs and their drivers

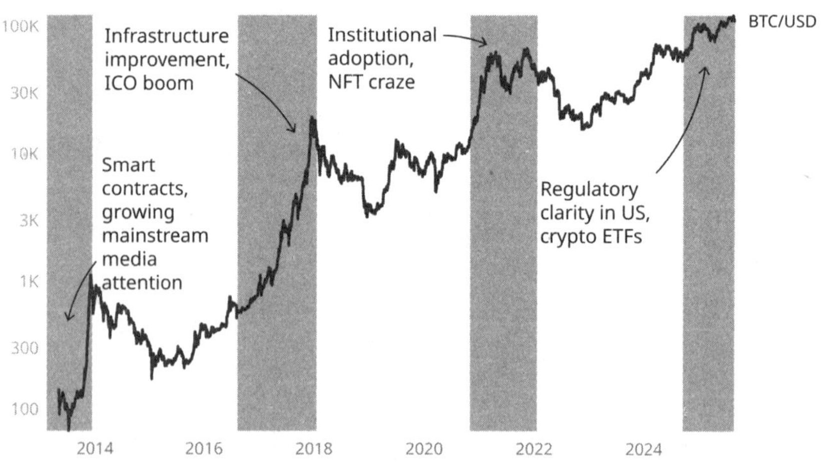

Attention: The BTC price development is presented on a logarithmic scale.

Chart: Igor Pejic • Data from: BTC price data from CoinGecko

entire history. What is not a constant is the reward. Participants in the network (called miners) race to find the solution to a mathematical puzzle. The first to find it is rewarded with fresh Bitcoins. Today, that reward stands at 3.125 coins per block. But this amount is cut in half roughly every four years. From some point in 2028, the winner will get only 1.5625 coins per block, which will again be reduced in 2032, and so on. Ergo, the supply dries out over time. By approximately 2140, there will be no more new coins.

The maximum amount of all Bitcoins ever in circulation is capped at 21 million, which makes Bitcoin a disinflationary asset. Natalie Brunell, the host of *Coin Stories*, points out that the circulation cap is why "Bitcoin is highly correlated with liquidity. And if you look at all the signposts for where liquidity is going, especially in a highly indebted global economy that needs to print in order to sustain itself, then I would argue that Bitcoin is one of the best investments you can make."

This is the backdrop against which crypto maximalists build their argumentation that the halving is supercharging scarcity by choking off supply. They have even come up with a mathematical rationalization for it, a metric that measures Bitcoin's scarcity. You divide the total existing stock (i.e., the circulating supply) by the annual production flow (i.e., newly mined Bitcoins per year). This is called the stock-to-flow ratio, or S2F.

The stock-to-flow argumentation sounds plausible at first. You can even chart the correlation of the ratio with the Bitcoin price development and it might appear there is a link. But while the 21 million cap is the reason Bitcoin has value in the first place, it doesn't make S2F a good method for forecasting its price movements.

First of all, S2F does not take into consideration demand. An asset can be extremely rare, but if there is no demand for it, scarcity won't matter. The appreciation of any asset is always driven by the same situation: Demand outstripping supply. S2F looks only at the supply side of this equation.

Moreover, linking Bitcoin rallies to the halving ignores two facts of Bitcoin mathematics. First, the halving can be forecast quite precisely. It is not like we wake up in a world in which, all of a sudden, the supply is cut by 50%. We know exactly how many coins will be in circulation at which point in time. No matter how far away the halving is, it is priced in. Second, of the 21 million Bitcoins that will ever be in existence, 19 million have already been mined. In the last cycle post-crash, we have seen an appreciation of about 350%. This stands in no relation whatsoever to the 10% of coins that still are to be mined.

So what is determining the price of Bitcoin, then? This chapter's chart shows what fueled the last four crypto bull runs. Most of them had a technological and an external component. In 2014, the automation of blockchains broke new ground. With the rise of smart contracts on the Ethereum, blockchain business logic could be coded on the blockchain. At the same time, the first widespread media hysteria took hold. The next wave was caused by significant infrastructure improvements, but also by the hype around initial coin offerings (ICOs), the no-strings-attached investment vehicle of the crypto world. The next bubble was blown by a special type of crypto asset—the non-fungible token (NFT). But also by large-scale institutional adoption. The recent wave lives off numerous corporate giants entering the space, as well as increased regulatory clarity.

Note also that, though Bitcoin is significantly different from other crypto assets, it moves in lockstep with them. The technical bull run drivers have been smart contracts, ICOs, NFTs. The Bitcoin blockchain can run neither of those, yet it has benefited from each of the booms tremendously.

79

Regulatory Clarity Drives the Risk Down and the Volume Up

IMAGINE YOU ARE THE ISSUER of a cryptocurrency. Not some shady one that is used in the deep corners of the dark web to pay for drugs and hitmen, but one that is helping banks. Yet you don't know whether the coin you are issuing is a security or a commodity. You don't even know which regulator to turn to. The only thing that's clear is that no one has any regulatory frameworks in place, nor the willingness to create some. So you ask them for formal guidance, but your plea puffs out. Worse, you

CHART 79

US spot ETF net flows driving the Bitcoin price

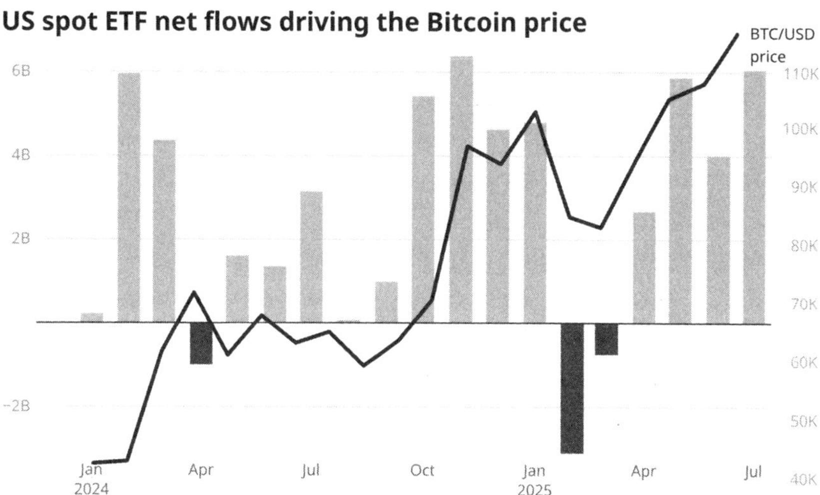

Chart: Igor Pejic • Data from: Glassnode

are hit with billion-dollar lawsuits by those very same regulators. The number one crypto exchange delists your token to comply with the new "rules," but at the same time the exchange itself is caught up in limbo so badly that it drags the SEC to the courts to obtain legal regulatory clarity. Meanwhile, states are suing the SEC about their authority in that matter. This chaos is bad for business. Utterly bad.

This was not a fictional nightmare scenario, but what Ripple and Coinbase actually lived through. They are just the two most prominent examples, but the entire cryptosphere suffered tremendously due to this "regulation by enforcement" approach, in which the only way to know what was allowed was to litigate.

The page was turned in 2024. First the House of Representatives passed the FIT21 Act, thereby ending regulation by enforcement. Then, in 2025, the GENIUS Act passed the Senate. It defines very specific rules on who can issue stablecoins, what the reserve requirements are, how to audit them, and much more. Even more important: The SEC, still under Chairman Gensler, greenlighted Spot Bitcoin and Ethereum ETFs. The Bitcoin price raced to a new all-time high. People who did not want to tinker with exchanges or wallets started pouring their money into crypto ETFs. Institutional investors, asset managers, and banks all lunged at this new opportunity as soon as it presented itself. Many of them did a brutal 180 on Bitcoin. Former critics now started offering them to clients. Natalie Brunell sums up the logic succinctly: "When it comes to banks, they're going to be heavily incentivized to offer products because a lot of their customer base is going to be demanding it. And if they don't offer it, people are going to change banks. So it's only natural that banks are going to be increasingly involved in the industry."

Alfred Taudes, who founded the Research Institute for Crypto-economics at the Vienna University of Economics and Business, also stresses the political dimensions. "A number of factors influences the Bitcoin price. The Bitcoin halving, demand, regulation, but also how politicians and business leaders see it. Donald Trump has announced a Bitcoin reserve and support for the Bitcoin mining community. Elon Musk is another prominent crypto advocate."

President Trump and Elon Musk were just the pinnacle of a powerful crypto wave that washed across all levels of politics. The president and his administration, the SEC, the Senate, the House, state and local elected officials. Those regulatory initiatives were important by and of themselves, but what really inspires confidence in investors is the clear bipartisan support for these forward-looking rules.

The American clarity around crypto assets is part of a larger trend. Most notably, the European Union passed the Markets in Crypto-Assets Regulation (MiCA) back in early 2023. It was permissive and a success to balance innovation with investor protection. MiCA did, however, put a heavy burden on large stablecoin activity to protect the stability of the financial system. Yet while MiCA was celebrated as a landmark, it was only the acts of the US Congress that moved the needle. As with tech in general, the EU provided a strong blueprint, but it is America where crypto's fate got decided.

> *"The US government adopting a pro-Bitcoin policy in several steps over the years has been remarkable to see and without a doubt it contributes to Bitcoin's longevity as a network. And it's not just the government. I always remind people and myself*

that in a representative government, the government is a representative of the populace and the will of that populace."

—NIK BHATIA, founder of the Bitcoin Layer, author of *Layered Money*, and adjunct professor at the USC Marshall School of Business

80

How Far Can the Value of Cryptocurrencies Climb?

DESPITE THE SUSTAINED UPS AND DOWNS, the overall trajectory of Bitcoin has known only one direction: Upward. As we've seen in the crypto market cycle, no matter how bad the collapses have been, the accumulation, growth, and bubble phases have always been better. But how long can this steep climb continue? Is the Bitcoin price about to hit its ceiling soon, given that yearly gains have already decelerated? There is a way to tell the potential. The price of each asset is set by supply and demand. In the case of Bitcoin, only one of these variables is unknown. There will never be more than 21 million Bitcoins in circulation. So how long the past price trend will continue comes down to one question only: How much money will investors still pour into the world's largest cryptocurrency?

You can't know for certain, but you can gauge the potential market by looking at how much money is invested in comparable asset classes. Some experts compare Bitcoin's market capitalization to that of the stock market. Interestingly, these comparisons are cited by both crypto believers and doomsayers, either as proof of how irrelevant or how undervalued Bitcoin is. Both are wrong. Bitcoin is frequently correlated with the stock market and is an investment asset rather than a currency. Yet it definitely does not behave like an equity. Holding it doesn't make you own part of a company. It doesn't pay you dividends. It doesn't give you voting rights. And the price is neither driven by the utility value of

Gold vs. Bitcoin market cap in $B

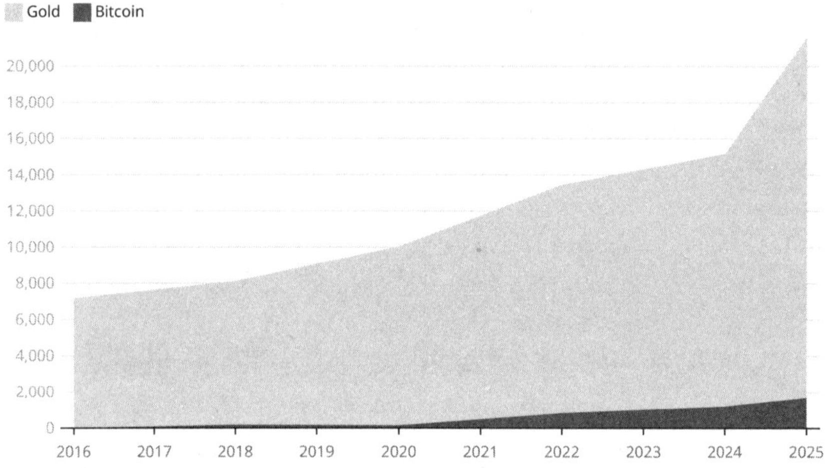

The market cap refers to the March figures of each respective year.

Chart: Igor Pejic • Data from: IGWT

the industry, nor the competitors' new products, nor a company's earning potential. Hence, both asset behavior and investor interest are fundamentally different. There is a far better comparison.

Bitcoin has been defined many times as digital gold. Its supply is limited, it is difficult to mine, and it cannot be copied or created artificially. The argument most frequently made against Bitcoin can be made against gold too—namely, that both are worth only as much as somebody is willing to pay for them. The shiny metal has close to no utility value. If you own real estate, you can live in it or rent it out. If you own stocks, you own part of a company. Fiat money is linked to the GDP of a country. Gold, on the other hand, keeps its value solely by hoping that somebody else will buy it in the future. Sure, gold can be worn around your neck, but so can silver and many, much cheaper, metals.

By looking at the money locked in gold, you get a rough understanding of the potential market demand addressable by cryptocurrencies in the long run. My chart at the top of this subchapter shows that, currently, there is roughly 12 times more money in gold than in Bitcoin. That means a lot of catching up is still ahead, but don't forget the insane speed of the crypto world. As Ronit Ghose observes: "Crypto speed-runs things. Developments happen there in one or two years that stretched over decades in previous social and financial history." Does that mean Bitcoin will certainly rise by a factor of 12 and pass the one-million-dollar mark? There are many hurdles to clear before that could happen. Above all, Bitcoin's price first has to start behaving like that of gold rather than stocks. Yet what the comparison to the gold market cap clearly demonstrates is that there is still plenty of market opportunity for Bitcoin. And there is a lot more capital locked in other precious metals. Those are all scarce and display similar characteristics to cryptocurrencies. Moreover, there are millions of investors that bring in fresh capital not currently invested in gold and the like. Despite all of that, Bitcoin's price still might stagnate or even fall, but it is unlikely to do so due to a saturation effect. The growth trajectory is nowhere near its end.

"Bitcoin is like digital gold, and I absolutely believe it will reach the market cap of physical gold as more institutions and individuals start to understand and appreciate the underlying technology."

—ANTHONY SCARAMUCCI, founder and managing partner of SkyBridge Capital and former White House communications director

81

The Fairy Tale of Decentralization

THERE IS NO DOUBT BITCOIN OCCUPIES a special place among crypto assets. Not because it was the first one. Nor because its market cap outshines the combined value of all others. But because it has a degree of decentralization unmatched by any other blockchain.

Share of Bitcoin blocks mined based on mining pools

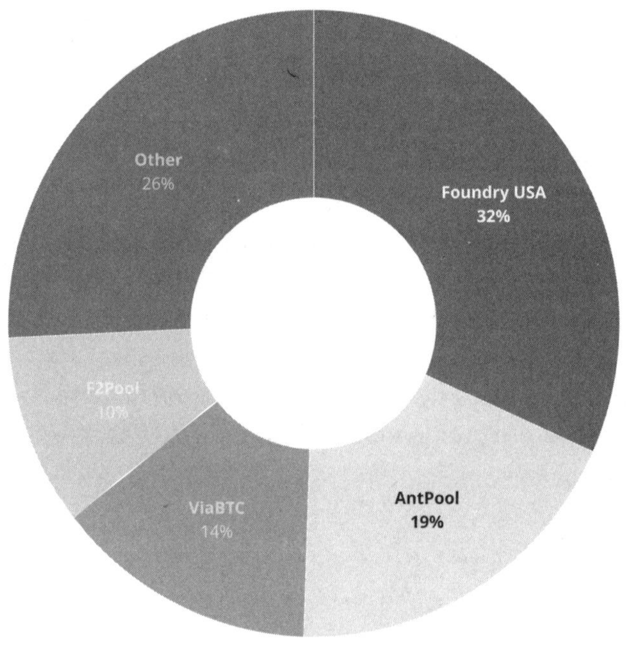

The number of blocks mined during H1 2025.

Chart: Igor Pejic • Data from: Zeus Mining

Yet even the king of crypto is plagued by concentration trends on all levels. A few custodial exchanges and wallets are holding more and more private keys—i.e., keys that can unlock customer funds. And the likes of Coinbase and Binance are growing bigger, not smaller. Thanks to the surge of crypto ETFs, asset managers like BlackRock and their custodians are in charge of ever more crypto wallets, while institutional investors such as MicroStrategy are relentlessly ramping up their Bitcoin reserves.

Unlike with other crypto assets such as Ethereum or Solana, owning the coins does not give you a say in the Bitcoin network. A process called mining does. Miners own high-performance computer chips and contribute their power to the network. The more power they contribute, the higher their so-called hashrate. Mining hashrate concentration is increasing too.

For individual miners, it is all but impossible to have a steady and predictable income stream. Of the thousands of miners, only one gets to win a huge reward every 10 minutes. So they join mining pools and bundle their hashrates. The pool wins frequently and distributes the reward to all miners. This is where the real concern lies. The two mining pools Foundry USA and AntPool now command more than 50% of the power in the Bitcoin network. This oligopoly evokes the specter of a 51% attack, whereby the majority of the network bends the rules and transactions to its will.

Contrary to popular belief, a 51% attack would not allow the conglomerate to rewrite past transactions, nor to change the core protocol by which Bitcoin works. It could, however, allow a dominant entity to manipulate the blockchain by reversing recent transactions, censoring blocks, or enabling double-spending. The impact is limited, but sufficient to make Bitcoin's value drop to zero if trust in the network is destroyed. And this is precisely why such an attack most probably will never happen. Why should a dominant player steal Bitcoins, when this very act would make all Bitcoins worthless?

None of the previously mentioned risks is a bright red flag that should make you dismiss Bitcoin. None of the scenarios is likely. But some are possible. Thus, you must factor in all these scenarios in your risk/reward calculations. It is not the utility value but the decentralization ethos that gives Bitcoin its value. Any successful attack, regardless how small, could send a crypto asset from hero to zero. Most importantly: There must not even be an actual attack. The sole fear that it *could* happen can trigger panic. Subsequent mass sell-offs would do the rest.

82

Realizing Crypto Gains in the Traditional Financial System

FOR MOST OF THE TIME, the route to crypto wealth was straightforward. If you wanted to ride the crypto market cycle, you bought Bitcoin. Or Ethereum. Or another altcoin. If you felt like gambling or monetizing a hype, you purchased coins at an ICO or added an NFT to your assets, or you got into whatever the latest industry trend was. Whatever you did, you did it within this new alternative financial system. This rule no longer stands.

Today, investors have many possibilities to ride crypto's success without ever leaving the traditional financial system. They can invest in companies whose entire corporate value hinges on that of Bitcoin because their main strategy is to hoard it (e.g., MicroStrategy). Or they can go for exchanges, which are showered with trading fees in every crypto bull run (e.g., Coinbase). Or they could even buy shares in a company that issues coins itself (e.g., Circle). For every strategy, there is at least one public company that can help you realize it. You can buy stocks

CHART 82

The impact of the GENIUS Act on crypto investments

Chart: Igor Pejic • Data from: Investing.com

from audited companies instead of dabbling with wallets, private keys, and the risks of frauds, scams, and thefts.

Not convinced yet? The returns when investing through the traditional financial system in crypto can sometimes be even higher than buying and holding digital assets directly. Consider the chart in this chapter. When the Senate passed the GENIUS Act in July 2025, the entire crypto industry breathed a sigh of relief. The law allows banks, as well as non-banks, to officially issue their own stablecoins. Stablecoins are also a crucial pillar for classic decentralized coins. They serve as a bridge between the traditional financial system and the crypto world. And while Bitcoin and other crypto assets jumped on the news, it was nothing compared to the way Circle's stocks soared. Circle is a stablecoin issuer itself, so this comes as no big surprise. But Circle was part of something bigger, a wave that lifted many other crypto-related companies more than it lifted the big coins themselves. Holders of Coinbase stock, for example, had quite a ride upon the news that the GENIUS Act succeeded on the Senate floor.

This episode reveals how intertwined crypto assets have become with the real economy. And this is good news for holders of crypto assets. Public equities provide a much needed on-ramp into the crypto realm. This means more investors. And more investors boost investment volumes, which eventually boosts the value of crypto assets.

Circle went public shortly before the GENIUS Act was passed and it soared by 750% within only three weeks. Its success proved to be a blueprint for other well-known crypto companies like Gemini to target a classic IPO. That doesn't mean, however, that the traditional crypto route, the ICO, is dead. Many companies still seek to raise capital without the scrutiny and overhead costs. And many investors prefer to hold coins directly, because they have only one possible point of failure rather than two. If, say, you invest in MicroStrategy, you are not just taking the currency risk of Bitcoin, but also the risk that there might be issues with the company and its management.

Hence, what we are seeing is a hybrid world in which traditional and decentralized models coexist and even melt into each other. For investors, this is all good news, as they get to choose from a plenitude of ways to invest in digital assets and the companies built around them.

83

Who Benefits from ICOs?

THIS CHAPTER'S TITLE ASKS who gains from ICOs. The answer in most cases: The issuers. Often it is *only* the issuers that benefit from new crypto projects.

And how could it be any different? A typical ICO goes like this: An idea for a new coin hits you. You write it up in a short document and wrap it in smart-sounding jargon and grandiose claims about disruption. A two-pager will do. You call it a white paper and place it onto a website with flashing zeros and ones. The text: More jargon. You run a marketing campaign on social media, Telegram, or wherever you find the broader crypto community. Perhaps you can get some industry heavyweights on board. Or even non-crypto influencers; it doesn't really

CHART 83

Initial Coin Offerings and their likelihood of getting listed

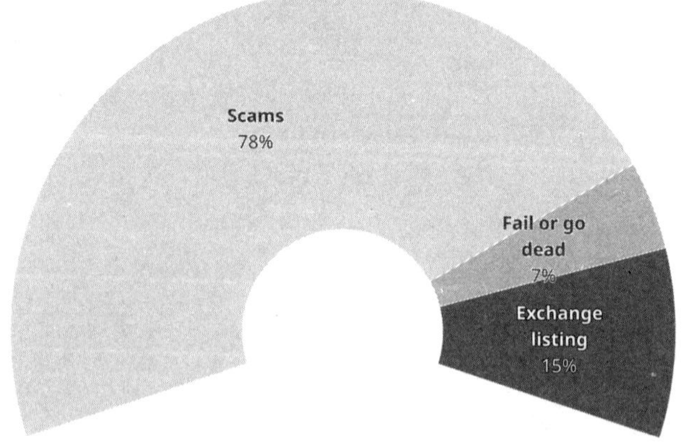

Chart: Igor Pejic • Data from: Satis Group

matter as long as they have reach. You incentivize them to promote your coin by giving them a part of your newly issued tokens. Be generous. Minting them doesn't really cost you anything. Designing the promotional campaign is often where most effort is invested.

Then set up the tokens and make them ready for distribution. Not yet the real application you promised in the white paper, just the coins. For issuing the coins, there is no need for a new blockchain. Simply use Ethereum or Solana and build the tokens on top. It is not rocket science. Define pricing and funding goals, and start selling. Then actually build the solution eloquently described in the white paper. Or don't. You've already pocketed your investors' fiat money, so why spend it on building a coin that might fail? That *is likely to* fail, given past data.

It is no surprise, then, that a study by Satis Group found eight out of ten ICOs to be outright scams. Many of the well-intentioned ones never made it to an exchange. Put differently: They never achieved any significance. That leaves only 15% of projects that even remotely had a chance to earn any return for investors. And for that to happen, many other things have to line up.

To be fair, over the last couple of years some investor protection mechanisms have been put in place. In the EU, ICOs require a prospectus light and issuers must properly disclose and prove their identities. In the US, the SEC has gone after countless ICOs for unregistered sales of a security. The Wild West of the late 2010s is over, but the key problem remains intact. Investors hand over money to somebody who likely has neither the qualifications nor the motivation to build the spaceship he said he would.

In case you still believe you can find asymmetric investment opportunities in ICOs, I did collect some traits that successful ICOs share. Empirical studies show that in successful projects the duration of the token sale tends to be shorter. Moreover, the share of tokens on sale tends to be smaller. A large number of experts and a larger development team correlate with higher success in both funding and subsequent performance. Another study found that there was one determinant of ICO success that stood above all else—namely, institutional investor backing. Superior screening and coaching abilities weed out most of the bad apples.

ICOs backed by crypto exchanges are particularly appealing. These are so popular they even have their own name—Initial Exchange Offerings (IEOs). It is the best way to make sure that the token will be listed at least on one exchange and investors will have a possibility to buy it.

84

Not-So-Stable Stablecoins

INVESTORS LIKE THE RETURNS OF CRYPTO investments. They don't like the volatility. So wouldn't it be great if you could have one without the other? In the early 2020s, more and more investors thought they had found that holy grail. Stablecoins. They loved the sound of it. Stable. No more ups and downs as with Bitcoin and Ethereum. One coin is one dollar. And while there was no value appreciation, you could lock those coins and receive high rewards for it. A risk-free stroll into crypto world. What could possibly go wrong? The holders of a coin called Terra (UST) can tell you.

But before we look at UST, let's understand why anybody would invest in a coin that is designed to have no appreciation. There are a

CHART 84

Stablecoin fluctuations exemplified by USDT

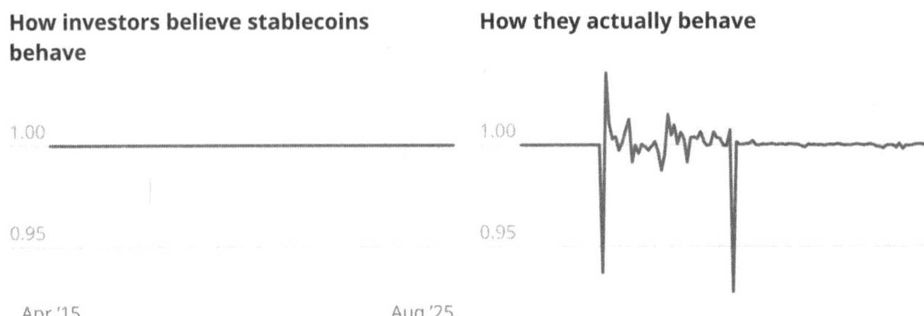

Chart: Igor Pejic • Data from: CoinMarketCap

couple of reasons. Companies use stablecoins for cheap and fast monetary transactions. People living in high-inflation countries might find it difficult to get their hands on US dollars to protect their savings. Stablecoins are easily accessible. Others might use stablecoins for tax reasons. But above all, private investors keep their money in stablecoins because they can earn—often attractive—yields. Now let's return to the fate of the UST stablecoin.

UST and Luna were two sister coins. By a complex mechanism of mining and burning, Luna tokens made sure UST would keep its peg to the dollar. The company had no reserve to uphold this peg. Instead, this task was done completely by an algorithm that managed the supply of the token. However, on May 7, 2022, a massive UST sell-off took place. It is still unclear whether this was triggered by the interest rate environment or a targeted attack, but the peg was lost. Suddenly, the price of one UST was $0.91. Seeing this gap, traders started to swap 91 cents' worth of UST for $1 of Luna. You can probably anticipate where this is going. The selling wave put more downward pressure on Luna. A complete meltdown followed. Exchanges took down the stablecoin. $50 billion in market value was wiped out in days. The dramatic crash cascaded through the market and countless crypto firms had to shut down their business.

The UST/Luna implosion caught many investors flat-footed. They believed that *stable*coins are stable, a flat line compared to the dollar. But in reality, they fluctuate constantly. Usually they fluctuate insignificantly. The *usually* is the problematic part, because as soon as the fluctuations get wilder, they are difficult to rein in.

Terra/Luna was a special kind of stablecoin that had no reserves whatsoever. This group is called algorithmic stablecoins. Today most coins are fiat-collateralized, meaning they can at least back a part of the coins in circulation by cash or Treasury bills.

As with ICOs, regulators have learned a lot, explains Alfred Taudes from the WU Research Institute for Cryptoeconomics: "It is fatal if a stablecoin loses its peg. That is why stablecoins are harshly regulated under the so-called MiCA regulation, a global trendsetter. Stablecoin issuers must back their tokens with 100% liquid reserves and disclose this regularly. Algorithmic stablecoins like Terra/Luna are forbidden in the EU." In the US, the GENIUS Act goes in the very same direction of liquidity requirements and excluding algorithmic stablecoins from the system, though not banning them. But it will be some time until the new rules in the US will come into full legal effect.

At the time of writing, Tether (USDT), by far the largest stablecoin, has a long history of problems with proving its backing and its liquidity. In 2021, the Commodity Futures Trading Commission fined it $41 million for making false claims about its reserves. The Commission found that Tether could only back 27.6% of its coins in circulation by cash and cash equivalents. Tether also has never been audited by any reputable accounting firm. It failed to meet the MiCA transparency requirements and is delisted in Europe, but still available in the US. Thus, American investors need to be particularly vigilant until any transitionary periods with the GENIUS Act are over.

And even once the gap is closed in a couple of years, there is an eternal lesson for investors: There is no free lunch. Every above-average yield comes with a risk. If anybody suggests otherwise, don't buy it.

85

Letting Digital Assets Work in Autonomous Protocols

WHEN THE MYSTERIOUS SATOSHI NAKAMOTO published his white paper that would forever change the world of money, he did not simply want to create a new asset, but an entire alternative financial system. No central banks. No commercial banks. No governments or regulators. But little did Satoshi know about the potency this new decentralized world would reach years after he started Bitcoin and dropped off the map. ICOs revolutionized investing and fundraising. Smart contracts created digital commodities. Stablecoins became the global seamless rails for transaction settlement. But one core area of any financial system was missing: Lending. Then DeFi came along. DeFi is short for *decentralized finance* and refers to autonomous protocols that let you replicate complex processes of the traditional financial world by algorithms only.

CHART 85

Capitalizing on Decentralized Finance (DeFi)

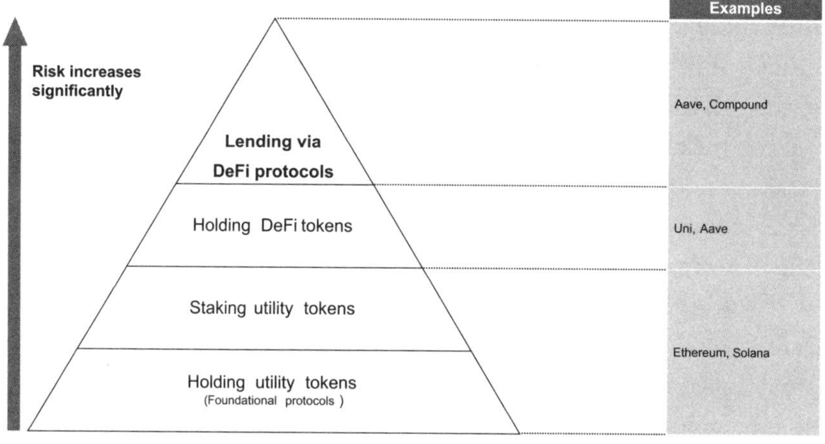

Chart: Igor Pejic

For loans and interest payments, DeFi means you can lock blockchain-based assets in a virtual vault as collateral and define rules as to what happens with those assets under which conditions. Want to move the collateral to the wallet of the lender if the credit-taker misses a payment? Want to automatically sell the collateral once the Bitcoin price falls under $100k apiece? No problem for DeFi. And there is no need for licensed banks, notaries, or any operational staff.

So, while waiting for their crypto-asset value to go up, investors can park them in DeFi lending protocols and earn passive income along the way. But DeFi lending comes with a host of risks. In fact, it comes with many more risks than stablecoins. Stablecoins face one major threat—namely, the loss of its peg to the dollar. This is something that can be managed by the issuer holding sufficient cash reserves and being independently audited. In contrast, there are at least two vital risks woven into DeFi. One is the market risk of the coins in question. Values might plunge precipitously. The second is smart contract risk. All these autonomous lending protocols depend on complex code. Smart contracts are routinely hacked and there is no way the Main Street investor can tell the robustness of a protocol.

At the top of this chapter you see a pyramid of the most popular ways to earn returns in the DeFi world. The higher up, the greater the risk. The bottom of the pyramid is made up of the foundational blockchains like Ethereum that enable the entire DeFi system. Those are lifted automatically when DeFi rises. Hacks and vulnerabilities are very unlikely if investors just buy the tokens and hold them. One step above on the risk ladder is when you don't just hold the tokens but stake them. Staking means you temporarily hand them over to the blockchain (or a staking pool), thereby helping it to generate new blocks. It is slightly riskier because you give away control over your assets while they are staked. You are compensated for that additional risk by receiving a yield.

If staking yield isn't enough to get you excited, you can buy and hold DeFi tokens directly. These tend to have a higher volatility than the foundational tokens. And if you lock DeFi tokens in autonomous lending protocols, you get even higher yields percentagewise. But this is the top of the risk pyramid. The value of the staking yield in dollar terms depends on how well the underlying DeFi token is doing. And the DeFi token value depends also on that of foundational utility tokens. There are many things that have to fall into place. They might sometimes, but certainly not always.

Considering that investing should be a long-term endeavor, the probability that at least one of these risks will materialize rises exponentially over the years. You are accepting a big downside, without the possibility of a stellar rise. This is an asymmetric investment, too, but one where the risk/reward ratio is turned upside down. The odds are stacked against you. Earning a yield of 5–10% does not seem so appealing anymore when you factor in the likelihood of total loss.

> *"It is common practice that the source code of DeFi applications is made publicly available on GitHub and described in detail in the documentation. There are also companies that are specialized in auditing smart contracts. Scientists are working on mathematical proofs that can prove the code is correct. And yet you can never be 100% sure."*
>
> —ALFRED TAUDES, professor at Vienna University of Economics and Business and founder of the WU Research Institute for Cryptoeconomics

86

NFTs and the Question of Utility Value

BROADLY SPEAKING, THERE ARE TWO TYPES OF ASSETS. Those that are interchangeable with similar assets and those that are not. A dollar is worth as much as every other dollar. The same applies to similar stocks and bonds. But your house is not the same as your neighbor's house. No two used cars are exactly the same. The *Mona Lisa* cannot simply be swapped for *The Last Supper.* Those assets are all non-fungible. You cannot trade them on a like-for-like basis.

Though Bitcoins are not 100% fungible (each coin has its recorded trading history), they behave like other true fungibles. That's why they can work as a monetary system. Ethereum made it possible to record non-fungible tokens (NFTs) on a blockchain as well. This could be a digital piece of art or a collectible, a jacket for a video game character, or a patent.

In 2021 and 2022, an NFT mania broke out. Digital pictures and collectibles raked in up to $69 million apiece. Reputable auction houses,

CHART 86

Categories of asset types

	Fungible assets	Non-fungible assets
Digital assets	o Cryptocurrencies o Tokenized securities o Stablecoins	o Cultural NFTs/ collectibles o Metaverse real estate o Commercial rights
Physical assets	o Stocks o Bonds o Cash	o Art o Real estate o Vehicles

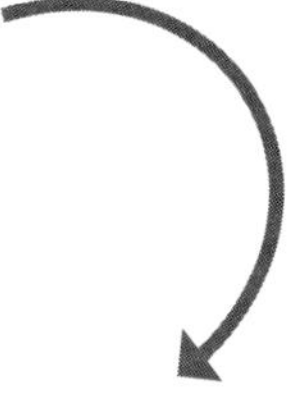

Chart: Igor Pejic

museums, and soccer clubs turned into issuers. NFTs even invigorated imaginations of the dormant metaverse idea. The frenzy ended rather abruptly by mid-2022 when rising interest rates sucked out the oxygen for speculative assets. Trading volumes plummeted as did the values of almost all NFTs.

The NFTs that drove the hype were pure speculative assets. There was no utility value that would have justified any price, let alone millions of dollars. An SUV might be non-fungible but you can get around with it. Commercial real estate can be rented out. These assets can create value. When speaking about today's tech world, Tim O'Reilly draws an interesting parallel to the finance industry before the 2009 crash, where valuations were no longer rooted in reality. "They were creating financial instruments to sell to the public rather than building useful housing. They were disconnected from reality. And I think that's true of a lot of today's Silicon Valley; it has been for the last 10 years. You can have bubble returns, but big crashes are coming when eventually reality catches up."

Digital or not, non-fungible assets by nature are subpar investments. They lack liquidity and interchangeability. If there is only one piece of something, there is no market for it. The price hinges on one buyer. If you have a great oil painting for which you paid $10 million, there is no guarantee you will even find a buyer that offers $1 million. NFTs suffer from this problem even more than physical assets. At least a rare painting's value is determined partly by decades of auction history, museum exhibitions, established art critics, and material condition reports. It can drive traffic to museums. NFTs, on the other hand, don't have any historic continuity or intermediaries. Often their values have not even been driven up by an irrational fear of missing out, but by one person with multiple wallets selling it to himself. You could replicate the business model of physical art and try to rent out the NFT to museums, if there was anybody willing to pay for digital exhibitions.

Non-fungibles with utility value are better alternatives because they have a floor price based on the future value they can generate. I know for how much I can rent out an apartment or how many spoons or socks a machine can produce per hour. But exiting such an investment is still tricky when the demand is limited. This is bad in the physical world, but much worse in the digital one. Digital assets are one of the most reactive asset classes. The super quick NFT meltdown is the best case in point. You simply don't have the time to search for buyers in the on-chain world.

87

Are Bits and Bytes the Evolution of Brick and Mortar? Buying Your House in the Metaverse

WE JUST SAW THAT NFTS WITHOUT UTILITY value are terrible investments. But what if you replicate the value of a house or land from the physical world into the digital world? What about buying lots of land in the metaverse? You can't physically live on them, but metaverse fans will tell you that you can build a business on those lots. You can develop the land and, for example, build a theme park or a digital museum and charge other people's avatars to use it.

I have mentioned the metaverse throughout the book, almost exclusively as an example for a failed technology. At the peak of the metaverse

CHART 87

Price development for phyiscal vs. digital land

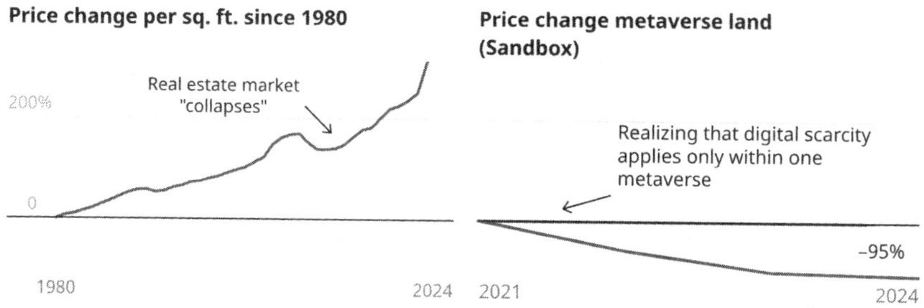

Values represent medians. No inflation adjustment. Sandbox was chosen for illustration because it is the longest-running major metaverse. But except for NFT Worlds, the trend is similar for all other major metaverses (Otherdeeds, Decentraland, Somnium Space, Voxels, Worldwide Webb, Topia Worlds).

Chart: Igor Pejic • Data from: US Census Bureau, CoinGecko, Dune Analytics, CoinLore, own calculations

hype, some crypto entrepreneurs would proudly be telling me how their real estate in the metaverse was appreciating faster than their apartment in Manhattan. That is a bright red flag on the speculation barometer in addition to all those other red flags we have seen in previous chapters. But to be prepared for new technological waves (or a possible comeback of the metaverse), we must learn from past failures just as much as successes. So, was the metaverse killed by miserable applications, or was the very idea of it flawed?

Let's pretend for a moment that things went the other way, that there had been some successful metaverse worlds akin to mega popular computer games like *The Sims* or *Grand Theft Auto*. Let's pretend that hundreds of millions of users flocked to this world and they really built a fully-fledged economy. This can, after all, still happen. In such a scenario, wouldn't metaverse real estate behave like its physical counterpart? The blockchain, after all, creates digital scarcity and it is possible to limit the availability of land.

That was exactly the storyline metaverse zealots sold and investors bought. Their greatest success was to popularize the metaphor "virtual land." It is powerful because it makes us think of those NFTs along the lines of physical land and conclude that they behave in a similar fashion. But there are tremendous differences. Above all, there are two major things that give real estate its value but that are missing in the metaverse: scarcity and location. In the metaverse, you can create artificial scarcity of land. But who can guarantee that there will be no future protocol updates in order to add more parcels? Planet Earth has natural limitations. Mountains, water, harsh climates, and the limited surface. They are tougher to overcome than a 51% hurdle in a network voting. More importantly: While you can limit the number of plots, you cannot limit the number of metaverses.

As for the location, consider that parcels of metaverse land are priced higher if they are close to the center. This makes sense in the real world. Getting from the suburbs to downtown takes time. Living in a far-flung place cuts you off from schools and hospitals. Your avatar doesn't have such problems. You can teleport yourself to everywhere you want. So why would it be better to live closer to the center?

Once these realizations dawned on the market, digital real estate plummeted 95% in value from its heyday. Many trend hunters were hurt badly. Now compare that to the bursting of the real estate bubble. The years 2008 and 2009 were bad for house owners, but after that, values started going up again, only this time at a faster pace than ever before.

I talked a good deal about scenario planning for the future, but make sure you also think through alternative scenarios of failed technologies in the past. Could the path have looked differently with other market dynamics? If so, it might pay to keep that technology on your radar.

VIII

MANAGING RISK

I REMEMBER SITTING THROUGH A LONG NEGOTIATION with an insurance startup a couple of years ago. I was looking for new partners that would bring in more customers for my company and thought that insurtech seemed to be a good fit. It was successful by most measures. Seven-figure valuation, startup awards, strong media presence, eloquent founder. The narrative was good too. They sought to automate health-care invoice submissions and reimbursement with AI. Actually, they called it "algorithms." This was still before the GenAI hype cycle kicked in. But at its core, the idea was that machine learning would create and fine-tune a mechanism that could replace human clerks. During the talk, I noticed some inconsistencies when they were talking about the speed and accuracy of the software. So I wanted to see it and check myself. I was put off. The warning bell in my head started to ring louder. At the same time, I didn't want my hunch to be correct. So much effort and potential would be wasted. Still, I continued to press on for quite some time. Then it slipped out. The software did not exist yet. Rather, founders and freelancers were hammering the invoices manually into Excel sheets. Their road map foresaw a prototype the coming year. The road map was one PowerPoint slide. That was it.

The story goes to the core problem with assessing risk in the tech sector. The "fake it until you make it" mindset is so prevalent because it is very easy to fake it in an industry that is so complex and guarded about its inner workings. You would expect size to correlate with transparency and trustworthiness. We will see in the following subchapters that it does not. At the same time, FOMO is exerting immense pressure to act, causing many lapses in sound judgment.

Tech investors have to be able to live with a high level of uncertainty, not only when selecting an asset but also when deciding whether to stick with it. Yet they have to understand where they can accept uncertainty and where not. The potency of the technological solution should not be a black box.

In this part, I distinguish between avoidable and calculated risks. If you accept a higher volatility for the promise of higher returns, that is a calculated risk. Accepting such risks might or might not yield the best results, but it is a conscious strategy. It can be quantified and managed. Avoidable risk, on the other hand, is putting your investment in jeopardy without getting an adequate upside in return.

Nobody is immune to these kinds of risks, including the largest venture capitalists and corporate decision-makers. Frauds, scams, and hype. But it is about more than just misjudging a company. Regulatory crackdowns, wars, and other macroeconomic conflicts all fall into the avoidable risk category. Usually, none of these come overnight. Spending time and brainpower on risks is not the most glorious endeavor, but if you don't, even being the best stock picker will not make you wealthy. Luckily, you can avoid most of these risks by building a vigilant mindset.

This part also presents techniques to contain calculated risk, one of which is to develop a more realistic mindset to combat the appeal of FOMO and media frenzies. Getting risk under control is the key to every successful investment strategy. And eliminating avoidable risks from your portfolio is a prerequisite for realizing technology alpha.

88

Frauds and Scams

WHEN INVESTORS THINK ABOUT RISK, they first and foremost ponder the likelihood of an asset going down in value. Hardly ever do they lose sleep over Ponzi schemes, scammers, or the safety of the platform they are buying the asset from. That is a pity, because eliminating these avoidable risks is even more impactful than managing the tricky market risk. It is a fact that investment crimes are exploding. It is also a fact that the vast majority of investment crimes revolve around new technologies. The FBI's Internet Crime Complaint Center reports that investment crime now by far beats any other crime category on the internet. Within less than five years, it went from literally nonexistent to $6.6B per year, more than the four runner-up categories combined. This is a figure that does not even include VCs losing money to cheating startup founders or

CHART 88

Investment fraud dominating crime types in complaint loss

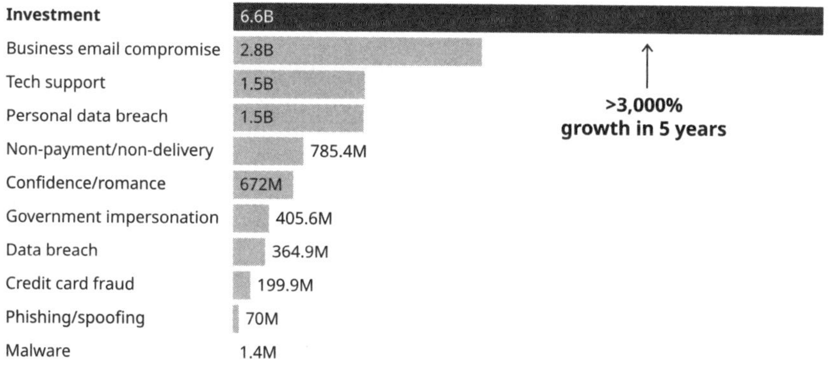

2024 figures

Chart: Igor Pejic • Data from: Multiple FBI Annual Internet Crime Reports

publicly traded companies doctoring their balance sheets. The damage done by those is many times higher, yet usually exploits the same psychological principles.

So why are frauds and scams particularly prevalent in the tech world? To begin with, the only thing larger than the promises of tech founders is investors' appetites to be part of the next iPhone or NVIDIA. At the same time, it is difficult to check the technology that is being sold. Algorithms are kept more secret than the contents of Area 51. Complexity is skyrocketing. And tech trajectories are exponential. This makes it easy to exaggerate the future potential of any asset and deploy psychological pressuring techniques.

One asset class is driving investment fraud more than any other: cryptocurrencies. Sometimes investors pay a broker who never actually purchases crypto tokens. Other times the tokens are bought but not stored adequately, so they get stolen. And very often, investors buy worthless tokens that have been hyped up in a pump-and-dump scheme, in which a group of insiders stimulates trading activity around a token until outsiders get in. Then they dump their tokens and the price collapses.

You can never completely eliminate the risk of frauds and scams. The best due diligence wouldn't have given you insight into Enron's accounting practices, nor would you have suspected Wells Fargo employees to be opening up fake bank accounts. But watching out for red flags—say, in the way new tech investments are marketed—quickly eliminates the vast majority of investment blunders.

Often high-profile cases of fraud and collapse lead to better oversight and better investor protection. Anthony Scaramucci, the former White House communications director and one of the most prominent crypto bulls, remembers how large-scale fraud eventually ended up helping the industry: "While I would not want to relive it, I don't regret all the bad crypto actors of the past. The collapse of FTX allowed the crypto industry to weed out the scams and frauds, and ultimately emerge stronger. It has made us focus on utility and hold ourselves more accountable to ensure something like that never happens again." I share Scaramucci's optimism, but make sure to be among the later beneficiaries of such blowups, not the early martyrs.

89

Beware the Media Frenzy

IN SEPTEMBER 2021, Charlie Javice was more than a shooting star in the tech world. JPMorgan Chase had just acquired her startup for a whopping $175 million and made her a managing director. Her app, called Frank, assisted students in finding loans to foot their college bills. It did so for an incredible number of five million students. Frank had turned its 28-year-old entrepreneur into a media darling even before her lucrative exit. Business media showered Javice with accolades such as including her on the illustrious *Forbes* 30 Under 30 list, celebrating her ability to scale her startup at record speed.

The most glorified entrepreneurs are good at scaling. Some scale investments into customers. Others scale them into profits. And far too

CHART 89

Forbes 30 Under 30 track record

many scale money into fraud. It turned out Frank's five million customers were closer to 300,000. The delta: Fabricated by Javice. Eventually, she was convicted and sentenced to 85 months behind bars.

Javice is neither the only, nor the most prominent, trendy tech fraudster that ended up standing in the dock. Samuel Bankman-Fried (known as SBF), at age 30, was America's 41st richest man. Two years later, his net worth was down to zero and he was sentenced to 25 years in prison for running multiple fraudulent schemes at his crypto exchange, FTX. Elizabeth Holmes was lauded as the first self-made female billionaire and a visionary in blood testing technology. Seasoned investors showered her biotech startup Theranos with $700 million as she touted her novel medical devices that could run hundreds of blood tests with a single drop of blood. The only problem was, the machines didn't work. More often than not they produced errors, missed diseases, and, worst of all, produced false positives nonstop. Holmes was sentenced to 11 years behind bars for investor fraud and conspiracy. The jury found she had straight-out lied about the capability of the medical devices and also falsified documents to support those lies.

Javice, Holmes, and SBF have more in common than high-profile tech investor fraud. They were all young, talented storytellers and the media was wooed by them. In fact, all three of them were featured on *Forbes*'s prestigious lists. This chapter's chart shows how they are symptomatic of a larger pattern of hyped-up entrepreneurs with stellar growth curves.

For every dollar the *Forbes* 30 Under 30 raised from investors, they were charged with two dollars of fraud. The problem lies not with *Forbes* or its list. Whether it was SBF, Holmes, or Janice—media of all hues swooned. And this created immense fear of missing out. Investors were opening up their wallets as fast as they could, throwing due diligence overboard. The founders were on the cover of all these prestigious magazines, so what could possibly go wrong?

The problem for investors is that the media works with a different logic. Investors and journalists are both enthralled by high yields, but investors also want that yield to occur with a high likelihood. And for a sound investment, it is absolutely vital that the risk and the downside potential are limited. Journalists, on the other hand, know that a favorable risk/reward ratio is not what will sell newspapers and generate clicks. Rather, short-term stellar gains make the headlines. And what sells really well is a relatable narrative. It is gripping to read the story of a blond college dropout, so afraid of needles that she sets out to revolutionize blood testing. It is so compelling that we want it to be true and disregard the red flags.

April Rudin, who understands the interplay between wealth management, tech, and the media like hardly anybody else, says that "media discussions are often dominated by a certain active trader mentality, centered around people that actively want to talk about how much money they made off NVIDIA, let's say, rather than the quiet and patient millionaire next door." And what was true for traditional media is even more true for social networks and other digital channels. "What is driving social media are clicks and eyeballs. Influencers in particular are paid by those metrics, not on the actual success of the investments they discuss. And to the algorithms it looks like they're popular, which gives them even more visibility."

Good investors not only disregard the media frenzy about a technology or a company, but all the personal anecdotes and the feel-good stories that serve to sell them. As Rudin puts it: "To become immune to this bias, the best strategy is educating yourself on how the news is made and amplified."

90

Building Contrarian Positions Into Your Portfolio

NONE OF US WOULD DENY THAT COMPANIES like Amazon or Microsoft are great businesses. But are they good investments? Value investors look at the fundamentals of a company to find out whether the market has correctly priced a stock. As I have argued throughout the book, this strategy might work well for traditional companies, but less so for tech companies.

CHART 90

Spotting divergence as a chance

Market perception

Your perception	Good	Average	Bad
Good	Hold	Buy (weak)	Buy (strong)
Average	Sell (weak)	Hold	Buy (weak)
Bad	Sell (strong)	Sell (weak)	Hold

Table: Igor Pejic • Data from: Concept adapted from Aswath Damodaran

For the latter group, the approach must rather be to catch tech waves and understand before most other investors what their impact will be.

Catching tech waves early implies that there is a mismatch between your perception and the perception of the market. You will have a different view on the outlook of technologies, industries, and companies, as well as a different view on the timeline.

If you are right, those mismatches are where you realize technology alpha. And if you consciously pursue a strategy of increasing your investment in areas with a high divergence, it can actually be a good way to manage risk for buzzy investment themes and trendy targets.

Going against the crowd ensures that you don't buy hypes at the peak and that you are not swayed by media frenzies. Also, adopting such a contrarian mindset will make it easier for you to hold on to an investment when the hype goes sour and when expert opinions turn into disappointment.

Chart 90 is a visual representation of how to spot points of divergence between your assessment and the market's. It is not rocket science, yet it is a highly helpful matrix when used routinely. It reminds you of the importance of divergence in building your portfolio. This is not to say that your entire portfolio should be made up of contrarian bets. The market is right about many things much of the time. Plus, you can't be smarter than the market everywhere. That's why a winning portfolio always also has a passive component, with contrarian positions only in those places where you feel extremely confident about your assessment.

But for going against the crowd in the first place, you must be psychologically attuned to the stresses and demands that contrarian strategies bring with them. Scott Hartley, the founder of Everywhere Ventures, notes that Peter Thiel is a great example of a contrarian investor and a good illustration of the mindset it takes to succeed as one. "He is an extremely independent thinker who is rigorous about the truth, even when it's unpopular. I think he effectively observes overruns in the status quo where things have gone too far, and he has the courage to take a counterbalanced stance to those core beliefs. It is therefore almost by definition unpopular, and because it's unpopular it means he's first, and because he's first it means he's already front-running those market corrections. Rather than value investing, maybe one could call it truth-seeking investing, even when it's unpopular." If you don't have this attitude, it is very difficult to go against the majority opinion, and even trickier to stick with it.

91

Combating Tech Anchors and Other Cognitive Biases

THE WORLD OF INVESTING BRIMS with psychological traps. Action bias, overconfidence bias, illusion of control, loss aversion, FOMO, and the list goes on. You would expect a discipline that is so based on figures and mathematical models to be purely rational, but nothing could be further from the truth. All of these mechanisms sway our individual decisions *and* general market sentiment so dramatically that the psychologist Daniel Kahneman won a Nobel Prize in Economics for challenging the notion of rational decision-making due to such mental shortcuts.

Technology investors should also beware of a cognitive bias called the anchoring effect. The chart demonstrates how it works. It shows the stock price development for Wirecard, a former German fintech star and media

CHART 91

Anchoring effect illustrated via the Wirecard collapse

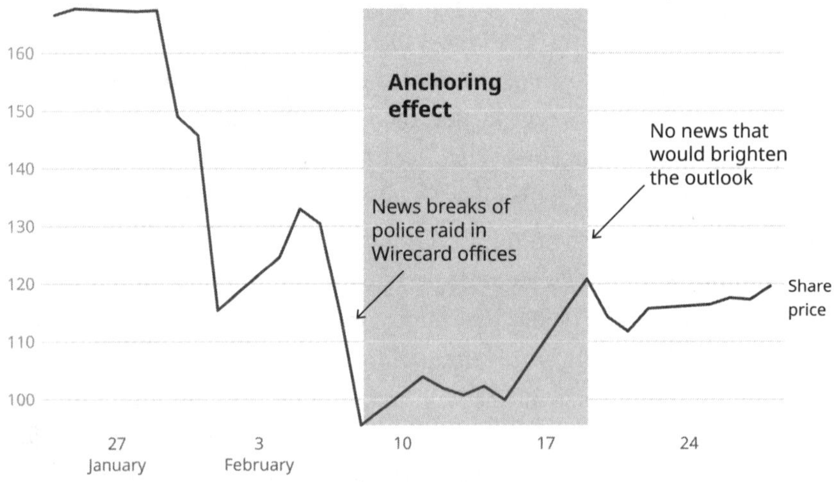

Share price development from 2019, in Euros.

Chart: Igor Pejic · Data from: Investing.com

darling. The digital payment processor was hailed as Europe's answer to PayPal and other Silicon Valley heavyweights. But in 2019, news broke that there was a police raid in one of Wirecard's offices. This seemed to confirm suspicions short sellers and investigative reporters at the *Financial Times* had been having for quite some time. They claimed that billions of Euros in cash shown on the balance sheet never even existed. Following the raid, the stock price dipped from €130 per share to below €100. But here is the really surprising movement: Within the following two weeks, the price recovered and reached some €120 again. During these days there was no new information that would have justified renewed investor optimism. The police had not issued a statement dispelling the allegations. No new auditor report strengthened Wirecard's case. The reason people started buying the stock was that they thought it was a bargain. Not because they did a detailed fundamental analysis. They bought it because it had previously stood in the region of 200 Euros. This all-time high had become their frame of reference, their mental anchor. Needless to say, that decision didn't end well for them. Wirecard collapsed the following year.

Anchoring effects come in all forms. Sometimes the all-time high becomes the anchor. Other times we still remember the IPO price or simply a nice round number with no particular significance. When Bitcoin raced past the $100,000 mark, a new anchor was set. It was easy to remember. Most frequently, however, our brains peg the worth of an asset to the price we paid for it in the past. Anchoring is a natural mental shortcut. Humans need a value against which they can quickly compare the current price of an asset, a reference point that is available instantly. Investors have to assess the value of equities constantly, so we must be capable of making good-enough decisions without spending excessive time and energy on a full, comprehensive analysis.

The anchoring bias is strongest in situations of high uncertainty and low expertise, which perfectly describes technology investing. The inner workings of tech companies are clandestine and complex. Traditional metrics and intrinsic valuations are of limited use. We cannot simply resort to P/E ratios or tangible assets, so many investors assess the price of a stock in the light of their anchors.

There is a simple technique to avoid falling for the anchoring bias without a fully-fledged analysis every time. Ask yourself if anything significant has changed in terms of fundamentals, in technology trajectories, or regulation. Is there a reason why the hypotheses you had initially are not valid anymore? If not, then the price coming down might be a buy signal, regardless of all-time highs or the price when you purchased it. If there was a change, it is time to dig deeper.

92

Mitigating the Impact of Stock Market Cycles

ALL EQUITY INVESTING CARRIES MACROECONOMIC RISK. Whether your strategy is to pick a technology, sector, or company—a rate cut by the Fed or a sudden recession can make you much richer or poorer (on paper). Whereas everybody is a genius in a bull market, hardly anybody

CHART 92

The history of US bear and bull markets

Average cycle length and daily returns since 1942 of the S&P 500 index

■ Bull market   ■ Bear market

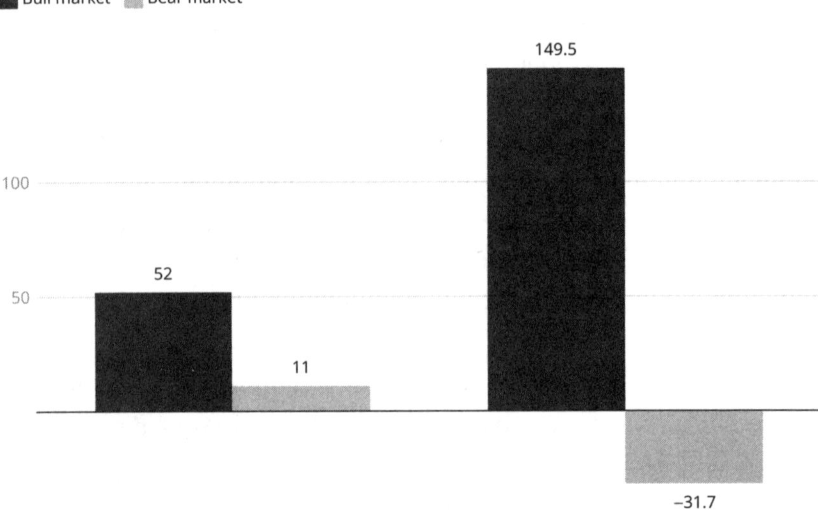

Daily average cumulative total returns from 4/29/1942—3/31/2025.

Chart: Igor Pejic • Data from: First Trust, *Bloomberg*

is a winner in a bear market. As we have seen in chapter 10, technology stocks have historically been more responsive to business cycles than other sectors. They performed best in expansions. In recessions, only real estate did worse.

The good news is that to protect your portfolio from this macro-volatility, you don't have to time the market, but only spend time in the market. Stay in long without touching your investments and over time recession and expansion phases work in your favor. In other words: The longer your investment horizon, the more you will automatically benefit from the asymmetry of bull to bear markets. Look at the chart and you will understand why this works. Average bull markets last longer than bear markets. Almost five times as long. As a result, markets grow more in good times than they contract in bad times. While investors historically lost 32% in downturns, they gained 150% when the market had a run.

Hence, mitigating stock market cycle risk is the most straight-forward thing to do. Yet for many investors it is difficult to carry through the simple strategy of staying invested. This is where cognitive biases get in the way again. The recency bias makes us put more weight on recent events than on decades of historical data and proven patterns. Loss aversion makes us feel more pain losing money than we feel joy for an equivalent gain. Herd mentality makes us copy the behavior of a larger group, in times of exuberance as well as gloom. And overconfidence bias makes us believe that we have more skill and acumen than other investors.

The fear of losing money during a market crash should be tempered by the historical fact that the market's propensity for growth is significantly greater than its capacity for loss. And just as with combating the anchoring effect, the key is a change in mindset. Don't equate the value of an investment with its current stock price. Alex Tapscott, the CEO of CMCC Global Capital Markets, puts it best: "There's a difference between investing and gambling. Gambling is buying something because you hope it will go up in value, and you'll be able to earn a return for risking some capital. Investing is knowing what you're buying and having reasons for owning it."

That is why it is so vital to clearly distinguish between tech cycles and stock market cycles. It is the former that should be triggering a shift in your strategy, not the latter. Stock market cycles are more transient and of shorter nature than technology cycles. They change the price of an equity, but not its underlying value. Tapscott cites the example of digital assets. Many people become depressed when Bitcoin and others go down in value. They think that they've lost money. "That is a gambling mentality. In an investing mentality, if the underlying value is the same or has not changed, then the fact that the price has gone down is actually a great thing. I get to buy more at a reduced price. And that is the difference in investing and gambling."

93

Is Dollar-Cost Averaging Really a Good Strategy to Combat Volatility?

THERE ARE A FEW PIECES OF ADVICE in the investing world that manage to go unchallenged. Diversify. Stay in for the long haul. And dollar-cost average (DCA). We've discussed diversification and investment horizons at length, but what is DCA and is it a good technique to slash risk?

DCA is a strategy by which you invest a fixed amount in regular intervals into an equity or a crypto asset. Thus, if you put $100 into the same company every month, some months you will get more shares for it and some months less. The idea is to take the component of timing out of your investment decisions. You make sure that you never buy at the peak, nor at the bottom. Rather, the acquisition price averages out over time. So, is this really good advice?

The purely mathematical answer might surprise you. While DCA lets you acquire more shares in recessions when prices are down, an initial lump-sum investment yields more shares eventually. Compare the fictional scenario of somebody investing $25,100 in the S&P 500 index in 2002. Twenty years later, that investment would have grown 3.4 times. Had the person opted for a DCA approach in which he put $100 per month in the same index, the multiplier would only be 2.5. Obviously, DCA also precludes you from taking advantage of under-priced equities. Had the person invested a lump-sum after the crash in 2009, the investment would have grown by 5.2 times.

But what if you are of particularly bad luck and buy just at the peak? Wouldn't you be very happy if you had opted for DCA instead? It actually depends on the asset. I calculated a similar scenario for Bitcoin. With its volatility, the sharp falls, and the even stronger

CHART 93

Dollar-cost averaging vs. lump-sum strategies

Method	Investment start	Investment end	Total investment	Final value	Multiplier
S&P 500					
Lump-sum	January 2002	November 2022	$25,100	$85,555	**3.4X**
Lump-sum after crash	February 2009	November 2022	$25,100	$131,540	**5.2X**
Dollar-cost averaging	January 2002	November 2022	$25,100	$62,478	**2.5X**
Bitcoin					
Lump-sum at peak	November 2021 (peak)	August 2025	$4,600	$8,569	**1.9X**
Lump-sum at bottom	June 2022 (bottom)	August 2025	$4,600	$16,525	**3.6X**
Dollar-cost averaging	November 2021 (peak)	August 2025	$4,600	$5,829	**1.3X**

The assumption for DCA is a $100 monthly investment, whereas the lump-sum is invested entirely on the first day of the investment start.

Table: Igor Pejic • Data from: S&P 500 investment from Tengku Muhammad Elzafir Habsjah and Indra Surya Permana. Own calculations for Bitcoin.

appreciation, Bitcoin is representative of tech assets in general. It turns out that even if you bought Bitcoin in November 2021, shortly before it crashed, less than four years later you would have outperformed an investor who had dollar-cost-averaged.

Studies from reputable financial institutions have reached similar conclusions. A paper by Vanguard proves the superiority of lump-sum investments in two-thirds of the cases. Once again, time in the market beats timing the market. Nothing is as powerful as returns and compound returns. But the attractiveness of DCA depends on the industry and asset class. If you have assets with a long-term upward trajectory like tech stocks or cryptocurrencies, DCA is not the best risk management strategy.

In reality, however, for many investors a lump-sum will not be on the table anyway. An unexpected inheritance or severance package might give you this option, but generally few people have large piles of cash sitting around idly. Investable assets have to be earned first. And this is why DCA provides an extremely helpful method for wealth creation. It enforces discipline to regularly put aside a part of your income and invest it.

Moreover, DCA protects investors from biases. By having a system on autopilot, they don't make decisions based on market conditions and emotions but by a set of rules that allow for little wiggle room. Plus, your mind is not resorting to psychological anchors because there is no one purchase price. While there might not be a mathematical argument for DCA, there definitively is a behavioral one.

Carl Richards, author of the bestseller *The Behavior Gap*, spent decades exploring how Main Street investors think about money. He argues that volatility should be embraced as a chance, not as a risk. "In fact, with any volatility it's best to be systematic about it. If I just set my buy signal as not something to do with the market movement, but my buy signal is Tuesday, the fifteenth, I always buy on the fifteenth. Then I will naturally take advantage of ups and downs in a way over time that benefits my average price of acquisition." He explains that in the early years it is all about accumulating shares, not dollars. The dollars will follow over time.

94

Regulatory Peril

REGULATION IS ANOTHER DOUBLE-EDGED SWORD. We have seen how regulatory clarity has made unprecedented investment amounts flow into the cryptosphere and thereby lifted prices and propelled progress. But very often regulation restricts innovation. When CRISPR technology gave us a marvelous tool for gene editing of living organisms, governments' first reaction was to tell scientists and companies what they were *not* allowed to do. There was no shortage of specters raised, from designer babies to genetically engineered crops. Progress was choked off. Artificial intelligence has never been in the focus of regulators until it became a mass phenomenon in 2022. Today, some applications are outright forbidden. Others require testing, documentation, transparency, and

CHRAT 94

The Brussels Effect and the threat to Big Tech

The Digital Markets Act spreading to major markets

Map: Igor Pejic • Data from: CEPA

sometimes registration with the authorities. Data privacy and protection laws limit access to the training material needed to advance large language models.

In every country there is a constant tug and pull between more business-friendly politicians and those obsessed with state control. And while the advance of technology cannot be halted, regulation can decelerate it and have a serious impact on the bottom line.

The European Union is most notorious for its harsh regulations, but it is more than that. The EU likes to call itself a regulatory superpower because the rules it imposes are routinely copied by lawmakers across the world. Hence, it pays to track the agenda of the European Commission. The EU passed a highly powerful set of rules on data protection (GDPR). To the dislike of digital advertisers, other governments were quick to copy it. The second Payment Services Directive (PSD2) served as a blueprint for open banking precepts around the world, the main catalyst of the fintech world. This power has been dubbed the "Brussels Effect."

Currently, the EU's Digital Markets Act (DMA) is causing a lot of headache to Big Tech. It is punishing gatekeepers of tech platforms if they lock out competition. Think search, social media, app stores. The map in this chapter highlights the regions where the DMA has already sparked similar regulation. Countries like the UK, Canada, and Mexico are putting the same type of pressure on Big Tech. And while the US has no big bill akin to the DMA, there is a rising spirit of holding tech giants accountable. The Department of Justice and the Federal Trade Commission are increasingly litigating against digital gatekeepers. And the stakes in the US are even higher. It is the only place where the breakup of tech giants could be mandated.

The resistance against technological progress and its agents is ramping up and spreading quickly throughout different geographies. It is hitting companies in the form of harsher regulation. At the same time, Big Tech is increasingly regarded not simply as an economic powerhouse, but a strategic asset in a new brewing superpower clash.

This all makes the future even less predictable for tech investors. One way to control the risk of detrimental regulation is to balance Big Tech positions in your portfolio, regardless of how much you believe in them.

These can be hit hard from one day to the next, even by the mere prospect of new rules. The same is true for sectoral ETFs because, to a large degree, these are also tied to the fortunes of Google and its peers. You can soften the impact of a possible regulatory crackdown by adding B2B and tier-two tech companies to your portfolio. Don't be fooled by the name. Tier-two tech stands for heavyweights with market caps in the hundreds of billions. They give stability yet stay out of newspaper headlines and the tweets of ambitious politicians. It's companies like Oracle and SAP that have built a dominant position in their fields, while at the same time they have a chance to harness the promises of technological progress.

"Through politics or the existing institutions of state, humans can push back and slow technological transformation or individual companies that are perceived to have become too important. In some countries, like China, the state is above all else, but we've seen similar things in the US as well. This golden age of tech is not a straight line as society might push back, because any change leads to winners and losers. Even if over time there are more winners than losers, the 'losers' feel it in the short term and they can mobilize politically, whether it's through regulation or taxation. AI is particularly at risk since it is a big disruptive force for both blue-collar and white-collar employment. The neoliberal consensus, which gave rise to this tech—it's broken down."

—RONIT GHOSE, Global Head of Future
of Finance, Citibank

95

Geopolitical Tensions and Core Tech Infrastructure

I DON'T BELIEVE THAT THE NEOLIBERAL consensus is broken, but it is in a lot of trouble. Across the world, politics are becoming more nativist and protectionist. Tariffs are making their comeback and leaders seek to re-shore supply chains. Yet, highly complex tech products don't quite play along. They, more than anything else, rely on things like rare earths and deep workforce expertise. From drones to computer chips, supply chains are branching out across the continents. At the same time, states are once again forming into blocs. Hostility is rising. In short: Geopolitical risk should be back on tech investors' radars.

CHART 95

Global market share of semiconductor foundries

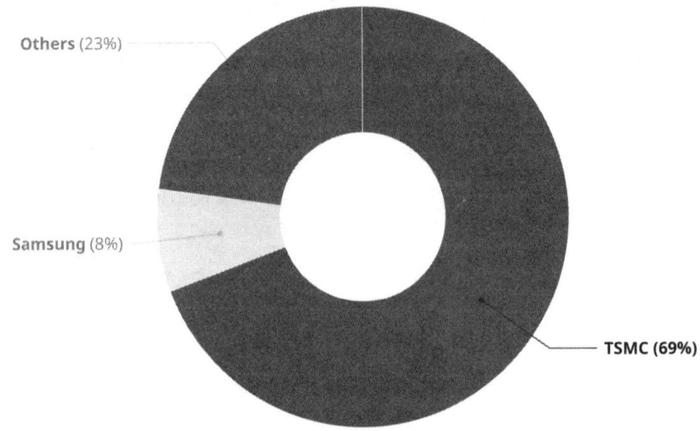

Q4 2024 figures based on foundries' revenues, thus not including chips used by themselves.

Chart: Igor Pejic · Data from: Manufacturers' financial statements as provided via TrendForce

Semiconductors are the best case in point. They are the material from which computer chips are made and therefore the foundation of the digital world. The vast majority of the world's computer chips are produced by one rather small island: Taiwan. More precisely, they are produced by one company named TSMC. To produce the chips that go into everything from your iPhone to the drones buzzing across war zones, first, semiconductor wafers have to be enriched with billions of transistors. This forms the raw material from which computer chips are then fabricated. This happens in so-called semiconductor foundries. TSMC is such a foundry and it creates 69% of the world's chips, which has turned it into one of the world's 10 most valuable companies. TSMC is a dream for every investor. Their position is firmly entrenched, with high entry barriers protecting the business. Foundries' fabrication plants—called fabs—take extremely long to build. And even once built, it is almost impossible to catch up in chip quality. But one factor could turn the dream into a nightmare: Geopolitical risk.

Taiwan could easily become the theater for the superpower clash between the US and China. It is an island of historic and geographical importance for China. Taiwan has been threatened with an invasion for a long time, so it came up with a strategy to make itself an indispensable cog in the chip supply chain. If America depended on the chips, armed conflict could be avoided. So what's the conclusion for investors? Is TSMC too good to be true? Or is it a wild card?

Stephen Foerster, professor of finance at Ivey Business School and author of *In Pursuit of the Perfect Portfolio*, argues that, from the standpoint of modern portfolio theory, such scenarios shouldn't make you discard companies like TSMC. "The ultimate diversification is across all geographies, all sectors, and all asset classes. If you believe in efficient markets, then all risks, including geopolitical risks, should already be priced into securities." Put differently, the market knows about the possible invasion scenario and has priced it in. The stock is cheaper than it would be without a looming conflict. And diversification across multiple territories is better than within one country.

There is, however, another way to think about geopolitical risk. A contrarian one. In the beginning of the book I talked about scenario planning and concluded that, rather than getting the future right, investors should build their portfolio in such a way that they end up winning in multiple possible futures. So what would a contrarian approach look like in terms of semiconductors? To answer that, think of who would benefit if TSMC tanked. It doesn't even have to come that far. How could the US build the semiconductor capabilities at home to phase out its reliance on Taiwan? Fabs are capital-intense, but that can be solved. The issue is that they require so much experience and that they take forever to be churning out chips at a splendid quality, which is needed to win the AI race. Hence, you can't build them from scratch. That's where Intel comes in.

If you look at the market share in the chart, Intel is nowhere to be found. But these figures downplay Intel's real strength. Intel is a fully integrated company that does what TSMC does. It has its own fabs. But then it doesn't (primarily) sell its chips to companies like NVIDIA or Apple. NVIDIA specializes solely in the design of the hardware. It doesn't have manufacturing. Intel, on the other hand, produces the chips *and* does the highly complex blueprints for the chips in-house. It is like TSMC and NVIDIA combined. The US government saw that strategic importance of Intel and in August 2025 it took a stake in it as part of its onshoring effort for chip manufacturing. Then NVIDIA invested in Intel and the price shot up. So every risk is also an opportunity if you do your scenario planning properly.

96

Should We Get More Pessimistic?

THE ROOT CAUSE OF RISK IS NEITHER VOLATILITY, nor regulators, nor possible wars. It is our appetites and expectations. As soon as I seek above-average returns, I am engaging in a strategy that might yield below-average returns. The problem is not that investors want to beat the market per se, but that most of them expect to have *excessive* returns. As this chapter's chart shows, the expectations are plainly unrealistic.

CHART 96

Expectation gap: Investors vs. financial professionals

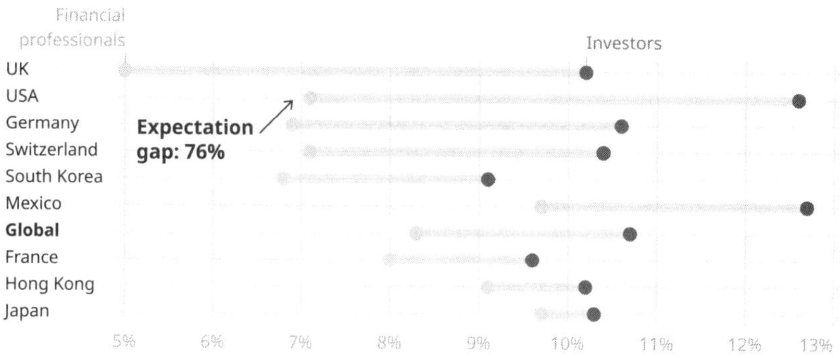

Countries sorted according to expectation gap (declining). 2025 survey results.
Chart: Igor Pejic • Data from: Natixis

The US and the UK are leading the list by far. It is unsurprising that financial professionals are more conservative, but the gap is stunning. In the US, there is a 76% difference between the returns envisioned by financial professionals and the general investor.

The gap is the largest in countries in which investing and financial news are most present in the public discourse. April Rudin reminds us that "people's expectations are primarily shaped by the world around them. The media plays a big role. It hypes up celebrities, influencers, and even You-Tubers as trustworthy sources. They seem successful, though often in reality they actually make more money from clicks than from the stocks they promote. It's the image of success that we see that shapes our expectations."

Unrealistic expectations will leave many investors disappointed, but will they also leave them poorer? There are good reasons to believe they will. First, high expectations lead to excessive risk taking and often it leads to portfolios bursting with speculative assets. Second, investors with stellar expectations will frequently be turning over their portfolio. This incurs trading fees that eat away returns. Much worse, sky-high expectations invite short-termism. This exposes you to all the risks we have already discussed, including catching the wrong phase in stock market cycles, crypto market cycles, or hype cycles. Many investors will try to time the market instead of consistently following through on a long-term strategy.

That's why the most effective risk management strategy is to calibrate your expectations. If you are targeting above benchmark returns, ask yourself where this delta is supposed to come from. Do you have superior stock valuation skills? Do you have unique insights into an industry or a company? Did you find a unique historic stock market pattern? Are you willing to dig into technologies and their industries deeper than others? Are you better at weeding out losers? If there is no strategy that gives you an edge, you are simply willing to load irrational risks into your portfolio. This way you might get lucky sometimes, but you most certainly will underperform the market over longer stretches of time.

IX

FINAL THOUGHTS

In the book we have seen that much of investing wisdom applies to tech as well: Let time work for you and don't draw conclusions too quickly. Stick to your strategy, even when times get tough and the frenzy is the loudest. Diversify your portfolio. Be skeptical of actively managed funds. Cut down fees.

We have also discussed the numerous critical specificities of tech, especially those based on tech's volatile, dynamic, and unpredictable nature. Investors have to scrutinize technological trajectories, the business models, and, above all, initial customer reactions. They should utilize the new investment vehicles and asset types offered by the tech world.

But with everything you've learned, keep in mind that every investment philosophy relies on implicit assumptions. In this book, I had a couple of them myself: Things move in cycles. Macro cycles are secondary to tech cycles. History, though not a guarantee, is a good signpost of the future. Success is measured in monetary terms.

All those assumptions are true. Except for those rare cases where they are not. And while you need such assumptions to build your tech investing strategy, make sure you will survive if you do encounter a rare instance in which their validity breaks. Plan for these scenarios. Build resilient positions in your portfolio.

This final part of the book shines light on some of my underlying assumptions and their possible limitations. It shows, for example, that technology does not rise and fall in a vacuum. It is dependent on other sectors and especially on the macroeconomic picture. The macro can accelerate or halt tech cycles. It can even choke them off completely for some time.

History is our major source for learning and recognizing patterns. People who find important patterns are rewarded. Over time, others apply those patterns too. Then people betting against them are considered fools until they turn out to be right and are rebranded as "contrarian geniuses." Another cycle. Understanding when a pattern ends is just as important as spotting it in the first place. Pattern shifts are rare, but can be fundamental. We will look at one such shift, triggered by the rise of the digital world.

In the course of the book, it should have become clear that there is no shortcut to technology alpha, neither through experts, consultants, nor fund managers. You will have to put in the effort, do your own research, and apply your own reasoning to make emerging technologies work for you. The book equips you with the tools and the broader picture to start your own analysis. This final part shows you that, while depth is good, range is indispensable. Technological progress is so intertwined that being a biotech or AI investor is not enough. You have to track and understand tech trajectories outside of your core zone of interest.

Finally, I urge everybody to regard tech investing as more than merely an exercise in increasing personal net worth. Most of us are not philanthropists. We invest for monetary gains. But the outcome of investing doesn't have to be exclusively financial. Money flowing into technology can improve the human condition on a larger scale than any other investment. If more people put their money into technology companies, innovation and adoption will accelerate. Productivity will rise. This will make the world more prosperous and just. It will make the future come more quickly.

97

Beyond Tech: The Macroeconomic Environment

NO MATTER HOW PROMISING A TECHNOLOGY IS, or how well a company is managed, macroeconomic trends can have a terrifying effect on your investment. Chart 97 ranks the worst trading days in recent Microsoft history. Six out of the 10 weakest days have their sole root cause in economy-wide shocks. And of the other four days, two were partly driven by a market recession. Tech stocks are high beta. They react to market swings stronger than other equities. Thus, if we drew up the table with the worst trading days for other tech giants, it would look similar for most of them. Covid, the financial crisis, Fed rate hikes. They all left their marks.

We have seen in chapter 10 how quickly and significantly the economic climate can influence technology companies. Macroeconomic cycles usually have a shorter-term impact than the phases of technology cycles. Yet they cannot be neglected. Recessions will often slow down tech trajectories, thus not just slashing shareholder value but also pushing back payday. The macro might not decide what will eventually happen, but when it will happen. Tech cycles should be at the core of your strategy, yet always be aware of how the macro impacts them.

The macro is more than just the business cycle. If you look in more detail at the individual macroeconomic indicators, they can help you with scenario planning. Scott Hartley of Everywhere Ventures stresses that understanding trends like the labor market or purchasing power make it easier to draw your conclusions of how a technology will be adopted. Even for the long run. He gives a concrete example. "You may see that strong economic output is increasing per capita GDP, and purchasing power, let's say in India. And then you can consider a coming technology, like Starlink. It is going to supercharge internet connectivity globally. The combination of these two forces mean over a billion people will have more money to spend and accessible internet, perhaps

CHART 97

The 10 worst trading days for Microsoft

Days in gray indicate crashes triggered by macroeconomic factors, those in bold are *solely* caused by macroeconomic impacts.

	Date	Change %	Explanation
1	March 16, 2020	**−14.74%**	**Covid-19 market crash**
2	January 22, 2009	−11.71%	Weak earnings report and market-wide recession
3	July 19, 2013	−11.40%	Disappointing earnings report disclosing problems with Windows and Surface tablets
4	April 28, 2006	**−11.38%**	**Fear of Fed tightening monetary policy**
5	March 12, 2020	**−9.48%**	**Day after WHO declared Covid-19 a global pandemic**
6	January 27, 2015	−9.25%	Mixed earnings report
7	September 29, 2008	**−8.72%**	**Height of the global financial crisis after Lehman Brothers collapse**
8	July 24, 2009	−8.26%	Weak earnings report and market-wide recession
9	December 1, 2008	**−7.96%**	**Deep freeze in credit markets and intensified concerns about global recession**
10	October 22, 2008	**−7.83%**	**Market-wide chaos as multiple financial institutions face bankruptcy and governments intervene**

Period considered: 2006—2025.

Table: Igor Pejic • Data from: Data on stock performance from Investing.com

for the first time. The impact of this is likely to be not only a rise in e-commerce, but also probably higher bandwidth e-commerce, such as over live video. Technology does not exist in a vacuum, so it is essential to understand the macroeconomic tailwinds, because economics and demography drive a lot of consumer behavior."

With the rise of digitalization since the 2000s, and even more so with the rise of AI since the 2020s, tech is not just impacted by macroeconomic trends. It is driving them. AI investments and returns are the backbone of the entire capital market. Productivity boosts are redefining employment. Electricity-gobbling data centers have economy-wide consequences on energy supply and demand. Business cycles and technology cycles are becoming more aligned. Imagine the progress of AI algorithms starting to become disappointing. Disillusionment sets in. Chain reactions would follow and could tank the entire stock market with all sorts of other unforeseeable spillover effects. It might easily trigger a recession.

98

Beyond Statistics: What Historical Data Can't Teach Us

THE LEGENDARY INVESTOR SIR JOHN TEMPLETON once declared: "The four most dangerous words in investing are: 'This time it's different.'" This adage is perhaps one of the most quoted in investment literature. It is commonly used as a warning against ignoring history. What hardly ever gets quoted is that Templeton also said that 20% of the time those four words are correct. Paradigmatic shifts in technology, markets, or the global economy can change the investing game in lasting ways.

Carl Richards says we have to distinguish between individual risk and system-level risk. "You have to ask the question, 'Did something fundamentally change?' Is what has been valid in the past still valid in the future? And that's a whole another ball of wax because then we are speaking of system-level risk." Changes on the system level can have all kinds of profound consequences. They can impact patterns on all levels. They can even alter the metrics we use for assessing an investment. "We admonish people that the last four words of any great investors are 'this time it's different' because we have generally decided that the system works. But that should not keep us from asking whether the system broadly is at risk or if the system is changing. That seems like a reasonable argument these days."

There is no shortage of reasons why the rules of the investment world by which we played for so long might be changing today. We derive

What if this time really is different?

Return ratio of growth stocks to value stocks (high ratio equals growth stock outperformance)

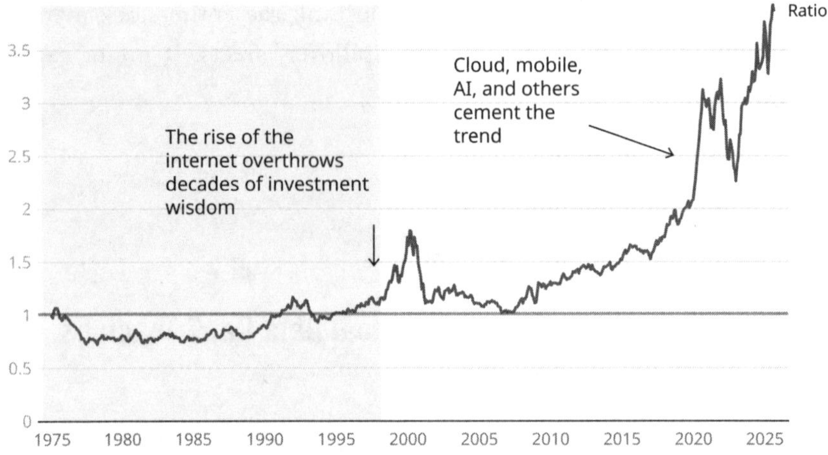

The performance is measured by comparing the MSCI USA Growth Index with the MSCI USA Value Index.

Chart: Igor Pejic • Data from: MSCI

those rules from historic data. And while that historic data stretches across decades, it is still uniform, meaning it covers only one paradigm. Data collection rarely starts before WWII, for good reason. Different mechanisms were in force during the wars. And very often, historic assessment only stretches to after the end of the Cold War. But that also means that we have derived our patterns from a neoliberal, unipolar world with the US as the undisputed superpower. A world more or less at peace, in which the expansion to emerging markets and ultra-low interest rates were fueling growth.

We have yet to see whether any of the current geopolitical changes will affect the rules of the investing game. But there has been one watershed development that has already altered the game: Digitalization.

Since the early 20th century, there have been two competing investment philosophies: Value investing and growth investing. One looked at the price of companies, the other at the growth potential. When you compared the outcomes of the two approaches, value investing ended up as the winner much more frequently than growth investing. That dramatically changed with the new millennium. Chart 98 displays how the two philosophies compared to each year. A value of one means they have delivered similar results. Everything below that shows value investors were ahead. If the value is higher than one, it indicates that growth stocks beat value stocks. The years preceding the dot-com bust marked a turning point in history. Ever since, value stocks as a group have underdelivered. Wisdom that applied for more than half a century suddenly didn't work for the largest, most valuable stock group, because value investing tools and principles like reversion to the mean fail when assessing tech companies. Big and Small Tech will always look expensive on paper.

Value investors will tell you that there will be market reversals. But the dominance of growth stocks soared with every new tech wave that built a new layer of digitalization. Mobile. Cloud. Blockchain. AI. The ratio in favor of growth investing went exponential. That is not to say that there will be no more reversals. Yet after every reversal like the dot-com bust, tech came back stronger after some time. Sometimes things really are different.

99

Beyond Advice: Curiosity, Range, and Your Own Research

IN THE WORLD OF TECH INVESTING, there is no single authority that can tell you where things are headed to. We have seen how every group that likes to think of itself as having superior knowledge routinely fails to be ahead of the market: tech experts (chapter 44), active fund managers (chapter 62), professional investors (chapter 88), and the media (chapter 89). But in every group, there are also people who get technologies, timing, and companies right consistently. The most impressive thing: Many times, these people are among the first to bet on a sudden, radical change of a tech's trajectory nobody else saw coming, because those resulted from an outside game changer.

CHART 99

Unexpected, outside game-changers of tech trajectories

Dormant tech area	Outside game changers	Game changer coming from	Problem solved
Genomics	Cloud-based AI services	Computing	Costs + capacity
Artificial intelligence	GPUs	Gaming	Capacity
Mobile payment	Introduction of Apple Pay	Smartphones	User adoption
Electric vehicles	High-capacity lithium-ion batteries	Consumer electronics	Costs + capacity
Cloud computing	Launch of AWS	Online retail	User adoption (business model)

Table: Igor Pejic

This chapter's chart shows why it is critical to have as many tech segments on your radar as possible. In the left column you see a number of technologies that were dormant for a long time, meaning that there were corporate pilots, plenty of scientific research, and fully commercialized products. Yet those technologies did not become mainstream because one piece in the puzzle was missing. That piece came from the outside. The revival of electric vehicles only became possible once consumer electronics came up with high-capacity lithium-ion batteries. GenAI needed GPUs that were developed for computer gamers. Genomics could only advance further once AI brought down costs for deciphering the massive volume and complexity of genomic data. The list is long. Sometimes it is not even an external tech trigger, but an external player that makes an existing technology commercially viable. Think Apple for mobile payment or Amazon for cloud computing. Cross-domain progress is frequently overlooked. It accounts for many game changers but is tricky to spot. Why? Career ladders are more quickly climbed with deep experience in one domain, which makes it difficult to build range.

Good for tech investors who are willing to leave their comfort zone and move into this gap.

Most of the people I interviewed for this book had a supernormal curiosity and remarkable range, from digging into research papers to flying halfway around the globe to visit companies. It's the source of much of their success. But one person stood out in the willingness to go to great lengths for self-education. Esther Dyson is a leading angel investor with a focus on health, digital technology, biotechnology, open government, and outer space. And if that doesn't seem like enough range, she has also been a journalist, a bestselling author, founding chairman of ICANN (Internet Corporation for Assigned Names and Numbers), and a philanthropist. The best part: She even trained as a cosmonaut in Star City outside Moscow. Dyson told me that you should also consider knowledge to be a form of return for your investment. "I invest in many things, but above all I invest for an education. I joined boards for an education." Dyson became a board member of 23andMe to learn about genetics. And she invested in various space companies to learn about space. And then she invested six months of her life to train in Star City. Even if you are not planning to don an astronaut suit any time soon, you should take her reasoning to heart: "That's why for me it's important to feel happy about something I invested in, even if I lose money, because I will have had the opportunity to understand that industry and market. You learn more from your mistakes, by figuring out what went wrong. If everything goes well, maybe you just got lucky."

Building range is not just an analytic matter. You have to build what Christian Busch calls a "serendipity mindset." In the highlighted quote, Busch explains why unexpected inputs increase our odds of seeing the big picture before it actually appears. Openness and curiosity have to become part of your everyday mindset.

> *"If you want to connect the dots before others do, the most important thing is to create more dots to connect. That means exposing yourself to broader sets of inputs—different industries, geographies, even hobbies. The taxi driver who overhears a conversation about Bitcoin and digs deeper isn't lucky just by accident; he's built a reflex to engage rather than dismiss. The*

*difference between successful and unsuccessful investors is never
just randomness, but about creating 'smart luck.' It is being open
to unexpected triggers but also developing the discipline to test and
size your bets."*

—CHRISTIAN BUSCH, business professor at the University of
Southern California and author of *The Serendipity Mindset*

100

Beyond Money: Nonfinancial Reasons to Invest in Tech

"GREED IS GOOD" thundered Gordon Gekko at a shareholder meeting in
the 1987 hit movie *Wall Street*. His argument was that individual greed
lifts the collective economy. Self-interest drives growth and progress. If
you invest, the money doesn't sit idly in your bank account but is used
to stimulate companies that innovate, produce, and employ people. In
pursuit of the highest returns, investors back the best and most efficient
companies. Gekko's line had reignited a debate that goes back to at least
the days of Adam Smith, the father of all modern economics. I would
like to add another facet to this debate: If investing for profits is good,
is investing for tech profits better? Economics gives us a clear answer.

Back in 1957, the economist Robert Solow set out to answer one of
the most fundamental questions of his discipline: Where does economic
growth come from? He built a model about the increase in output of
an economy and found that only 13% of it could be accounted for by an
increase in labor force and capital input. Thus, the economic benefits that
Gordon Gekko was alluding to make up only a fraction of the 13%. But
what about the other 87%? They became known as the Solow residual.
It basically stands for the effects of innovation and technological progress. In other words, tech advancements are responsible for almost all
of the economic growth of a country. Wherever you look around you,
evidence of it pops up. Thanks to machinery like tractors and genetically

Where does economic growth come from?

Quantifying the Solow residual to explain the increase in output per worker

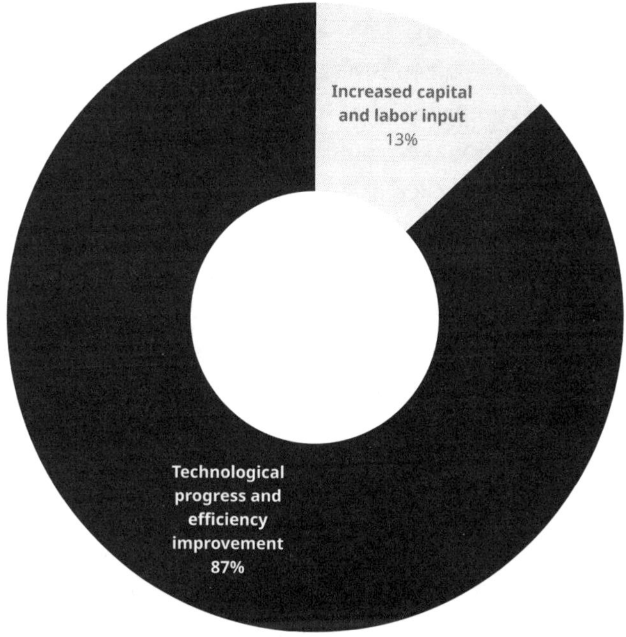

Chart: Igor Pejic • Data from: Robert Solow

engineered crops, only a handful of people are needed to produce enough food to feed the world. Robots keep warehouses running 24/7. Ride hailing apps reduce idle times for cab drivers. GPS navigation shortens their routes. And even the other 13%—capital and labor input—are aided by advancements of tech. Medical technology helps people stay healthier and thus remain part of the workforce for longer. Computers and the internet help in educating the workforce and connect graduates quicker to the right jobs. ETFs and cryptocurrencies boost the supply of capital. ICOs and crowdfunding let innovative companies grow at record speed.

Tech investments are the true engine of modern progress. They speed up the clock of innovation and make the world better, sooner. Not every technology is equal, though. And as a tech investor, the size of your returns should not be the only decision factor. Greed might be good, but it must never be unhinged. You can back technologies that let you scroll through your neighbor's cat pictures . . . and plunge teenagers into depressions. You can bet on smart fridges becoming the next big thing because they will solve your problem of running out of milk . . . and your retailer's problem of not knowing that you like to drink your milk at 2:30 A.M. Or you can invest in biotech companies that eradicate disease. Or space companies that let us reach for the stars and become a star-faring civilization. Or you can put your funds in the quest for a general artificial intelligence or an efficient quantum computer, which will help humanity in literally all areas. You have more good and bad possibilities at your disposal than any previous generation of humans. It's your choice. Make it wisely.

What better way to close this book than with the words of an internet pioneer that has championed sustainable innovation throughout his career. Tim O'Reilly fought against the misuse of platform market power, advocated for open data, and built an education platform that, up to this day, serves as an indispensable knowledge catalyst. Via Alpha-Tech Ventures, O'Reilly continues to fund a new generation of companies that want to change the world for the better. He invests in founders with a big dream to do good, rather than in those promising exclusively financial gains. Whether investing in public or private markets, every tech investor should pay heed to his words: "A lot of good things can come from putting your money in new technology. My advice is, invest in things you want to see exist. They'll make the world a better place."

Acknowledgments

First of all, thank you, the reader of this book, for picking up *Tech Money* and investing your most valuable asset—your time—into these pages. I sincerely hope the ideas and lessons within will provide ample return.

I also owe a great debt to my interview partners: incredible individuals who sat down with me to share stories, insights, and expertise that took a lifetime to build. Despite being a complete stranger to most of you, you opened your doors and your archives. Some of you appear in these pages by name and quotation; others spoke candidly on background, without attribution. Yet the openness, intellectual robustness, and occasional skepticism of each of you pushed the arguments in this book to be clearer and more reliable.

I am profoundly grateful to Donya Dickerson, the best agent I could wish for. Without your stewardship, this book might have been finished in half the time, but it would have been only a tenth as good. Your ability to challenge, encourage, and protect the work all at once made all the difference, from our first conversation to publication and beyond.

A heartfelt thank-you goes to the entire team at Diversion, in particular to my editor, Dan Ambrosio. You grasped the vision for this book immediately and championed it from day one. The blend of your pragmatism and deep insight of the business book world was exactly what this project needed. *Tech Money* is sharper and more actionable because of your guidance.

To my family: Your support is the bedrock of everything I do. My parents provided me with the most vital form of capital—one that pays dividends in investing, life, and writing alike: a foundation built on patience and a work ethic taught entirely by example. I am forever grateful for the sacrifices you made for us.

Above all others, thank you to my wife, who more than tolerated my obsession with a project that has eaten up countless nights, weekends, and holidays for the better part of two years. Your love and support made this possible. And to my son, who pulled me back to reality when I was lost in spreadsheets and charts. Every time you mashed the keys while I was mid-thought or bounced a ball off my desk, you reminded me that the ultimate purpose of financial success is to serve a higher calling: the time we spend together and the life we build for those we love.

References

INTRODUCTION AND PART 1

Boeing (2025). Software Engineering Careers, https://jobs.boeing.com/software-engineering-careers#:~:text=We%20employ%20more%20than%205%2C000,1%2C500%20active%20software%2Drelated%20patents (last accessed: 2025, Aug 8).

Forbes - Paul Tassi (2022, Oct 7). Report: Even Meta's Own Employees Don't Want To Go To Own Metaverse, https://www.forbes.com/sites/paultassi/2022/10/07/report-even-metas-employees-dont-want-to-go-its-own-metaverse/ (last accessed: 2026, Jan 23).

JPMorgan Chase (2024). A Sneak Peek into JPMorgan Chase's Ignite 24, https://www.jpmorgan.com/technology/technology-blog/ignite-2024-communities (last accessed: 2025, Aug 8).

Meta - Nick Clegg (2021, Oct 17). Investing in European Talent to Help Build the Metaverse, https://about.fb.com/news/2021/10/creating-jobs-europe-metaverse/ (last accessed: 2025, Nov 5).

New York Post - Rikki Schlott (2022, Feb 5). Four ordinary people share how they got rich from crypto, https://nypost.com/2022/02/05/how-cryptocurrency-made-these-four-ordinary-people-rich/ (last accessed: 2026, Jan 23).

Outtalent (2025). Top 50 Companies, https://outtalent.com/us50/ (last accessed: 2025, Aug 8).

Reuters (2022, April 14) via *The Guardian*: Man who paid $2.9m for NFT of Jack Dorsey's first tweet set to lose almost $2.9m, www.theguardian.com/technology/2022/apr/14/twitter-nft-jack-dorsey-sina-estavi (archived at https://perma.cc/P68B-2GZS and last accessed: 2026, Jan 23).

Walmart (2022, March 15). Walmart Global Tech Accelerates Expansion with Plans to Hire Thousands of Technologists and Add New Locations, https://corporate.walmart.com/news/2022/03/15/walmart-global-tech-accelerates-expansion-with-plans-to-hire-thousands-of-technologists-and-add-new-locations#:~:text=Walmart%20Global%20Tech%20now%20includes,invest%20in%20our%20current%20associates (last accessed: 2025, Aug 8).

PART 2

Anthropic (2025, Feb 10). The Anthropic Economic Index, https://www.anthropic.com/news/the-anthropic-economic-index (last accessed: 2025, Nov 5).

Business of Apps (2025, Feb 17). Amazon Statistics (2025), https://www.businessofapps.com/data/amazon-statistics/ (last accessed: 2025, July 30).

CNBC—Greg Iacurci (2022, Oct 14). Here's the Inflation Breakdown for September 2022—in One Chart, https://www.cnbc.com/2022/10/13/heres-the-inflation-breakdown-for-september-2022-in-one-chart.html (last accessed: 2025, Nov 5).

CompaniesMarketCap (2024, Apr 3; 2025, Aug 6). Largest Companies by MarketCap, https://companiesmarketcap.com/ (last accessed: 2025, Nov 5).

Economic Research Council (2019, Nov 1). Top Ten Companies by Market Cap over 20 Years, https://ercouncil.org/2019/top-ten-companies-by-market-cap-over-20-years/ (last accessed: 2025, Nov 5).

Economist Intelligence Unit (2023, Nov 15). Big Tech Has Recovered in 2023, https://www.eiu.com/n/big-tech-has-recovered-in-2023/ (last accessed: 2025, Nov 5).

Financial Times (2024, Feb 24). Warren Buffett Admits Berkshire Hathaway's Days of 'Eye-Popping' Gains Are Over, https://www.ft.com/content/1a6f4bd9-b9c7-462e-8152-4ee52a41fbao (last accessed: 2025, Nov 5).

Fukuyama, F. (2006). *The End of History and the Last Man*. Free Press.

IMF via Statistics Times (2025, Aug 6). Projected GDP Ranking, https://statisticstimes.com/economy/projected-world-gdp-ranking.php (last accessed: 2025, Nov 5).

Innovation Frontier Project—Marshall Reinsdorf (2022, June 8). Is Inflation Still Low in the Digital Economy? https://innovationfrontier.org/is-inflation-still-low-in-the-digital-economy/ (last accessed: 2025, Nov 5).

Investing.com (2025). S&P 500 Information Technology (SPLRCT), https://www.investing.com/indices/s-p-500-information-technology-historical-data (last accessed: 2025, Nov 5).

Investopedia—Will Kenton (2025, Aug 20). The Rule of 72: Definition, Usefulness, and How to Use It, https://www.investopedia.com/terms/r/ruleof72.asp (last accessed: 2025, Nov 5).

Kenneth French Data Library and SPDR Americas Research (2025, Oct). Sector Business Cycle Analysis, https://www.ssga.com/library-content/products/fund-docs/etfs/us/insights-investment-ideas/sector-business-cycle-analysis.pdf (last accessed: 2025, Nov 5).

Macrotrends (2025). MSFT, GOOG, AMZN, AAPL, META, NVDA, TSLA, https://www.macrotrends.net/stocks/charts (last accessed: 2025, Nov 5).

Moore, Gordon E. (1965). Cramming More Components onto Integrated Circuits, http://cva.stanford.edu/classes/cs99s/papers/moore-crammingmorecomponents.pdf (last accessed: 2025, Nov 5).

Novel Investor (2025). Annual S&P Sector Returns, https://novelinvestor.com/sector-performance/ (last accessed: 2025, Nov 5).

Schwab (2025, June 6). Sector Views: Monthly Stock Sector Outlook, https://www.schwab.com/learn/story/stock-sector-outlook (last accessed: 2025, Aug 8).

SK Ventures (2023, Mar 21). Society's Technical Debt and Software's Gutenberg Moment, https://skventures.substack.com/p/societys-technical-debt-and-softwares (last accessed: 2025, Nov 5).

Statista (2025). Share of Value Added to the Gross Domestic Product of the United States in 2024, by Industry, https://www.statista.com/statistics/248004/percentage-added-to-the-us-gdp-by-industry/ (last accessed: 2025, Nov 5).

US Bureau of Labor Statistics (2025). Employment by Major Industry Sector, https://www.bls.gov/emp/tables/employment-by-major-industry-sector.htm (last accessed: 2025, Aug 1).

Vanguard (2025). Investment Portfolios: Asset Allocation Models, https://investor.vanguard.com/investor-resources-education/education/model-portfolio-allocation (last accessed: 2025, Nov 5).

Visual Capitalist—Dorothy Neufeld (2025, Mar 20). Charted: How Apple Makes Its $391B in Revenue, https://www.visualcapitalist.com/charted-how-apple-makes-its-391b-in-revenue/ (last accessed: 2025, Nov 5).

Visual Capitalist—Dorothy Neufeld (2025, Mar 24). Charted: How Microsoft Makes Its Billions, https://www.visualcapitalist.com/how-microsoft-makes-its-billions/ (last accessed: 2025, Nov 5).

Yahoo Finance (2023, May 3). Apple to Chevron: These Are Warren Buffett's Biggest Holdings, https://finance.yahoo.com/video/apple-chevron-stocks-warren-buffett-145312240.html (last accessed: 2025, Aug 1).

PART 3

Aerospace Security (2022, Sept 1). Space Launch to Low Earth Orbit: How Much Does It Cost? https://aerospace.csis.org/data/space-launch-to-low-earth-orbit-how-much-does-it-cost/ (last accessed: 2025, Nov 5).

Amazon (2025, Feb 6). Amazon.com Announces Fourth Quarter Results, https://ir.aboutamazon.com/news-release/news-release-details/2025/Amazon-com-Announces-Fourth-Quarter-Results/default.aspx (last accessed: 2025, Nov 5).

Amazon—Thomas Kohnstamm (2025, June 3). Everything You Need to Know About Project Kuiper, Amazon's Satellite Broadband Network, https://www.aboutamazon.com/news/innovation-at-amazon/what-is-amazon-project-kuiper (last accessed: 2025, Nov 5).

Atlantic Council—Ananya Kumar (2022, Mar 1). A Report Card on China's Central Bank Digital Currency: The e-CNY, https://www.atlanticcouncil.org/blogs/econographics/a-report-card-on-chinas-central-bank-digital-currency-the-e-cny/ (last accessed: 2025, Nov 5).

Axios—Ina Fried (2024, Aug 29). OpenAI Says ChatGPT Usage Has Doubled Since Last Year, https://www.axios.com/2024/08/29/openai-chatgpt-200-million-weekly-active-users (last accessed: 2025, Nov 5).

BBC (2012, June 28). Minitel: The Rise and Fall of the France-Wide Web, https://www.bbc.com/news/magazine-18610692 (last accessed: 2025, Nov 5).

Business of Apps (2025, Feb 17). Amazon Statistics (2025), https://www.businessofapps.com/data/amazon-statistics/ (last accessed: 2025, July 30).

Capital One Shopping Research (2025, July 23). Amazon Logistics Statistics, https://capitaloneshopping.com/research/amazon-logistics-statistics/ (last accessed: 2025, Nov 5).

CoinDesk—Cam Thompson (2022, Oct 13). It's Lonely in the Metaverse: DappRadar Data Suggests Decentraland Has 38 'Daily Active' Users in $1.3B Ecosystem,

https://www.coindesk.com/web3/2022/10/07/its-lonely-in-the-metaverse
-decentralands-38-daily-active-users-in-a-13b-ecosystem (last accessed: 2025,
Nov 5).

CoinMarketCap (2025). Decentraland, https://coinmarketcap.com/currencies/decentraland/
(last accessed: 2025, Nov 5).

CoinMarketCap (2025). The Sandbox, https://coinmarketcap.com/currencies/the-sandbox/
(last accessed: 2025, Nov 5).

Collins, Jim (2001) *Good to Great: Why Some Companies Make the Leap and Others Don't.*
HarperCollins.

Cooper, Michal J., Dimitrov Orlin, Rau P. Raghavendra (2001). A Rose.com by Any
Other Name. *The Journal of Finance*, Vol. 56, No. 6 (Dec. 2001), https://www.jstor
.org/stable/2697826?origin=JSTOR-pdf (last accessed: 2025, Nov 5).

Data Energy Institute (2025). Energy Charting Tool, https://www.energyinst.org/
statistical-review/energy-charting-tool/energy-charting-tool (last accessed: 2025,
July 31).

Electro IQ—Saisuman Revankar, Rohan Jambhale (2025, July 2). ChatGPT Statistics
by Market, User, Price and Performance (2025), https://electroiq.com/stats/chatgpt
-statistics/ (last accessed: 2025, July 31).

Focus online (2024, Nov 15). Bezahlbare Klima-Kraftstoffe könnten ab 2037 fossilen
Sprit ersetzen, https://www.focus.de/auto/news/neue-studie-zu-e-fuels-bezahlbare
-klima-kraftstoffe-koennten-ab-2037-fossilen-sprit-ersetzen_id_260450070.html
(last accessed: 2025, Nov 5).

Frontier Economics (2024, Sept 18). Scenarios for the Market Ramp-Up of E-Fuels in
Road Transport, https://www.frontier-economics.com/media/sbvdujwz/final-eng
-scenarios-for-the-market-ramp-up-of-e-fuels-in-road-transport-druck-18102024
.pdf (last accessed: 2025, Nov 5).

Gerstner, Brad (2022, Oct 24). Time to Get Fit—An Open Letter from Altimeter to
Mark Zuckerberg (and the Meta Board of Directors), https://medium.com/@alt
.cap/time-to-get-fit-an-open-letter-from-altimeter-to-mark-zuckerberg-and-the
-meta-board-of-392d94e80a18 (last accessed: 2025, Nov 5).

Gilder, George (1993, Sep 13). Metcalfe's Law and Legacy, *FORBES ASAP*, Sept. 13,
1993, 158.

Johnson, Jarvis (2023). I Spent a Week Alone in the Metaverse, https://www.youtube
.com/watch?v=KW64FiBoITg (last accessed: 2025, Nov 5).

Los Angeles Times—Jerry Hirsch (2015, Mar 19). Elon Musk: Model S Not a Car but a
"Sophisticated Computer on Wheels," https://www.latimes.com/business/autos/la
-fi-hy-musk-computer-on-wheels-20150319-story.html (last accessed: 2025, Nov 5).

McDowell, Jonathan (2025). Jonathan's Space Pages: Decadal Trends, https://
planet4589.org/space/stats/decpie.html (last accessed: 2025, June 17).

McDowell, Jonathan (2025). Jonathan's Space Pages: Satellite and Debris Population: Past
Decade, https://planet4589.org/space/stats/acdec.html (last accessed: 2025, June 17).

McDowell, Jonathan (2025). No Title, https://planet4589.org/space/stats/out/satpie.txt
(last accessed: 2025, June 17).

Meta—Nick Clegg (2021, Oct 17). Investing in European Talent to Help Build the Metaverse, https://about.fb.com/news/2021/10/creating-jobs-europe-metaverse/ (last accessed: 2025, Nov 5).

Metcalfe, Robert M. (1995, Oct 2). Metcalfe's Law: A Network Becomes More Valuable as It Reaches More Users, *InfoWorld* (Vol. 17, Issue 40), https://go.gale.com/ps/i.do?id =GALE%7CA17524205&sid=googleScholar&v=2.1&it=r&linkaccess=abs&issn =01996649&p=AONE&sw=w&userGroupName=anon%7Ec14c7b71&aty=open -web-entry (last accessed: 2025, Nov 5).

Moore, Geoffrey (2014). *Crossing the Chasm: Marketing and Selling Disruptive Products to Mainstream Customers*, 3rd Edition (Collins Business Essentials). Harper Business.

S&P Global—Iuri Struta (2025, Jan 22). GenAI Funding Hits Record in 2024 Boosted by Infrastructure Interest, https://www.spglobal.com/market-intelligence/en/news -insights/articles/2025/1/genai-funding-hits-record-in-2024-boosted-by-infrastructure -interest-87132257 (last accessed: 2025, Nov 5).

Statcounter (2025). Search Engine Market Share United States of America, Jan 2020– July 2025, https://gs.statcounter.com/search-engine-market-share/all/united-states -of-america/#monthly-202001-202507 (last accessed: 2025, Nov 5).

Statista (2025). Anzahl der Neuzulassungen von Elektroautos in Deutschland von 2003 bis Januar 2025, https://de.statista.com/statistik/daten/studie/244000/umfrage /neuzulassungen-von-elektroautos-in-deutschland/ (last accessed: 2025, March 2).

Statista (2025). Percentage of Population Using the Internet in the United States from 2000 to 2025, https://www.statista.com/statistics/209117/us-internet-penetration/ (last accessed: 2025, Nov 5).

The Byte via *Newsweek* (2022, Oct 14). Fact Check: Does Zuckerberg's '$1.2bn Metaverse' Only Have 38 Users? https://www.newsweek.com/fact-check-does-zuckerbergs -12bn-metaverse-only-have-38-users-1751905 (last accessed 2026, Jan 23).

The Verge—Alex Heath (2022, Oct 7). Meta's Flagship Metaverse App Is Barely Used by the Employees Building It, https://www.theverge.com/2022/10/6/23391895 /meta-facebook-horizon-worlds-vr-social-network-too-buggy-leaked-memo (last accessed: 2025, Nov 5).

The Verge—Casey Newton (2021, July 22). Mark in the Metaverse, https://www .theverge.com/22588022/mark-zuckerberg-facebook-ceo-metaverse-interview (last accessed: 2025, Nov 5).

The Verge—Clark Mitchell (2021, Oct 1). Google Says Bing Users Search for Google More Than Anything Else, https://www.theverge.com/2021/10/1/22703263/google-lawyer -argues-bing-used-find-google-top-search-defaults (last accessed: 2025, Nov 5).

Triple A (2024). Cryptocurrency Ownership Data, https://www.triple-a.io/crypto currency-ownership-data (last accessed: 2025, Nov 5).

US Department of Energy (n.d.). Timeline: History of the Electric Car, https://www .energy.gov/timeline-history-electric-car (last accessed: 2025, Nov 5).

Wall Street Journal—Jeff Horwitz, Salvador Rodriguez, Meghan Bobrowsky (2022, Oct 15). Company Documents Show Meta's Flagship Metaverse Falling Short, https:// www.wsj.com/articles/meta-metaverse-horizon-worlds-zuckerberg-facebook -internal-documents-11665778961?mod=hp_lead_pos3 (last accessed: 2025, Nov 5).

Wang, Brian (2024, Jan 19). How Will SpaceX Bring the Cost to Space Down to $10 per Kilogram from Over $1000 per Kilogram? https://www.nextbigfuture .com/2024/01/how-will-spacex-bring-the-cost-to-space-down-to-10-per-kilogram -from-over-1000-per-kilogram.html (last accessed: 2025, Nov 5).

Wharton School—Berry Libert, Megan Beck, Jerry Wind (2016, Apr 14). Network Revolution: Creating Value Through Platforms, People, and Technology, http:// knowledge.wharton.upenn.edu/article/the-network-revolution-creating-value -through-platformspeople-and-digital-technology/ (last accessed: 2018, May 15).

PART 4

Ahmed, Nur, Muntasir Wahed, and Neil C. Thompson (2023). The Growing Influence of Industry in AI Research, *Science* 379, no. 6635 (March 2023): 884–86.

Anderson, Philip, and Michael L. Tushman (1990). Technological Discontinuities and Dominant Designs: A Cyclical Model of Technological Change. *Administrative Science Quarterly*, Vol. 35, No. 4 (Dec. 1990), 604–33, https://www.edegan.com/pdfs /Anderson%20Tushman%20(1990)%20-%20Technological%20Discontinuities%20 and%20Dominant%20Designs.pdf (last accessed: 2025, Nov 5).

Brynjolfsson, Erik, and Andrew McAfee (2014) *The Second Machine Age: Work, Progress and Prosperity in a Time of Brilliant Technologies*. W. W. Norton & Company.

Capgemini (2023). Effective Investment in Generative AI for Marketing (last accessed: 2025, Oct 10).

CoinGecko (2025). Bitcoin BTC price, https://www.coingecko.com/en/coins/bitcoin (last accessed: 2025, Nov 5).

David, Paul (1989) *Computer and Dynamo: The Modern Productivity Paradox in a Not-Too-Distant Mirror. Economic Research Papers from University of Warwick, 268373*, https://econpapers.repec.org/paper/agsuwarer/268373.htm (last accessed: 2025, Nov 5).

Ebert, Christof, and Panos Louridas (2023). Generative AI for Software Practitioners, *IEEE Software*, Vol. 40, No. 4 (July 2023), 30–38, https://www.researchgate.net /publication/372212988_Generative_AI_for_Software_Practitioners (last accessed: 2025, Nov 5).

Electro IQ—Joseph D'Souza (2025, Jan 14). Blockchain Statistics, https://electroiq .com/stats/blockchain-statistics/ (last accessed: 2025, Nov 5).

Fenn, Jackie, and Mark Raskino (2008). *Mastering the Hype Cycle: How to Choose the Right Innovation at the Right Time (Gartner)*. Harvard Business Review Press.

Galaxy—Alex Thorn (2025, May 1). Crypto & Blockchain Venture Capital—Q1 2025, https://www.galaxy.com/insights/research/crypto-venture-capital-q1-2025 (last accessed: 2025, Nov 5).

Google Scholar (2025). Search for "Blockchain," https://scholar.google.com/scholar?q =blockchain&hl=en&as_sdt=0%2C5&as_vis=1&as_ylo=2017&as_yhi=2017 (last accessed: 2025, April 20).

Google Trends (2025). Search for "Blockchain," https://trends.google.com/trends /explore?date=all&q=blockchain&hl=en-GB (last accessed: 2025, April 20).

Illumina (2023, April 4). Press Release: Illumina's Revolutionary NovaSeq X Exceeds 200th Order Milestone in First Quarter 2023, https://emea.illumina.com/company /news-center/press-releases/2023/4b48580b-42d4-419b-8512-5adcbb069836.html (last accessed: 2025, Nov 5).

JPMorgan Asset Management (2025). Guide to Retirement 2025, https://am.jpmorgan .com/content/dam/jpm-am-aem/global/en/insights/retirement-insights/guide-to -retirement-us.pdf (last accessed: 2025, Nov 5).

McKinsey (2023, June 14). The Economic Potential of Generative AI: The Next Productivity Frontier, https://www.mckinsey.com/capabilities/mckinsey-digital/our -insights/the-economic-potential-of-generative-ai-the-next-productivity-frontier# introduction (last accessed: 2025, Nov 5).

National Human Genome Institute (2023, May 16). DNA Sequencing Costs: Data, https://www.genome.gov/about-genomics/fact-sheets/DNA-Sequencing-Costs -Data (last accessed: 2025, Nov 5).

National Library of Medicine (2025). GenBank and WGS Statistics, https://www.ncbi .nlm.nih.gov/genbank/statistics/ (last accessed: 2025, Nov 5).

PwC (2023). Perspectives from the Global Entertainment & Media Outlook 2023–2027, https://www.pwc.com/gx/en/industries/entertainment-media/outlook/downloads /PwC-GEMO-2023-PDF.pdf (last accessed: 2025, Aug 10).

Reuters—Noel Randewich and Medha Singh (2024, Feb 23). Nvidia Adds Record $277 Billion in Stock Market Value, https://www.reuters.com/technology /ai-leader-nvidia-rises-forecast-tops-wall-streets-lofty-goals-2024-02-22/ (last accessed: 2025, Nov 5).

Tetlock, Philip (2006). *Expert Political Judgment: How Good Is It? How Can We Know?* Princeton University Press.

Visual Capitalist—Dorothy Neufeld (2022, Mar 11). The Top Investment Quotes Every Investor Should Know, https://advisor.visualcapitalist.com/the-top-investment-quotes -every-investor-should-know/ (last accessed: 2025, Nov 5).

Visual Capitalist—Jeff Desjardins (2018, June 8). How Long Does It Take to Hit 50 Million Users? https://www.visualcapitalist.com/how-long-does-it-take-to-hit-50 million-users (last accessed: 2025, Nov 5).

Vox—Kelsey Piper (2025). You're Wrong About DeepSeek: What the Hot New Chinese AI Product Means—and What It Doesn't, https://www.vox.com/future-perfect/397539 /deepseek-artificial-intelligence-chatgpt-openai-china (last accessed: 2025, Jan 31).

WIPO (2025). PATENTSCOPE Simple Search "Blockchain," https://patentscope.wipo .int/search/en/result.jsf?_vid=P20-M98MCG-72585 (last accessed: 2025, April 20).

PART 5

AIAAIC (2023, Feb). Google Bard Makes Factual Error About the James Webb Space Telescope, https://www.aiaaic.org/aiaaic-repository/ai-algorithmic-and-automation -incidents/google-bard-makes-factual-error-about-james-webb-space-telescope (last accessed: 2025, Nov 5).

Bain & Company—David Harding, Dale Stafford, and Suzanne Kumar (2024, Apr). How Companies Got So Good at M&A, https://www.bain.com/insights/how-companies-got-so-good-at-m-and-a/ (last accessed: 2025, Nov 5).

Bal, Matthew (2024, May 23). Updated: Parallel Bets, Microsoft, and AI Strategies, https://www.matthewball.co/all/parallelbets (last accessed: 2025, Nov 5).

Bankrate—Brian Baker (2025, Sep 15). Trillion-Dollar Companies: 10 Most Valuable Mega-Cap Stocks, https://www.bankrate.com/investing/trillion-dollar-companies/ (last accessed: 2025, Nov 5).

BBC (2016, July 14). Nintendo Shares Up More Than 50% Since *Pokémon Go* Release, https://www.bbc.com/news/business-36791275 (last accessed: 2025, Nov 5).

Brookings—Samantha Gross (2019, Dec 11). The Saudi Aramco IPO Breaks Records, but Falls Short of Expectations, https://www.brookings.edu/articles/the-saudi-aramco-ipo-breaks-records-but-falls-short-of-expectations/ (last accessed: 2025, Nov 5).

Business of Apps—Nayden Tafradzhiyski (2025, Jan 22). *Pokémon Go* Revenue and Usage Statistics (2025), https://www.businessofapps.com/data/pokemon-go-statistics/ (last accessed: 2025, Nov 5).

Capital IQ: Qtd. in Bain & Company (2024)—see above.

CNBC (2024, Jan 24). Meta Passes $1 Trillion in Market Cap, https://www.cnbc.com/2024/01/24/meta-passes-1-trillion-in-market-cap.html (last accessed: 2025, Nov 5).

CompaniesMarketCap (2025, Nov). P/E Ratio for Saudi Aramco (2222.SR), https://companiesmarketcap.com/saudi-aramco/pe-ratio/ (last accessed: 2025, Nov 5).

Damodaran, Aswath (2025, Jan 9). R&D Statistics by Sector (US), https://pages.stern.nyu.edu/~adamodar/New_Home_Page/datafile/R&D.html (last accessed: 2025, Nov 5).

Dealogic: Qtd. in Bain & Company (2024)—see above.

Dimensional—Wes Crill (2023, Dec 7). Magnificent 7 Outperformance May Not Continue, https://www.dimensional.com/ca-en/insights/magnificent-7-outperformance-may-not-continue (last accessed: 2025, Nov 5).

EY Parthenon—Amiya Setu and Heith Rothman (2023, Sept 23). Why Some Acquirers Are Seeing a Big Boost in Shareholder Returns, https://www.ey.com/en_us/insights/strategy/how-mergers-and-acquisitions-can-create-value-defying-m-and-a-skeptics (last accessed: 2025, Nov 5).

Financial Times—Alexandra Heal (2025, June 11). Private Market Funds Lag US Stocks over Short and Long Term, https://www.ft.com/content/c21a5ca9-6175-498a-bf32-9c91e4366085 (last accessed: 2025, Nov 5).

GuruFocus (2025). Technology Select Sector SPDR ETF, https://www.gurufocus.com/etf/XLK/summary (last accessed: 2025, Nov 5).

Investing.com (2025). Historical Data, https://www.investing.com/equities/ (last accessed: 2025, Nov 5).

Lee, Cheng-Yu, and Bich-Ngoc Thi Le (2020). Technological Diversification and Firm Performance: The Contingency Effects of Independent Directors and Growth Opportunity. *Review of Integrative Business and Economics Research*, Vol. 10, Issue 2, https://buscompress.com/uploads/3/4/9/8/34980536/riber_10-2_04_m19-082_53-68.pdf (last accessed: 2025, Nov 5).

LSEG—Indrani De, Sayad Reteos Baronyan (2025, Jan 23). Do Valuations Correlate to Long-Term Returns? Examining US Equities Through Various Size and Style Indices, https://www.lseg.com/en/insights/ftse-russell/do-valuations-predict-long-term-returns-examining-us-equities-through-various-size-and-style-indices (last accessed: 2025, Nov 5).

LobbyFacts (2025). Meta Platforms Ireland and Its Various Subsidiaries, https://www.lobbyfacts.eu/datacard/meta-platforms-ireland-limited-and-its-various-subsidiaries?rid=28666427835-74#data-card-data-financial (last accessed: 2025, April 20).

Macrotrends (2025). https://www.macrotrends.net/stocks/research (last accessed: 2025, Nov 5).

Macrotrends (2025). Alphabet PE Ratio 2011–2025 | GOOG. + Meta Platforms PE Ratio 2011–2025 | META. + Palantir Technologies PE Ratio 2019–2025 | PLTR, https://www.macrotrends.net/stocks/charts/ (last accessed: 2025, Nov 5).

MIT Sloan—Gerard J. Tellis, Eden Yin, and Rakesh Nira (2011, June 22). How Quality Drives the Rise and Fall of High-Tech Products, https://sloanreview.mit.edu/article/how-quality-drives-the-rise-and-fall-of-high-tech-products/ (last accessed: 2025, Nov 5).

OpenSecrets (2025). Industry Profile: Internet, https://www.opensecrets.org/federal-lobbying/industries/summary?cycle=2025&id=B13 (last accessed: 2025, Nov 5).

Public Citizen (2024, Aug 21). Crypto Corporations Dump $119M into Attempt to Buy 2024 Elections, https://www.citizen.org/news/crypto-corporations-dump-119m-into-attempt-to-buy-2024-elections/ (last accessed: 2025, Nov 5).

Quartz—Joshua Wong and Joon Ian Wong (2022, July 21). We Finally Know How Much Nintendo Made from *Pokémon Go*, https://qz.com/819677/nintendo-pokemon-go-profits-we-finally-know-how-much-nintendo-made-from-pokemon-go (last accessed: 2025, Nov 5).

Reuters—Junko Fujita (2016, July 25). Nintendo Shares Dive as Company Plays Down *Pokémon GO*'s Earnings Impact, https://www.reuters.com/article/us-nintendo-pokemon-stocks-idUSKCN10504G/ (last accessed: 2025, Nov 5).

The Guardian—Alex Hern (2016, July 25). Nintendo Shares Plummet After It Points Out It Doesn't Make *Pokémon Go*, https://www.theguardian.com/technology/2016/jul/25/pokemon-go-nintendo-shares-tokyo-stock-exchange-niantic (last accessed: 2025, Nov 5).

The Guardian—Kalyeena Makortoff (2020, Jan 17). Google Owner Alphabet Becomes Trillion-Dollar Company, https://www.theguardian.com/technology/2020/jan/17/google-owner-alphabet-becomes-trillion-dollar-company (last accessed: 2025, Nov 5).

The Motley Fool—Stephen Wright (2024, Sept 11). 3 Simple Things Warren Buffett Looks For in Stocks to Buy, https://www.fool.co.uk/2024/09/11/3-simple-things-warren-buffett-looks-for-in-stocks-to-buy/ (last accessed: 2025, Nov 5).

Wooley, Kaitlin, Daniella Kupor, and Peggy J. Liu (2022, Aug 24). Does Company Size Shape Product Quality Inferences? Larger Companies Make Better High-Tech Products, but Smaller Companies Make Better Low-Tech Products. *Journal of Marketing Research*, Vol. 60, No. 3, https://journals.sagepub.com/doi/10.1177/00222437221124857 (last accessed: 2025, Nov 5).

Yahoo Finance (2017, Dec 13). How Facebook Dominated the Social Network World, https://finance.yahoo.com/news/facebook-dominated-social-network-world-163239781.html.

YCharts (2025). New Fundamental Chart, https://ycharts.com/charts/fundamental_chart (last accessed: 2025, April 20).

YCharts (2025). S&P 500 P/E Ratio (I:SP500PER), https://ycharts.com/indicators/sp_500_pe_ratio (last accessed: 2025, April 20).

Zhan, Xinrui, Yunqing Liu, and Xingxin Zhao (2024, June 25). The Impact of Technological Diversification on Innovation Performance: The Moderating Effects from an Agency Perspective, https://ssrn.com/abstract=4875721 (last accessed: 2025, Nov 5).

PART 6

Belgian Financial Forum—Sofie Verbeke (2024, Oct 9). Equity Crowdfunding as a New Type of Financing, https://financialforum.be/en/bfw-digitaal/life-after-equity-crowdfunding-analysing-the-financial-performance-of-equity-crowdfunded-firms-in-belgium-using-a-matched-sample (last accessed: 2025, Nov 12).

Bernstein, William J. (1996). Bequeathing Your Assets to Your Broker. *Efficient Frontier*, http://www.efficientfrontier.com/ef/996/broker.htm (last accessed: 2025, Nov 5).

Bloomberg and Janus Henderson qtd. in TiAm Fund Research (2019, April 9). Janus Henderson: How Do Tech IPOs Perform in Their First Year? https://www.fundresearch.de/aktien/How-do-tech-IPOs-perform-in-their-first-year.php#:~:text=The%20second%20is%20that%20the,a%20quadrupling%20within%20a%20year. (last accessed: 2025, Nov 5).

British Venture Capital Association (2023, July). Performance Measurement Survey 2022, https://www.bvca.co.uk/static/dee050a8-2e3f-46f6-bc68ce6fb8d89b96/BVCA-Performance-Measurement-Survey-2022.pdf (last accessed: 2025, Nov 12).

Charles Schwab (2023, Oct). Charles Schwab ETFs and Beyond Study, https://content.schwab.com/web/retail/public/about-schwab/schwab_etfs_and_beyond_study_2023.pdf (last accessed: 2025, Nov 12).

Damodaran, Aswath (2025, January). Historical Returns on Stocks, Bonds and Bills: 1928–2024, https://pages.stern.nyu.edu/~adamodar/New_Home_Page/datafile/histretSP.html (last accessed: 2025, Nov 12).

Fama, Eugene F (1969). Efficient Capital Markets: A Review of Theory and Empirical Work. *The Journal of Finance*, Vol. 25, No. 2, Papers and Proceedings of the Twenty-Eighth Annual Meeting of the American Finance Association New York, N.Y. December 28–30, 1969 (May 1970), pp. 383–417, https://www.jstor.org/stable/2325486 (last accessed: 2025, Nov 5).

Financial Times—Alexandra Heal (2025, June 11). Private Market Funds Lag US Stocks over Short and Long Term, https://www.ft.com/content/c21a5ca9-6175-498a-bf32-9c91e4366085 (last accessed: 2025, Nov 5).

Gallup (2025, May 13). Americans Still Turn to People for Financial Advice, https://news.gallup.com/poll/660467/americans-financial-advice-rooted-people.aspx (last accessed: 2025, Nov 12).

Harvard Law School—Kosmas Papadopoulos, Institutional Shareholder Services Inc (2019, June 28). Dual-Class Shares: Governance Risks and Company Performance, https://corpgov.law.harvard.edu/2019/06/28/dual-class-shares-governance-risks-and-company-performance/ (last accessed: 2025, Nov 12).

Harvest (2019, May 16). How Have Tech-IPOs Performed in Their First Year—A Base Rate Analysis, https://www.hvst.com/posts/how-have-tech-ipos-performed-in-their-first-year-a-base-rate-analysis-oK9TPv6p (last accessed: 2025, Oct 1).

ICI Investment Company Institute (2025, Oct 31). Release: Active and Index Investing, September 2025, https://www.ici.org/research/stats/combined_active_index (last accessed: 2025, Nov 5).

ICI Investment Company Institute (2025, March). Trends in the Expenses and Fees of Funds, 2024. *ICI Research Perspective*, Vol. 31, No. 1, https://www.ici.org/system/files/2025-03/per31-01.pdf (last accessed: 2025, Nov 5).

IFA Index Fund Advisors—Murray Coleman (2025, April 15). Active Fund Managers vs. Indexes: Analyzing SPIVA Scorecards, https://www.ifa.com/articles/spiva-report-active-vs-passive (last accessed: 2025, Nov 12).

IG—Charles Archer (2023). What Are the Average Returns of the FTSE 100? https://www.ig.com/uk/trading-strategies/what-are-the-average-returns-of-the-ftse-100—230511 (last accessed: 2025, Nov 12).

Journal of Financial Planning (2023). https://20882726.fs1.hubspotusercontent-na1.net/hubfs/20882726/2023_Trends_in_Investing_Report_FIN.pdf (last accessed: 2025, Nov 12).

Klausner, Michael, Michael Ohlrogge, and Emily Ruan (2021, Dec 20). A Sober Look at SPACs. *Yale Journal on Regulation*, 2022, Vol. 39, No. 1, https://papers.ssrn.com/sol3/papers.cfm?abstract_id=3720919 (last accessed: 2025, Nov 12).

Morningstar—Zachary Evens (2025, May 23). Fund Fees Are Still Declining, but Not as Quickly as They Once Were, https://www.morningstar.com/financial-advisors/fund-fees-are-still-declining-not-quickly-they-once-were (last accessed: 2025, Nov 5).

Morningstar—Manager Research (2024, October). Morningstar Global Thematic Funds Landscape 2024, https://marketing.morningstar.com/content/cs-assets/v3/assets/blt9415ea4cc4157833/blt6fb6a3f1b9107adb/680a4b98c7bd3455a8049363/Morningstar_Global_Thematic_Funds_Landscape_2024.pdf (last accessed: 2025, Nov 5).

NYU Stern—see Damodaran.

Portfolios Lab (2025, Nov 11). 50/50 Stocks/Bonds, https://portfolioslab.com/portfolio/clevqbo3700010smjc5htdn9y (last accessed: 2025, Nov 12).

Ritter, Jay R. (2025, July 2). Initial Public Offerings: Technology Stock IPOs, https://site.warrington.ufl.edu/ritter/files/IPOs-Tech.pdf (last accessed: 2025, Nov 12).

Ritter, Jay R. (2025, Oct 21). Special Purpose Acquisition Company (SPAC) IPOs, https://site.warrington.ufl.edu/ritter/files/IPOs-SPACs.pdf (last accessed: 2025, Nov 12).

SEC (1962, July 9). *Wharton School Report*, https://www.sechistorical.org/collection/papers/1960/1962_0709_WhartonSEC.pdf (last accessed: 2025, Nov 5).

Seedrs (2023). Portfolio Report Winter 2023, https://assets.seedrs.com/documents/seedrs2023portfolioreport (last accessed: 2025, Nov 12).

Sharpe, William (1964). Capital Asset Prices: A Theory of Market Equilibrium Under Conditions of Risk. *The Journal of Finance*, Vol. 19, 425–42, https://papers.ssrn.com/sol3/papers.cfm?abstract_id=4654611 (last accessed: 2025, Nov 5).

SPIVA Scorecard—see IFA Index Fund

Sun, Zheng, Ashley Wang, and Lu Zheng (2009, Sept). Do Active Funds Perform Better in Down Markets? New Evidence from Cross-Sectional Study, http://ssrn.com/abstract=1474083 (last accessed: 2025, Nov 5).

YCharts (2025, Aug 18). The 10 Best Performing ETFs Over the Last 10 Years (July 31, 2015, and July 31, 2025), https://get.ycharts.com/resources/blog/the-10-best-performing-etfs-in-the-last-10-years-ycharts-analysis/ (last accessed: 2025, Aug 31).

PART 7

Aslan, Aylin, Ahmet Şensoy, and Levent Akdeniz (2023, Jan). Determinants of ICO Success and Post-ICO Performance. *Borsa Istanbul Review*, Vol. 23, No. 1, (January 2023), 217–39, https://www.sciencedirect.com/science/article/pii/S2214845022000898?via%3Dihub (last accessed: 2025, Nov 12).

Caleb & Brown (2025, June 24). Bitcoin's Market Cycle, https://calebandbrown.com/blog/bitcoins-market-cycle/ (last accessed: 2025, Nov 12).

CFTC (2021, Oct 15). Release Number 8450-21, https://www.cftc.gov/PressRoom/PressReleases/8450-21 (last accessed: 2025, Nov 12).

CNBC—Ryan Browne (2022, June 15). Bill Gates Says Crypto and NFTs Are "100% Based on Greater Fool Theory," https://www.cnbc.com/2022/06/15/bill-gates-says-crypto-and-nfts-are-based-on-greater-fool-theory.html (last accessed: 2025, Nov 12).

CoinGecko (2025). Bitcoin BTC Price, https://www.coingecko.com/en/coins/bitcoin (last accessed: 2025, Nov 5).

CoinGecko—Tharmaraj Rajandran (2024, Aug 6). Metaverse Land Prices Plummet by Nearly 95% from Peak Values, https://www.coingecko.com/research/publications/metaverse-land-prices (last accessed: 2025, Nov 12).

CoinLore (2025, Aug 29). ETH Historical Prices / Price History Ethereum, https://www.coinlore.com/coin/ethereum/historical-data (last accessed: 2025, Nov 12).

CoinMarketCap (2025, Oct 22, and 2021, Oct 9). All Crypto Market Cap, https://coinmarketcap.com/ (last accessed: 2025, Oct 31).

CoinMarketCap (2025, Oct 31). About Coinbase Exchange, https://coinmarketcap.com/exchanges/coinbase-exchange/ (last accessed: 2025, Oct 31).

CoinMarketCap (2025, Oct 31). Cryptocurrencies Tracked by CoinMarketCap, https://coinmarketcap.com/charts/number-of-cryptocurrencies-tracked/ (last accessed: 2025, Oct 31).

Dune Analytics qtd in CoinGecko (2024)—see above.

Fisch, Christian, and Paul P. Momtaz (2020, June). Institutional Investors and Post-ICO Performance: An Empirical Analysis of Investor Returns in Initial Coin Offerings (ICOs). *Journal of Corporate Finance*, Vol. 64, 101679, https://www.researchgate.net/publication/342481501_Institutional_investors_and_post-ICO_performance_An_empirical_analysis_of_investor_returns_in_initial_coin_offerings_ICOs (last accessed: 2025, Nov 12).

Forbes—Q.ai (2022, Sep 20). What Really Happened to LUNA Crypto? https://www.forbes.com/sites/qai/2022/09/20/what-really-happened-to-luna-crypto/ (last accessed: 2025, Nov 12).

Fox Business—Suzanne O'Halloran (2025, May 20). JPMorgan CEO Jamie Dimon Clears Bitcoin for Bank, https://www.foxbusiness.com/markets/jpmorgan-ceo-jamie-dimon-clears-bitcoin-bank (last accessed: 2025, Nov 12).

Glassnode (2025, Aug 22). BTC: US Spot ETF Net Flows [USD], https://studio.glassnode.com/charts/institutions.UsSpotEtfFlowsNet?a=BTC&c=usd&resolution=1month&zoom=all (last accessed: 2025, Aug 22).

IGWT (2025, Nov 4). Chart Market Capitalization of Gold and Bitcoin, in USD bn, https://ingoldwetrust.report/chart-gold-bitcoin-marketcap/?lang=en (last accessed: 2025, Nov 4).

Investing.com (2025). Historical Data, https://www.investing.com/crypto/bitcoin/btc-usd-historical-data (last accessed: 2025, Nov 5).

Investing.com (2025). Historical Data, https://www.investing.com/equities/ (last accessed: 2025, Nov 5).

iShares (2025). IBIT: Bitcoin Exposure Made Easy, https://www.ishares.com/us/literature/product-brief/ibit-product-brief.pdf (last accessed: 2025, Nov 12).

Satis Group via International Banker—Nicholas Larsen (2018, Nov 12). ICOs and the Problem of Scams, https://internationalbanker.com/brokerage/icos-and-the-problem-of-scams/ (last accessed: 2025, Nov 12).

The New Frontier—Igor Pejic (2025, July 1). Circle Goes Public and Surges 750% in Less Than Three Weeks, https://igorpejic.substack.com/p/circle-goes-public-and-surges-750.

US Census Bureau, the US Bureau of Labor Statistic qtd. in Home Bay—Sam M. Huisache (2023, Sept 12). 2023 Data: The Price per Square Foot for U.S. Homes Has Increased 368% Since 1980, https://homebay.com/price-per-square-foot-2023/ (last accessed: 2025, Nov 12).

Visual Capitalist—Marcus Lu (2024, Feb 7). Visualized: Bitcoin Returns vs. Major Asset Classes, https://www.visualcapitalist.com/bitcoin-returns-vs-major-asset-classes/ (last accessed: 2026, Jan 23).

Yahoo Finance via *Business Insider*—Theron Mohamed (2024, Apr 18). Jamie Dimon Calls Bitcoin a "Fraud" and a "Ponzi Scheme"—and Says the Crypto Is Hopeless as a Currency, https://finance.yahoo.com/news/jamie-dimon-calls-bitcoin-fraud-131026597.html (last accessed: 2025, Nov 12).

Zeus Mining (2025). https://www.zeusbtc.com/blog/details/5768-top-5-best-bitcoin-mining-pools-compared-in-2025 (last accessed: 2025, Nov 12).

PART 8

Bakke, Chris qtd. in *The Guardian*—Arwa Mahdawi (2023, April 7). 30 Under 30-Year Sentences: Why So Many of Forbes' Young Heroes Face Jail, https://www.theguardian.com/business/2023/apr/06/forbes-30-under-30-tech-finance-prison (last accessed: 2025, Nov 12).

Bloomberg qtd. in Visual Capitalist—Dorothy Neufeld (2025). Visualizing 60 Years of Stock Market Cycles, https://www.visualcapitalist.com/60-years-of-stock-market-cycles/ (last accessed: 2025, Nov 12).

CEPA—Ronan Murphy (2025, Mar 19). Mapping the Brussels Effect, https://cepa.org/comprehensive-reports/the-brussels-effect-goes-global/ (last accessed: 2025, Nov 12).

Damodaran, Aswath (2024, Feb 8). The Seven Samurai: How Big Tech Rescued the Market in 2023! https://aswathdamodaran.blogspot.com/2024/02/the-seven-samurai-how-big-tech-rescued.html (last accessed: 2025, Nov 12).

FBI Annual Internet Crime Report (2023), https://www.ic3.gov/annualreport/reports/2023_ic3report.pdf (last accessed: 2025, Nov 12).

FBI Annual Internet Crime Report (2024), https://www.ic3.gov/AnnualReport/Reports/2024_IC3Report.pdf (last accessed: 2025, Nov 12).

First Trust (2025). History of U.S. Bear & Bull Markets, https://www.ftportfolios.com/COMMON/CONTENTFILELOADER.ASPX?CONTENTGUID=4ECFA978-D0BB-4924-92C8-628FF9BFE12D (last accessed: 2025, Nov 12).

Forbes (2025, Nov 11). Profile: Sam Bankman-Fried, https://www.forbes.com/profile/sam-bankman-fried/?sh=43d5242b4449 (last accessed: 2025, Nov 12).

Investing.com (2025). Historical Data, https://www.investing.com/equities/ (last accessed: 2025, Nov 5).

Muhammad Elzafir Habsjah, Tengku, and Indra Surya Permana (2023, Aug). Comparison of Long-Term Investment Strategies: DCA vs Lump-Sum Investing in the S&P 500 Index. *International Journal of Management Science and Application*, Vol. 2, No. 2, 19–25, https://ejournal.sultanpublisher.com/index.php/ijmsa/article/view/126 (last accessed: 2025, Nov 12).

Natixis (2025). Welcome to the Age of Diminished Expectations. 2025 Natixis Global Survey of Individual Investors, https://www.im.natixis.com/content/dam/natixis/website/insights/investor-sentiment/2025/individual-investor-survey/individual-investor-survey-full-report.pdf?utm_source=theideafarm.com&utm_medium=referral&utm_campaign=deficit-demographic-disasters (last accessed: 2025, Nov 12).

NPR—Bobby Alin (2023, May 30). Elizabeth Holmes Has Started Her 11-Year Prison Sentence. Here's What to Know, https://www.npr.org/2023/05/30/1178728092/elizabeth-holmes-prison-sentence-theranos-fraud-silicon-valley (last accessed: 2025, Nov 12).

TrendForce (2025, June 3). Global Foundries' Revenue, https://datatrack.trendforce.com/Chart/groupContent/61/global-foundries-revenue (last accessed: 2025, Nov 12).

US Department of Justice (2024, Mar 28). Samuel Bankman-Fried Sentenced to 25 Years for His Orchestration of Multiple Fraudulent Schemes, https://www.justice.gov/archives/opa/pr/samuel-bankman-fried-sentenced-25-years-his-orchestration-multiple-fraudulent-schemes (last accessed: 2025, Nov 12).

Vanguard (2023, Feb). Cost Averaging: Invest Now or Temporarily Hold Your Cash? https://corporate.vanguard.com/content/dam/corp/research/pdf/cost_averaging _invest_now_or_temporarily_hold_your_cash.pdf (last accessed: 2025, Nov 12).

PART 9

Investing.com (2025). Historical Data, https://www.investing.com/equities/ (last accessed: 2025, Nov 5).

LongTerm Trends (2025). Growth vs. Value Stocks, https://www.longtermtrends.net /growth-stocks-vs-value-stocks/ (last accessed: 2025, Sept 5).

Marks, Howard (2019, June 13). This Time It's Different, https://www.advisorperspectives .com/commentaries/2019/06/13/this-time-its-different (last accessed: 2025, Nov 12).

MSCI (2025). MSCI USA Value Index and MSCI USA Growth Index, https://app2 .msci.com/products (last accessed: 2025, Sept 5).

Solow, Robert M. (1956). A Contribution to the Theory of Economic Growth. *Quarterly Journal of Economics*, Vol. 70, 65–94.